A SITE OF CONVERGENCE

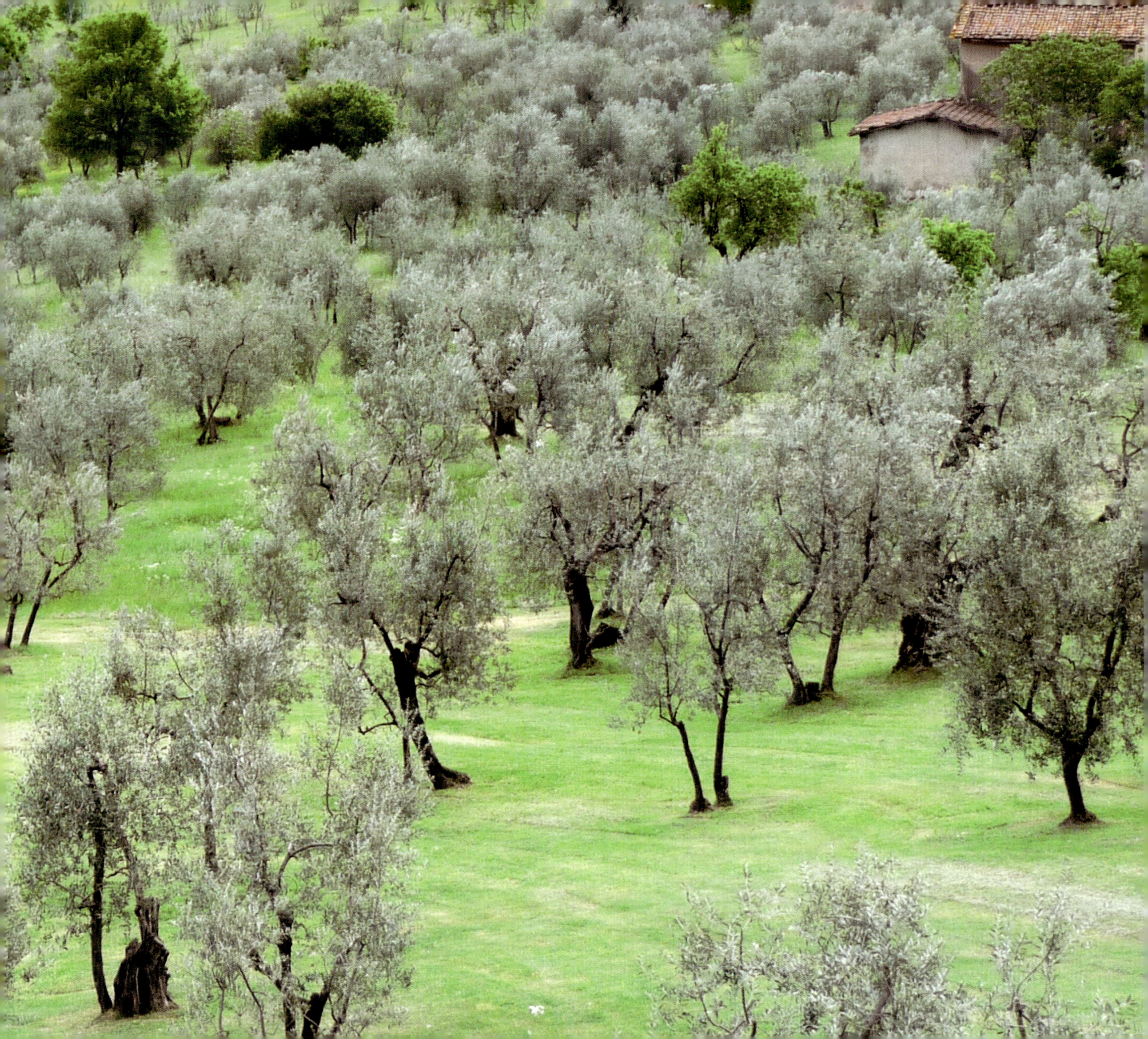

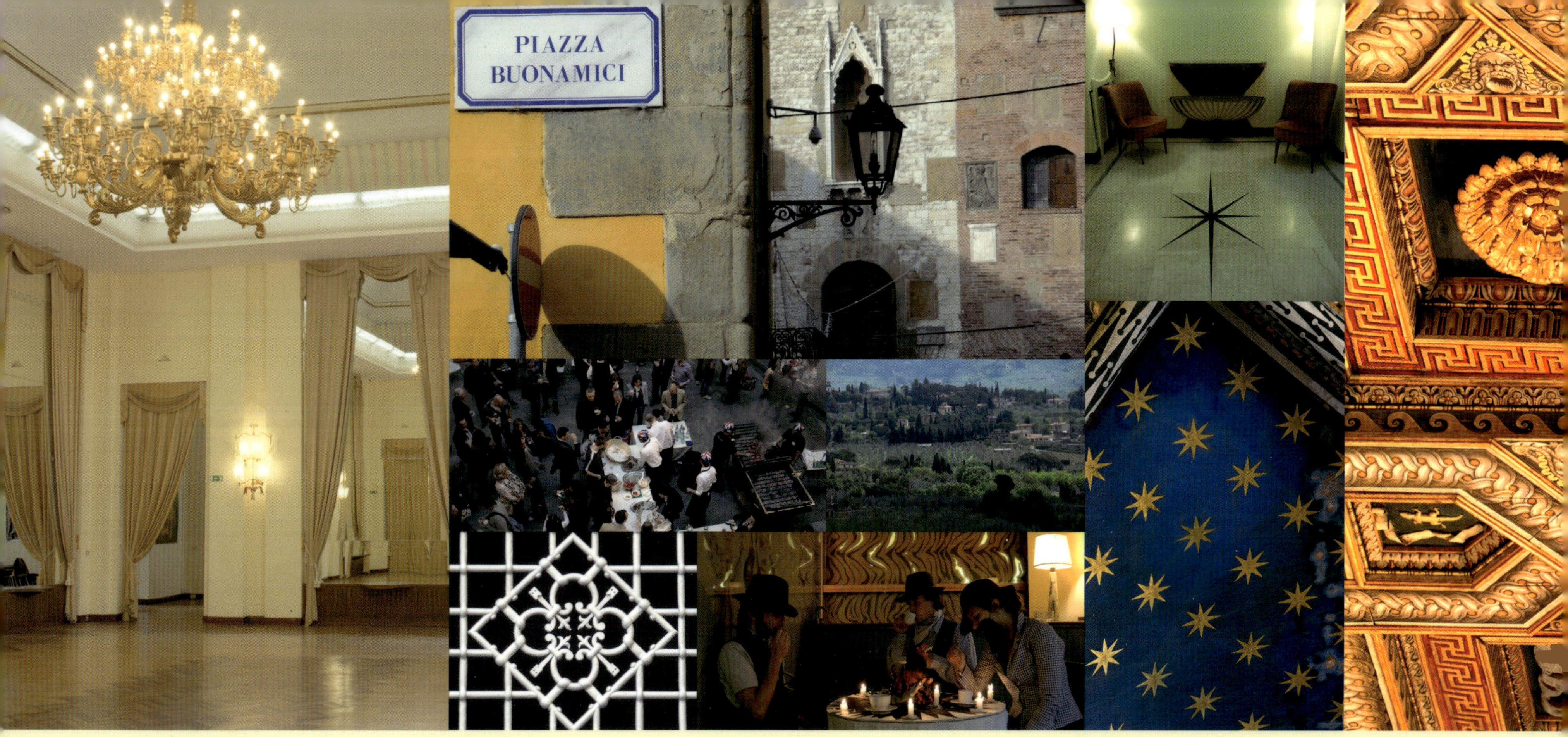

The Monash University Prato Centre, located in the heart of Tuscany, is housed in a landmark eighteenth century mansion—the Palazzo Vaj. This commemorative publication highlights the elegant spaces of the Palazzo Vaj as the context for exhilarating encounters with the city and people of Prato, art and artists, researchers and experts, teachers and students from around the world.

A Site of Convergence is the result of collaboration between writer and editor Cynthia Troup, and the late Jo-Anne Duggan, the Centre's first artist in residence. It is a tribute to the humanist vision that shaped the development of the Centre, and a celebration of Jo-Anne Duggan's photographic art.

Interweaving narrative, vignettes and splendid images, A Site of Convergence tells a fascinating and beautifully illustrated story of the fulfillment of an audacious dream to establish an Australian cultural and scholarly home in Italy, a home which has become, over the last ten years, a vibrant crossroad for cultural and intellectual exchange, as well as a significant site in its local Italian community.

Professor Ros Pesman, The University of Sydney

ISBN (print): 978-1-921867-18-7
ISBN (online): 978-1-921867-19-4

www.publishing.monash.edu/books/prato.html

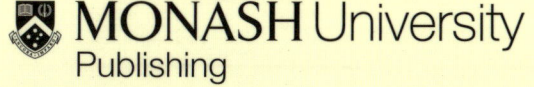

Murray, Philomena, 'European Studies—Looking to the Future', *Australian and New Zealand Journal of European Studies*, vol. 1 no. 1 (2009), pp. 1–13.

Tuccio, Silvana, 'Australian Cinema in Italy: *Squardi Australiani*', in *Australians in Italy: Contemporary Lives and Impressions*, edited by Bill Kent, Ros Pesman and Cynthia Troup (Clayton, Victoria: Monash University ePress, 2008; Monash University Publishing, 2010), pp. 261–71.

Prebys, Portia, editor, *Educating in Paradise: Thirty Years of Realities and Experiences of North American Colleges and Universities in Italy* (Rome: The Association of American College and University Programs in Italy, 2008).

NEWSPAPER AND MAGAZINE ARTICLES

'Accordo ufficiale per l'università dell'Australia', *La Nazione Prato*, 4 March 1999.

'Al via l'attività della Monash University', *Il Corriere di Prato*, 23 November 2000.

Barni, Fabio, 'Arriva l'università australiana', *Il Tirreno Prato*, 1 October 1999.

Bernacchioni, Camilla, 'Chi ha paura dei dinosauri delle tenebre?', *Il Tirreno Prato*, 16 September 2001.

Bernacchioni, Camilla, 'Palazzo Vaj, arrivano gli australiani', *Il Tirreno Prato*, 24 January 2001.

Bita, Natasha, 'Recipe for a Continental Campus', *The Australian*, 31 October 2001.

Bompard, Paul, 'Monash Finds Italian Home for Academy', *The Times Higher Education Supplement*, 14 September 2001.

Davison, Graeme, 'From Footscray to Florence: Francis William Kent, Historian, Educator, 30-3-1942–30-8-2010' [Obituary], *The Age*, 3 November 2010.

'Director for Monash University in Prato', *Monash Memo*, 12 July 2000.

Giannattasio, Nicola, 'Monash University porta Prato sulle trace dei dinosauri polari', *Il Corriere di Firenze*, 19 September 2001.

'Gli australiani sbarcano a Prato', *Il Tirreno Prato*, 28 December 1998.

'Grigliata per tutti alla Monash', *Il Tirreno Prato*, 22 May 2010.

Hooper, John, 'Made in Little Wenzhou, Italy: The Latest Label from Tuscany', *Guardian*, 17 November 2010.

'I giovani «Sguardi australiani»', *La Nazione Prato*, 15 October 2002.

'Inaugurata la sede della Monash, folla per i dinosauri', *Il Tirreno Prato*, 19 September 2001.

'La Monash in Toscana', *Il Globo*, 11 October 2000.

'La Monash s'insedia in Toscana', *Il Globo*, 6 November 2000.

'La Monash University prepara il debutto con una mostra e un grande convegno', *Il Tirreno Prato*, 8 May 2001.

'La Monash University sbarca Palazzo Vaj', *Il Corriere di Prato*, 18 November 2000.

'Law Semester in Full Swing at Monash University's Prato Centre in Italy', *Monash Memo*, 18 April 2007.

'L'università australiana a palazzo Vai', *Il Tirreno Prato*, 19 November 2000.

'L'università australiana Monash ha aperto a palazzo Vaj al posto dei Misoduli', *La Nazione Prato*, 18 November 2000.

Martinelli, Luca, 'Campus australiano in centro', *Il Corriere di Prato*, 26 September 2000.

'Monash Prato Centre Expands', *Monash Memo*, 8 February 2006.

'Monash University per la multicultura', *La Nazione Prato*, 16 May 2001.

'New Monash Europe Centre of Excellence Launched', *Monash Memo*, 2 August 2006.

Nucci, Fabrizio, 'Monash, il lato buono della globalizzazione', *Metropoli Prato*, 22 January 2010.

O'Grady, Desmond, 'Australian Initiative a First in Italy', *The Age*, 16 August 2000.

Pecorario, Lucia, 'Monash, che "affare" per la nostra città', *La Nazione Prato*, 21 May 2010.

Petrelli, Alessandra, 'Open Day alla Monash University', *Il Nuovo Corriere di Prato*, 21 May 2010.

'Pratesi & cinesi: ora ci prova la Monash', *La Nazione Prato*, 6 November 2007.

'Prato Centre Opened in Fine Style', *Monash Memo*, 26 September 2001.

'Prato Centre Reaches Out to the World', *Monash Memo*, 9 May 2001.

'Prato centro europeo della Monash', *Il Tirreno Prato*, 27 February 2008.

'Prato Supports Aboriginal Art Show', *Monash Memo*, 9 July 2003.

Rosenthal, David, 'Italian Palace of Ideas', *The Australian*, 23 May 2001.

'Sicurezza in auto, alla Monash il primo centro europeo', *La Nazione Prato*, 27 February 2008.

Spagnolo, Germano, 'La Monash s'insedia in Toscana', *Il Globo*, 6 November 2000.

'Una giornata alla scoperta della Monash, viaggio-guida nella nuova biblioteca Bill Kent', *La Nazione Prato*, 19 May 2010.

SELECT BIBLIOGRAPHY

INTERVIEWS
Loretta Baldassar, Melbourne, 23 December 2010.
Cecilia Hewlett, Melbourne, 23 November 2010.
Bill Kent, Melbourne, 3 June 2010.
Annamaria Pagliaro, [via telephone] Prato, 26 January 2011.
Leon Piterman, Melbourne, 28 January 2011.
Kit Wise, Melbourne, 17 February 2011.

MONASH UNIVERSITY ARCHIVAL DOCUMENTS
'An Opportunity to Invest in Australia's Historic and Future Links with Italy': Monash University Centre in Italy Investment Brochure, May 1999.
'Copy of Gazetted Prato Registration': Internal Memo and attachments to Professor Stephen Parker, from Helen Fletcher-Kennedy, Office of International Development, 11 June 2003.
'Draft Letter of Invitation' to Dr Guangyu Zhu, College of Fine Arts and Design, Wenzhou University, from Loretta Baldassar, Director, Monash University Prato Centre, 29 October 2010.
'Establishment of Monash University Centre in Prato: Request for Consideration by Council': Letter to Mr Phillip Siggins, Manager, University Secretariat, from Matthew Anderson, Executive Officer (Europe), 13 December 2000.
Kent, F. W., 'Viaggio nell'interpretazione della città': Essay Manuscript in English for Translation into Italian and Publication by the Comune di Prato, March 2004.
Letters to Australian Members of Federal and State Parliaments inviting them to 'The Grand Opening of the Monash University in Prato, Italy', from David Robinson, Vice-Chancellor and President of Monash University, 16 July 2001.
Letter to His Excellency the Honourable Sir James Gobbo, AC, Governor of Victoria, from David Robinson, Vice-Chancellor and President of Monash University, 22 August 2000.
Letter to Professor David Robinson, Vice-Chancellor, Monash University, from Vannino Chiti, President, Regione Toscana, 22 July 1998.
Letter to Professor F.W. Kent, Monash University, from Andrea Lulli, Councillor for Economic Development, Comune di Prato, 3 August 2000.
Letter to Professor F.W. Kent, Monash University, from Rory Steele, Australian Ambassador to Italy, 17 August 2000.
Letter to Professor F.W. Kent, Director, Monash Centre at Prato, from Ros Pesman, Pro-Vice-Chancellor, College of Humanities and Social Sciences, University of Sydney [no date visible].
Letter to Vannino Chiti, President, Regione Toscana, from David Robinson, Vice-Chancellor and President of Monash University, 27 May 1998.
Media Release, Monash University Museum of Art: *Judy Watson*, 9–19 April 2002.

'Monash in Europe 2010': Strategic Directions Statement, May 2005.
Monash University Accident Research Centre Annual Report 2009.
Monash University Prato Centre Directors' Reports, 2001–10 (to the Europe Steering Group, 2001–06; to the Prato Advisory Group 2007–10; to the International Committee 2007–10, which was called the International Advisory Group 2007–08).
Monash University Prato Centre Draft Artist in Residence Program Brief, October 2010.
'Monash University Prato Centre 2009': Advancement Lunch Presentation Booklet, 10 November 2010.
'Prato Lease': Facsimile to Mr Renn Wortley, University Solicitor, from Professor Bill Kent, Director, Monash University in Prato, 16 October 2000.
'Re: Legal Status in Italy and Leasing Contract in Prato': Facsimile to Mr Renn Wortley, University Solicitor, from Mario Borio and Gian Franco Borio, Studio Borio, Florence, 18 October, 2000.
Simmonds, Michael, 'Monash University Prato Centre—Selected Landmarks to 2009', May 2009.
Stichtenoth, Karen, Media Release, Monash University News and Events: 'The Italian Connection', 19 May 2005.

ARTICLES, BOOKS AND CATALOGUES
Becattini, Giacomo, editor, *Prato: Storia di una città*, vol. 4, *Il distretto industriale (1943–1993)*, (Florence, Le Monnier, 1997).
Bortolotti, Lando, and Giuseppe de Luca, *Come nasce un'area metropolitana: Firenze Prato Pistoia: 1848–2000* (Florence: Alinea Editrice, 2000).
Butler, Sally, 'Multiple Views: Pluralism as Curatorial Perspective', *Australian and New Zealand Journal of Art*, vol. 4, no. 1 (2003), pp. 11–28.
Duncan, Jenepher, and Linda Michael, *Love Me Love My Lump: Patricia Piccinini Photographs*, catalogue in English and Italian (Clayton, Victoria: Monash University Museum of Art, 2003).
Duncan, Jenepher, and Linda Michael, *Our Place: Issues of Identity in Recent Australian Art*, catalogue in English and Italian (Clayton, Victoria: Monash University Museum of Art, 2001).
Fiumi, Enrico, *Demografia, movimento urbanistico e classi sociali in Prato dall'età comunale ai tempi moderni* (Florence: Olschki, 1968).
Johanson, Graeme, Russell Smyth and Rebecca French, editors, *Living Outside the Walls: The Chinese in Prato* (Newcastle Upon Tyne: Cambridge Scholars Publishing, 2009).
Kent, Bill, 'Gaining a Foothold: Australian Cultural Institutions in Italy', in *Australians in Italy: Contemporary Lives and Impressions*, edited by Bill Kent, Ros Pesman and Cynthia Troup (Clayton, Victoria: Monash University ePress, 2008; Monash University Publishing, 2010), pp. 39–53.
Monash University, *Leading the Way: Monash 2020* (Clayton, Victoria: Monash University, 1999).

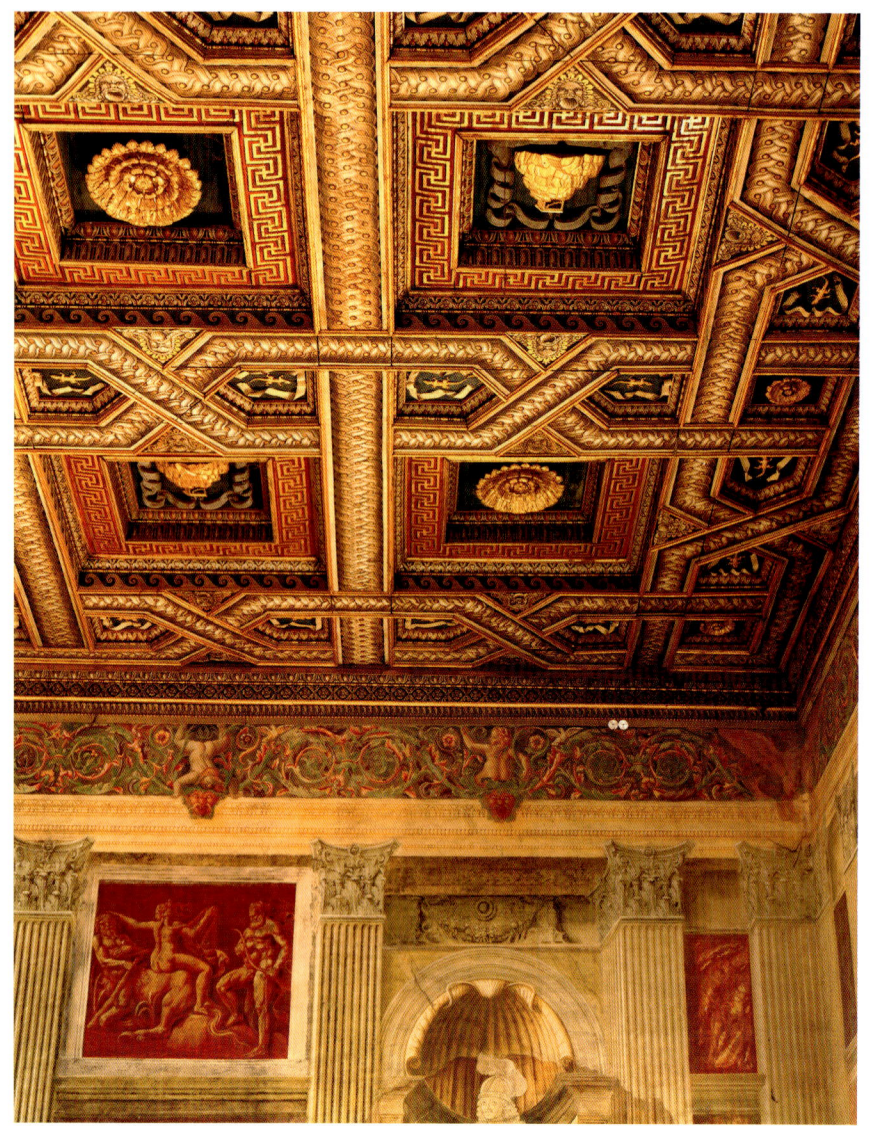
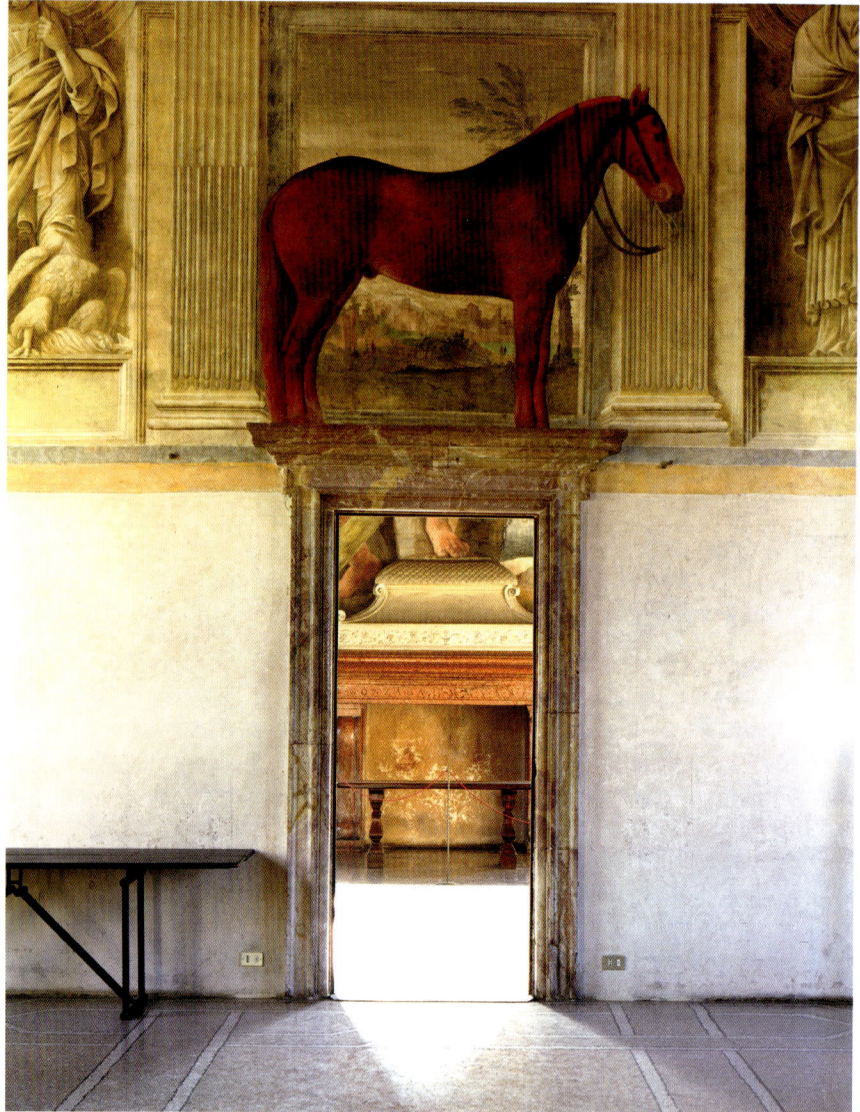

WONDROUS POSSESSIONS

Sala dei Cavalli (Room of the Horses) #1, #2, #3,
Palazzo Te, Mantua

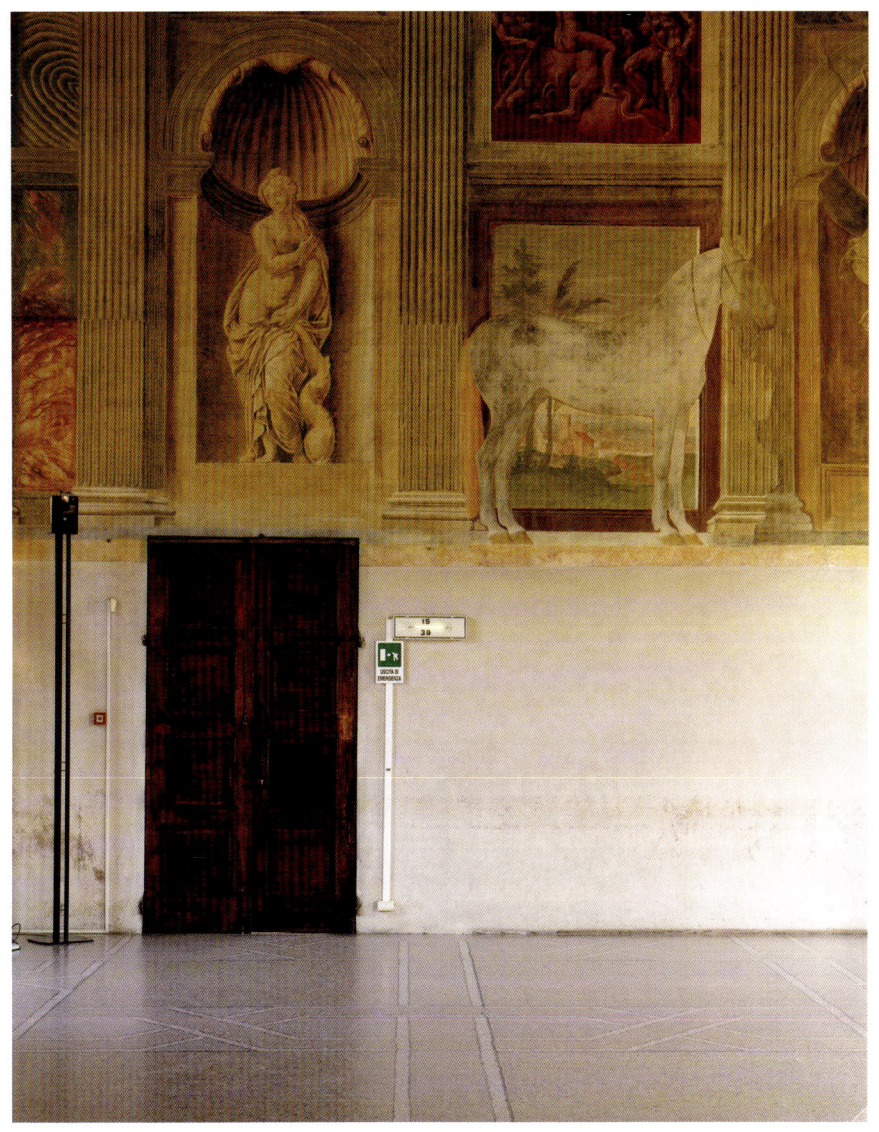

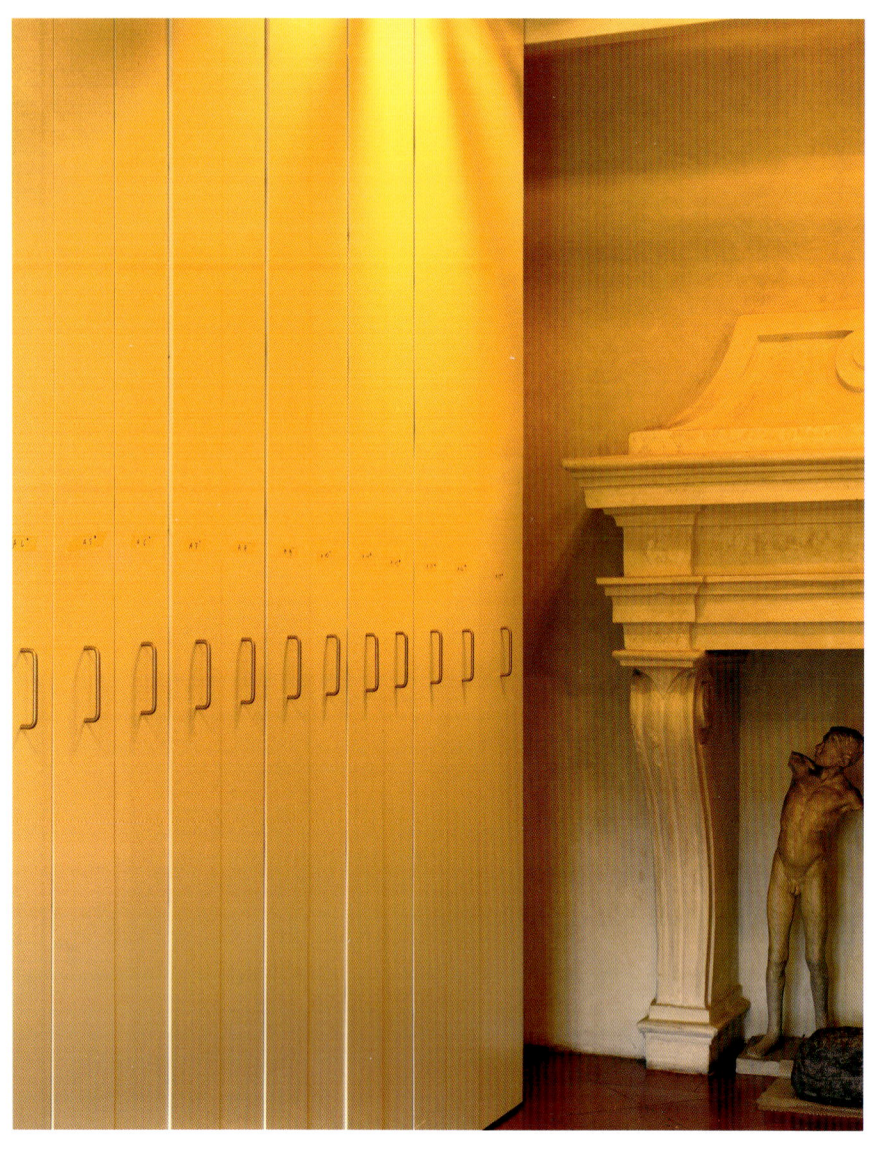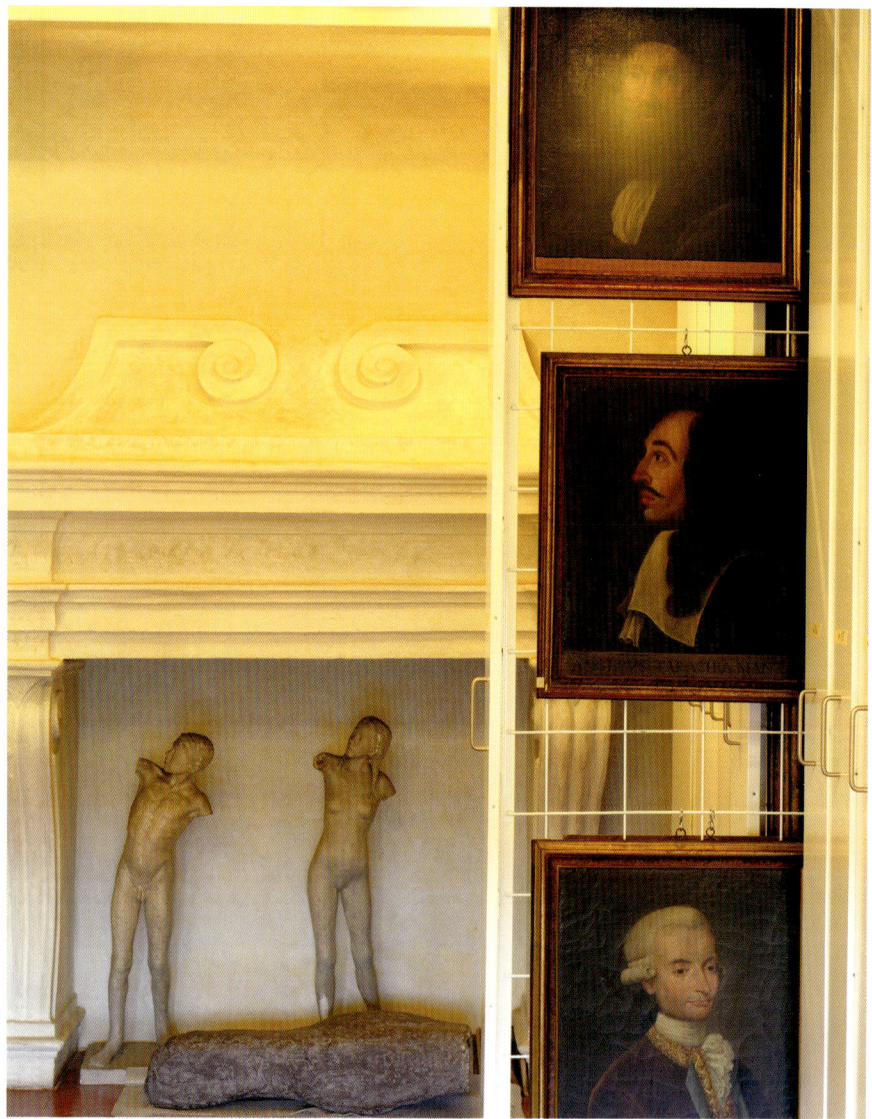

WONDROUS POSSESSIONS

Depositario (Depository) #1, #2, #3,

Palazzo Te, Mantua

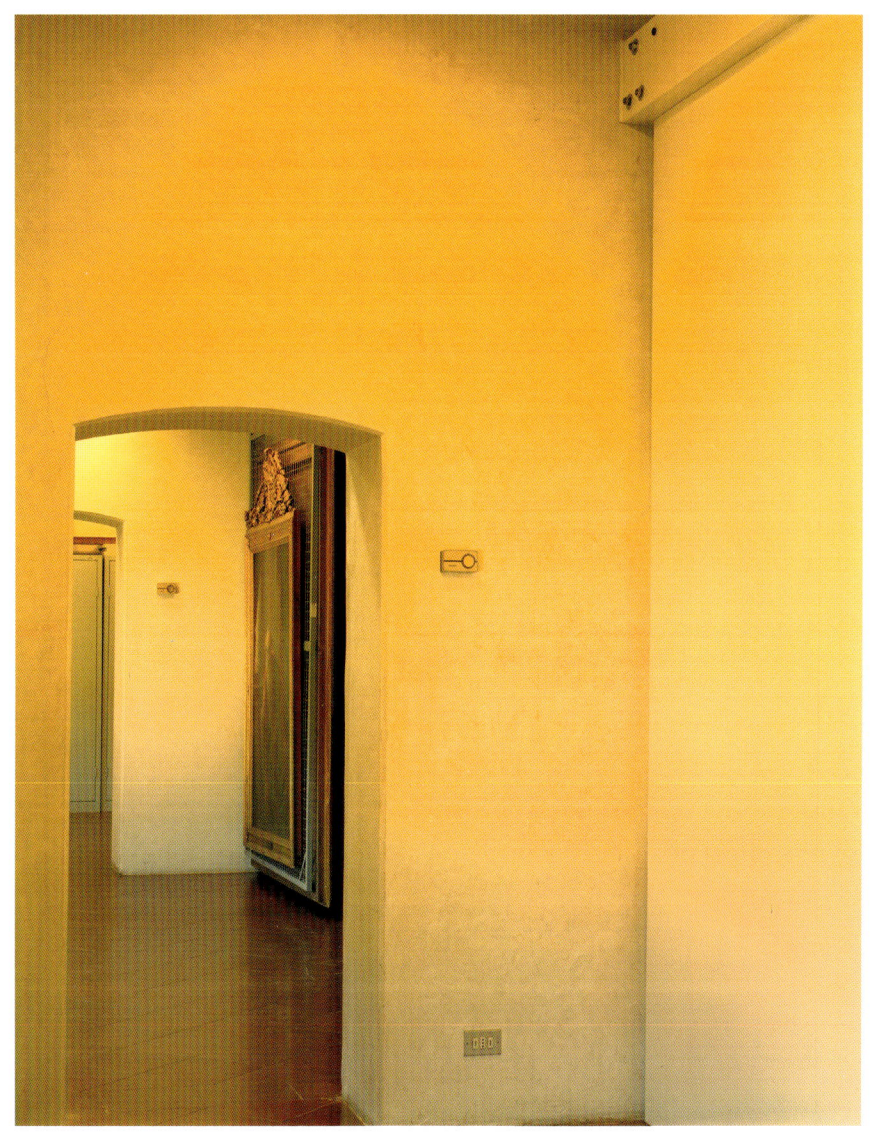

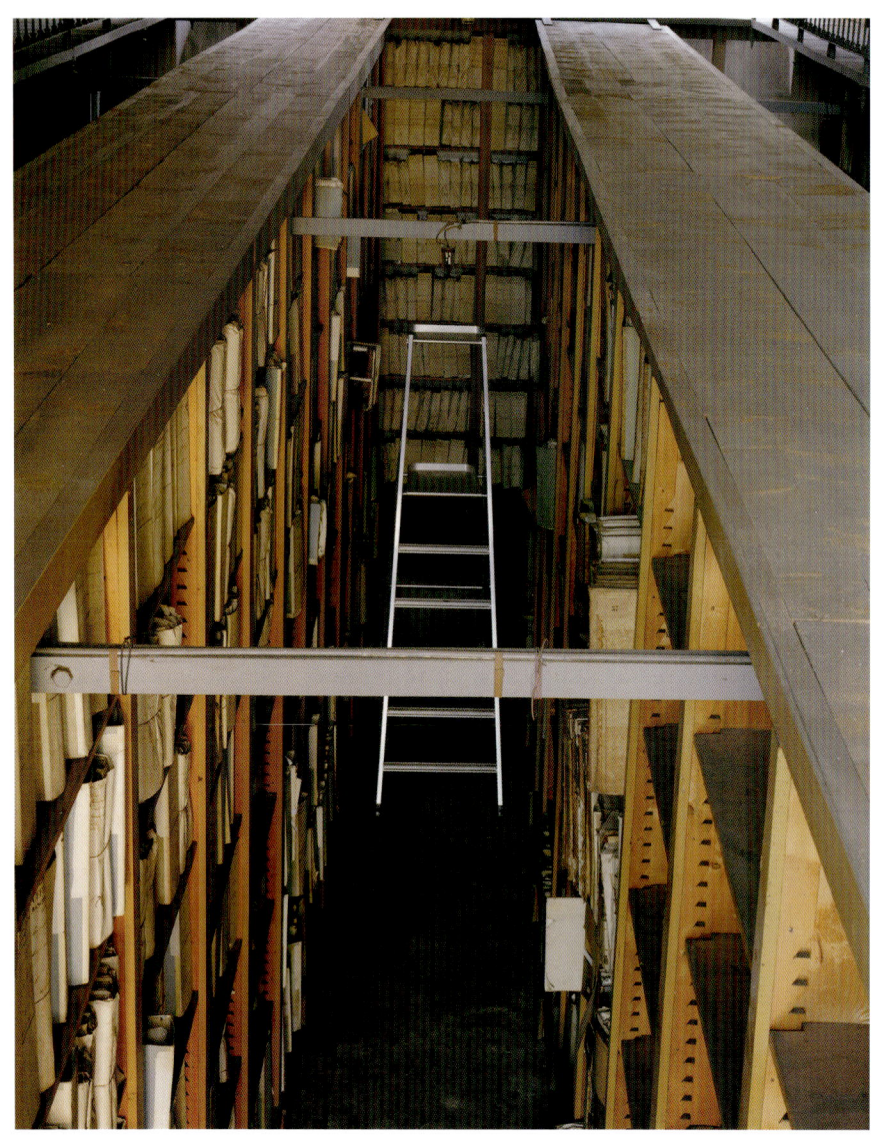
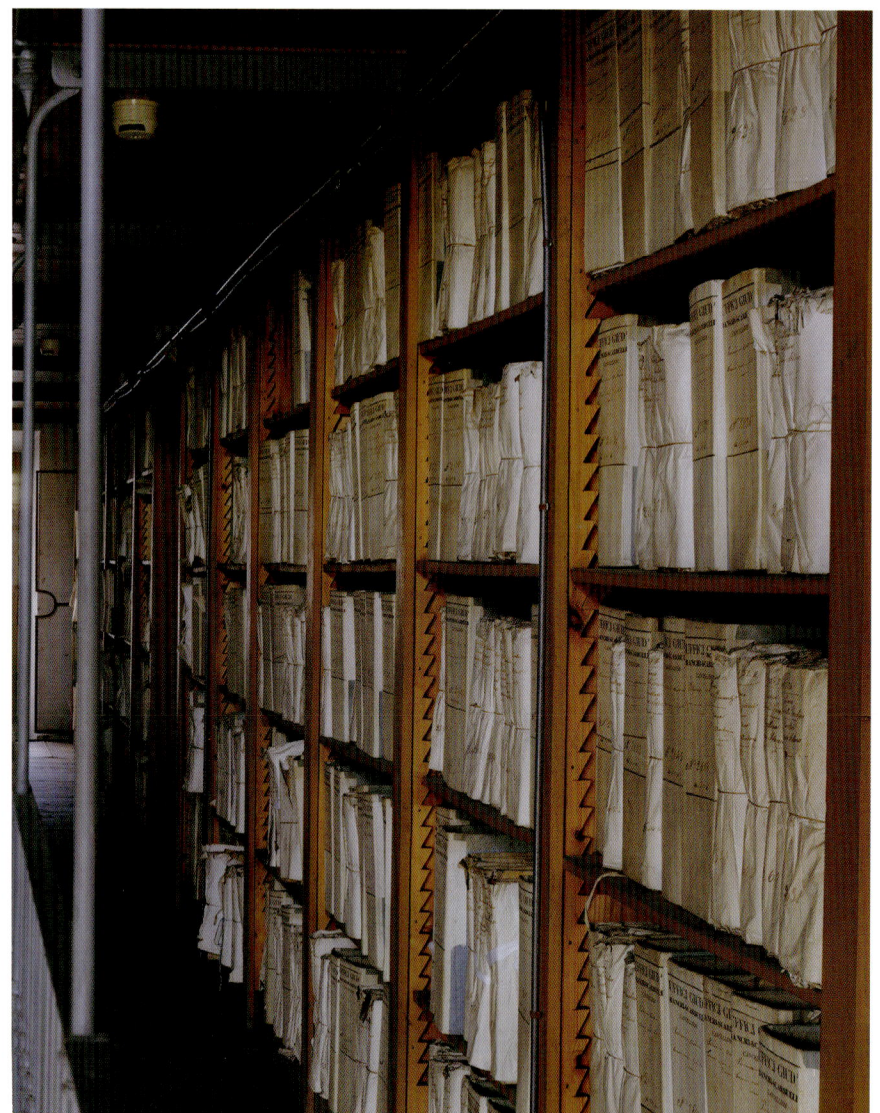

WONDROUS POSSESSIONS

Archivi (Archives) #1, #2, #3,

Archivio di Stato, Mantua

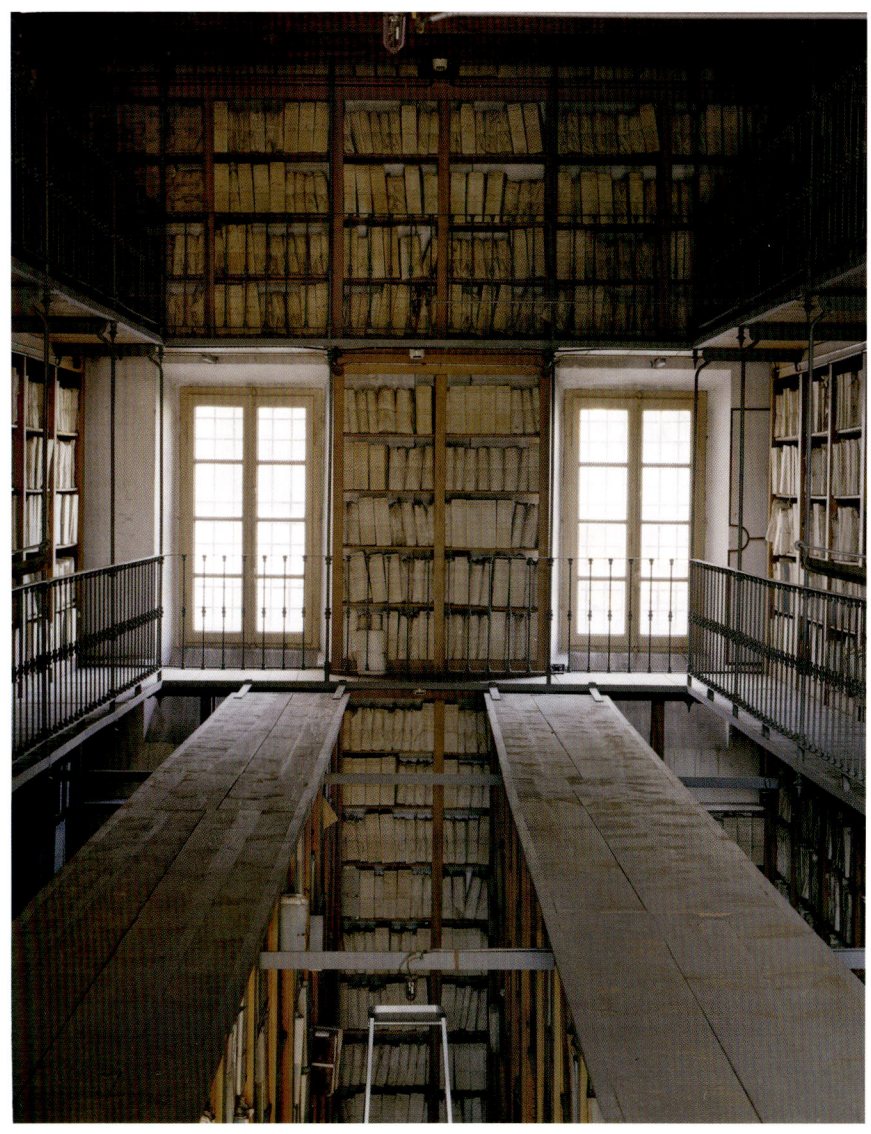

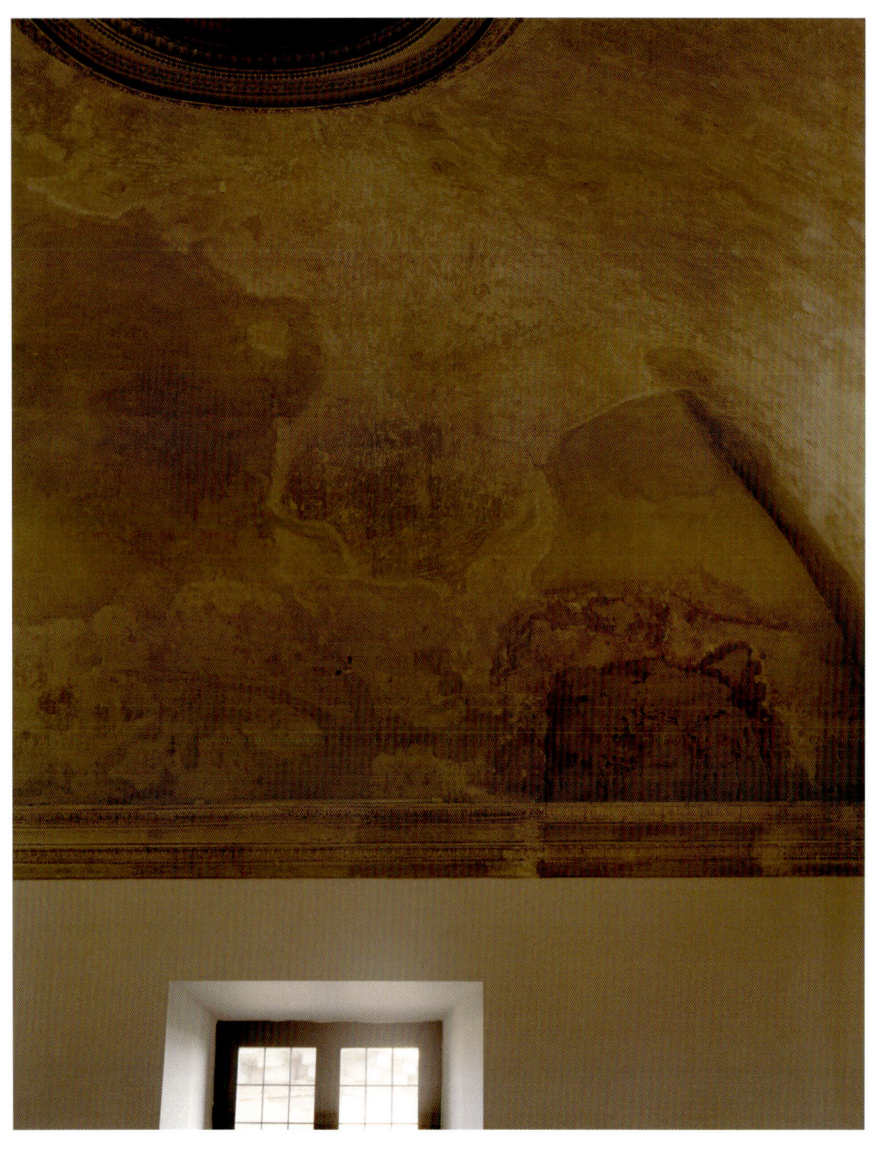 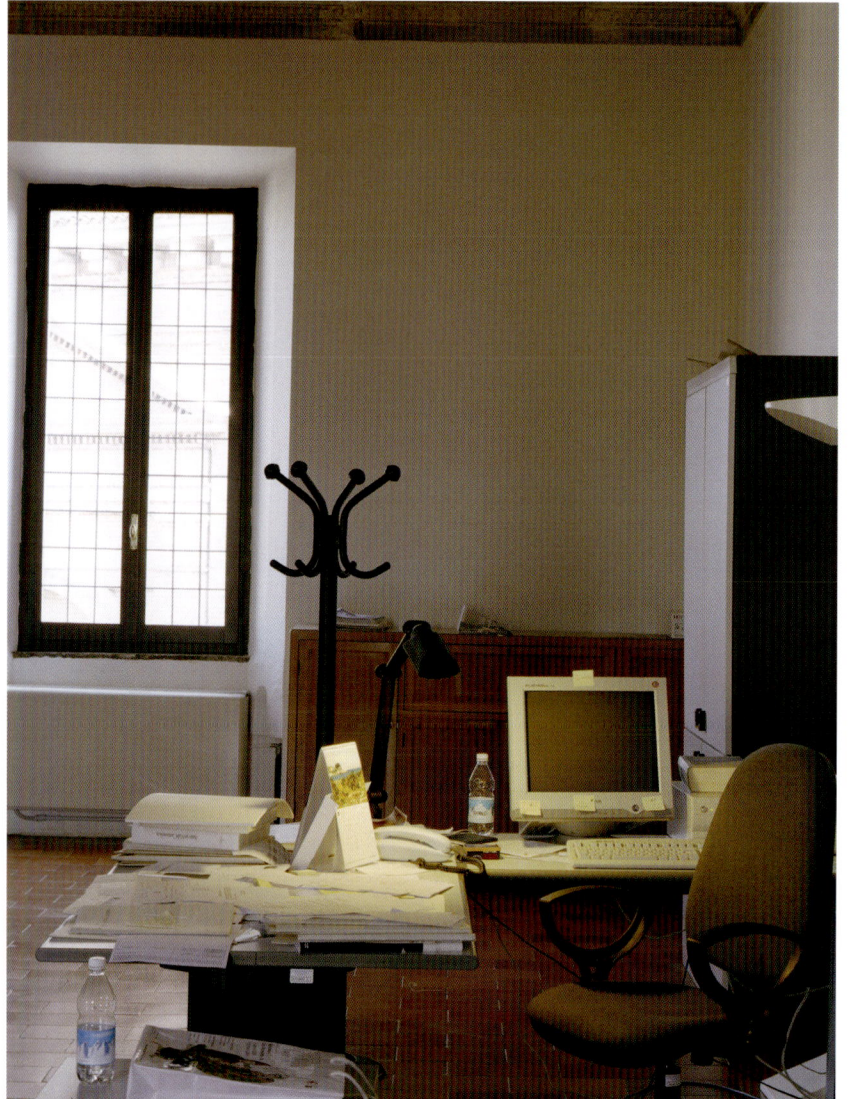

WONDROUS POSSESSIONS

Ufficio (Office) #1, #2, #3,

Palazzo Ducale, Mantua

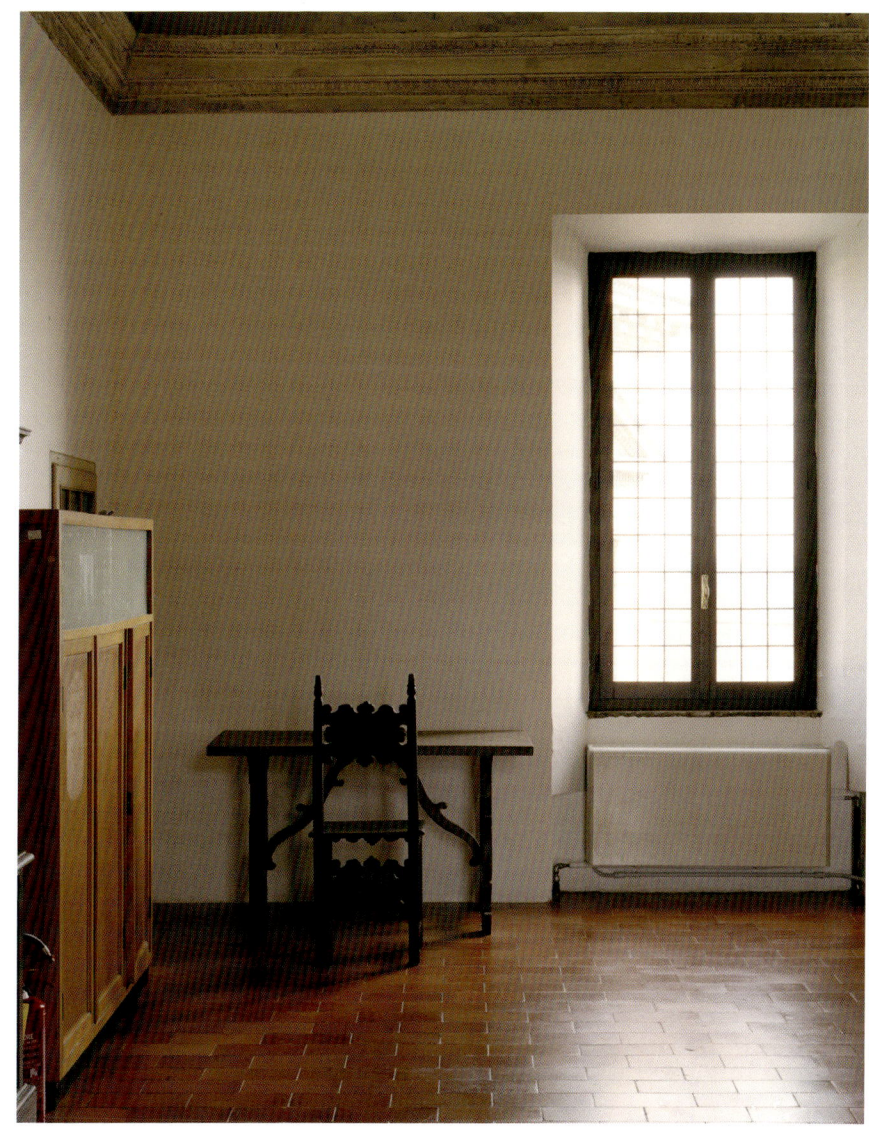

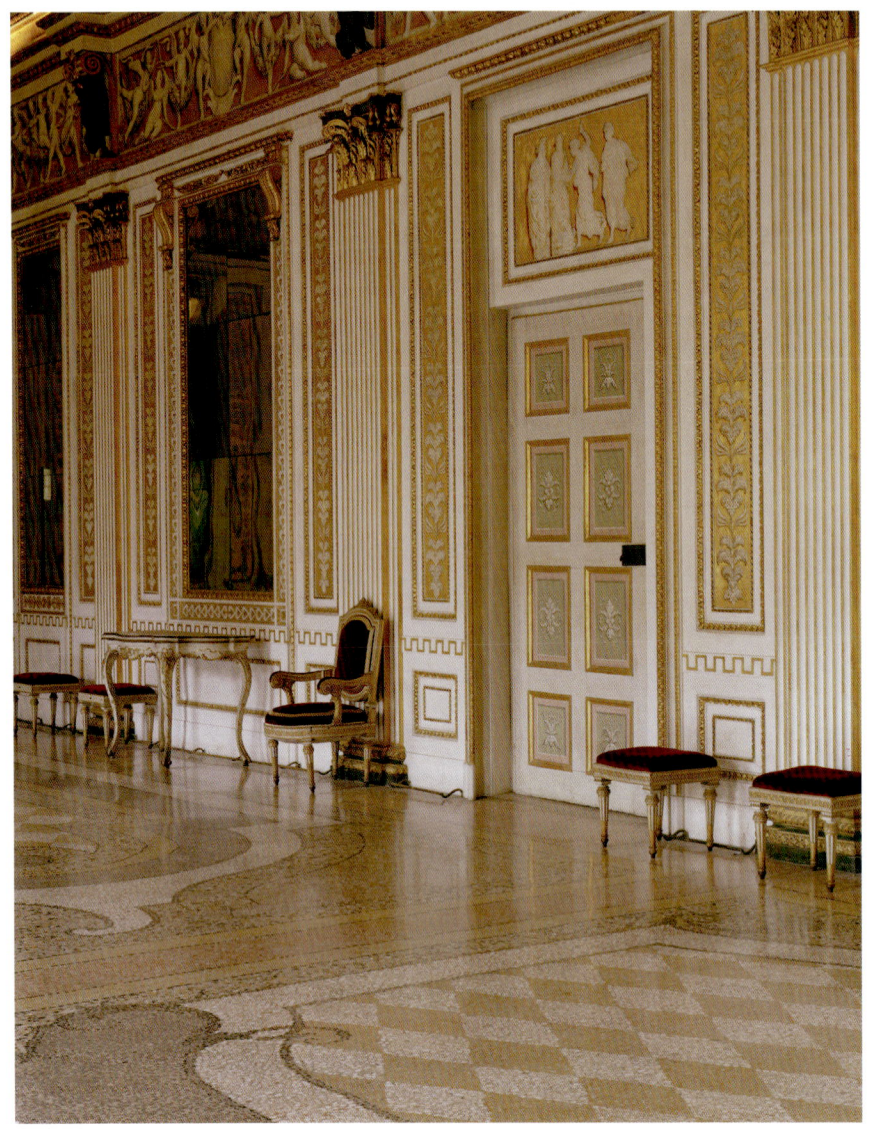
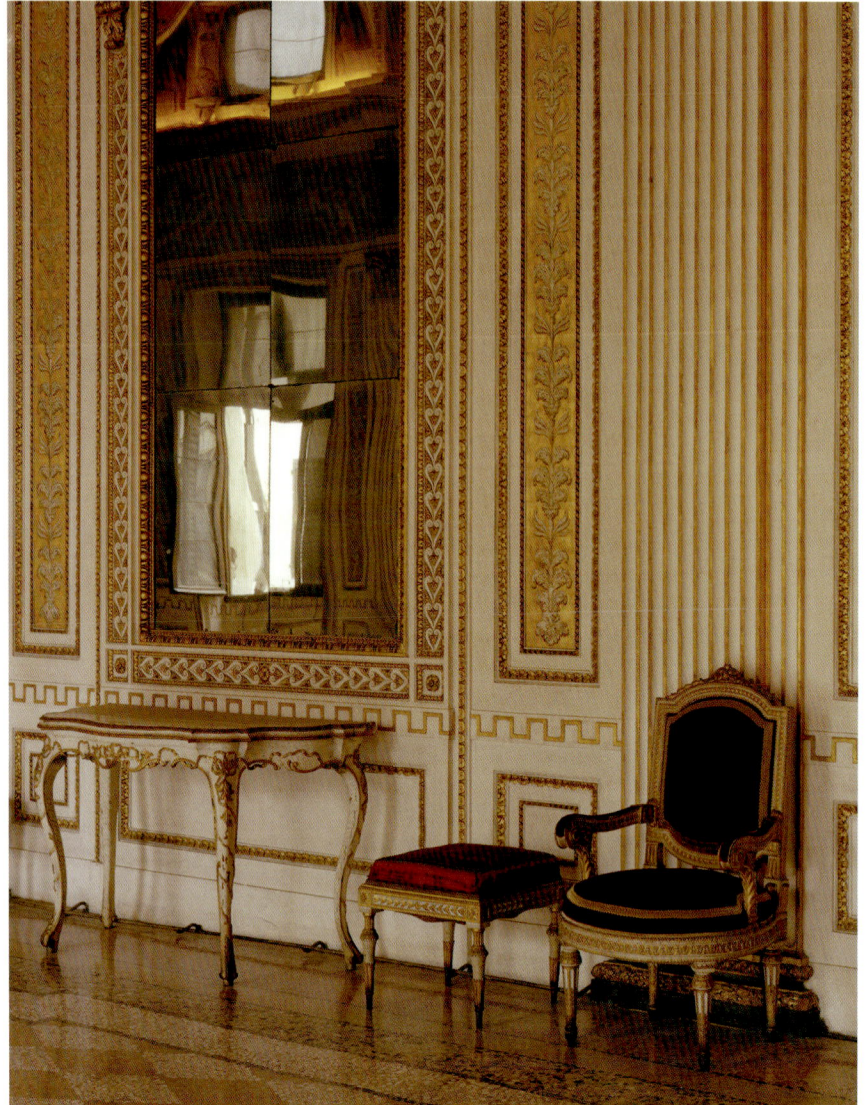

WONDROUS POSSESSIONS

1250mm x 1000mm chromogenic prints, 2010

Galleria degli Specchi (Gallery of Mirrors) #1, #2, #3,
Palazzo Ducale, Mantua

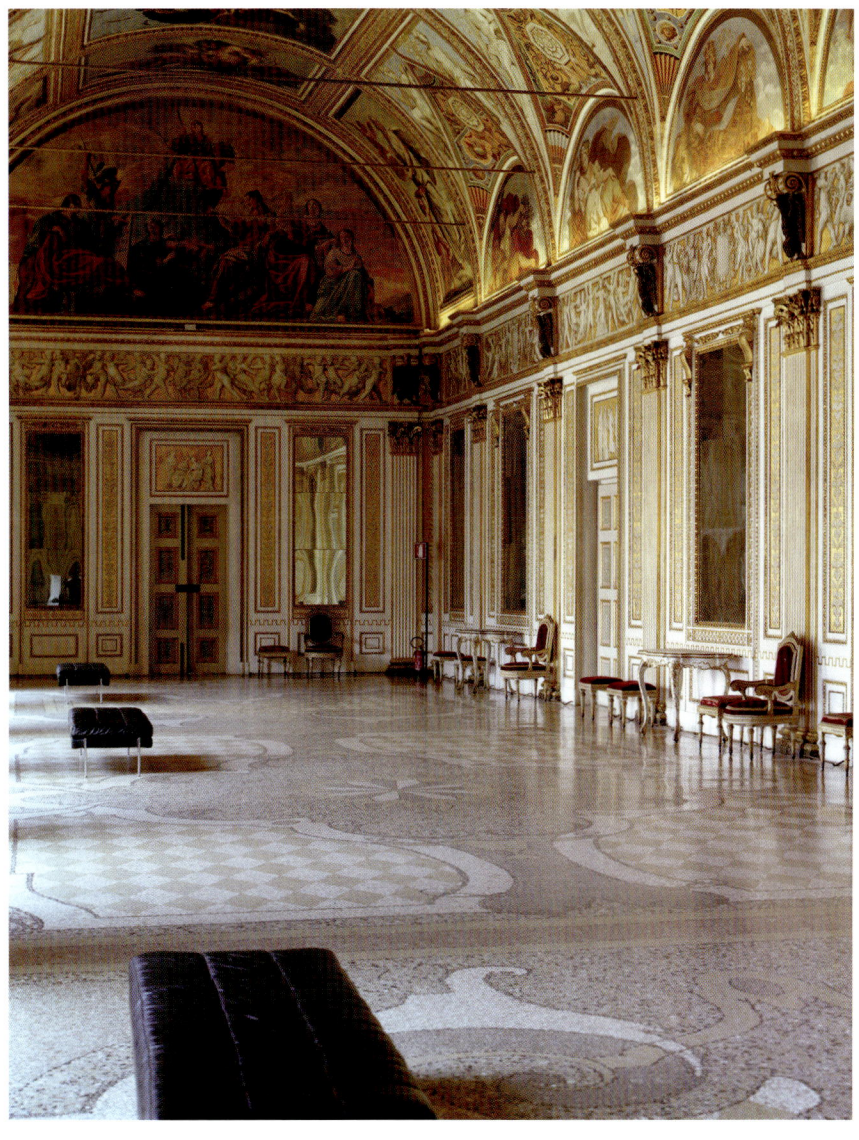

Making images in institutional contexts that reference Italy's history, culture and identity encourages reflection on the intricacies of artworks and our lived relationships with objects that no reproduction can possibly promote. It lends itself to changed questions about conventional theories and perceptions of 'historicity' and produces new understandings. All this rumination—a flow of scholarly, empirical, visual and creative research—is wedded to my practice of photography as an embodied way of thinking. On location, I first examine the complexity of the circumstances of viewing, to precisely consider the notions of time, knowledge, and desire that seem to coalesce in that place. Finally I consider colour, light, composition, angle of view, depth of field and exposure times, format and film stock, while planning for grain structure, paper surface, image size and manner of display.

Like the buildings studied for *Sites of Convergence #1*, Prato's Palazzo Datini—the fourteenth century palace now home to Prato's State Archives—sharpened my appreciation of the importance of ancient civic spaces constructed in the past to Italy's modern urban landscapes. For this reason, the origins of my more recent work hinge on my visits to Prato and Palazzo Vaj. While living in Prato I was able to gain access to museums and cultural institutions with an unprecedented efficiency; both in and beyond Tuscany I could undertake empirical research in places typically restricted to the public. As a consequence, my thinking became informed by new relationships with archivists and conservators whom I met through the Soprintendenze dei Beni Culturali, the government organisations charged with preserving Italy's cultural heritage. I learned that approximately 83 per cent of the offices of the Soprintendenze in Italy are located in historic buildings.

While continuing to pursue site-specific work, my definition of the museum or gallery environment broadened to include lesser-known Italian institutions, and spaces often hidden from the gaze of the non-specialist visitor. Not surprisingly, these too display with fascinating immediacy the layering of different historical fragments and remnants, all reminders of successive generations that can fire the imagination as much as the questioning mind.

The project *Wondrous Possessions* was closely informed by this research, and the insights that followed. The subjects of these images, the palaces constructed by the Gonzaga family in Mantua, and the ex-Jesuit convent which houses the State Archives of Mantua, are in essence 'universal possessions', part of a world patrimony of cultural riches, although as museums or archives they necessarily guard as much as they display the wonders of their collections. *Wondrous Possessions* seeks to evoke the calmly enigmatic atmosphere of these environments. More than my previous work, it is a form of tribute. I have aimed to immerse the viewer in the understated theatricality of settings that also witness the careful daily work of people dedicated to examining and interpreting the past. Such settings are themselves sources for the different perspectives so critical to developing conceptual ideas. The format of the triptych or diptych presents multiple viewpoints, overtly addressing the viewer's memory, curiosity and expectations; asking her or him to pursue some felt 'sense' of the overall spatial continuum that includes the long moment of looking in the present.

Wondrous Possessions was shown at Palazzo Vaj in May 2010, to coincide with the Monash Prato Centre Open Day celebrations. It is clear to me that taking my practice to Prato as a resident artist was instrumental in the creation of these images.

I was able to stay in Prato for the first 6 weeks of the exhibition, having received a grant from the Australian Foundation for Studies in Italy to make the new work that would be shown under the title *Sites of Convergence*. This was a large project comprising three sets of images: together they investigate the aesthetics of communal spaces, and their accumulated significance—across numerous lifetimes, and also across the geographical and cultural trajectories traced by stories of Italian immigration to Australia. The photographs of the first series (see page 24) were taken in Prato.

Within the compact radius of the *centro storico*, Prato is studded with magnificent 'sites of convergence', or sociality, which have served this public purpose more or less continuously for centuries: for example, the monumental frescoed refectory of the Cicognini College; the council hall and other rooms of the Palazzo Comunale; the monastery church of San Niccolò. These days, understandably, these sites are also conserved and promoted amongst the city's architectural or artistic treasures. It was a joy to discover them 'on the doorstep' of Palazzo Vaj, and, through the process of researching and creating the images, to try to examine the means by which these buildings hold in luminous balance the material detail of their historical value, and their adaptation to present uses. The images of *Sites of Convergence #2* and *Sites of Convergence #3* were taken in Australia; in Daylesford and Hepburn Shire, Victoria (#2), and in and around the town of Ingham, Queensland (#3), both areas with a heritage very strongly tied to particular Italian immigrant communities.

One of the unique advantages of a residency at the Monash Prato Centre is the opportunity for interaction with the scholarly, student and local communities that the Centre attracts. Daniella Lamberini's reflections on *Impossible Gaze* increased my awareness of my so-called 'antipodean point of view': a tendency to treat architectural space according to western European traditions identified with landscape painting, privileging depth and breadth. This is an anecdotal example of the wider intellectual influences that I became interested to absorb into my practice through living and working in Prato under the aegis of the Centre.

Often these influences emerged from conversations begun on the splendid staircase at Palazzo Vaj, or from memorable excursions. The commentary and critique so necessary to my methodology could take place spontaneously, as part of being 'based' at the Monash Centre. For instance, it was while at Prato that I visited the town of Arezzo for the first time, accompanying a group of Monash Art and Design students led by Bronwyn Stocks, a scholar of medieval and Renaissance Italian art. With the students, I was able to contemplate and discuss the masterful fresco cycle by Piero della Francesca in the San Francesco Basilica, drawn into the world of their meanings by Bronwyn's combination of excitement and expertise. At Prato's Luigi Pecci Centre for Contemporary Art, I had the rare chance to see works by contemporary German photographer Thomas Struth (I had studied and written about his work in my doctoral thesis of 2003–04), and encountered the work of Italian photographer Massimo Vitali for the first time, finding his mural-sized prints exhilarating in their description of the 'human terrain'. On such occasions, I was benefiting from the provocative array of artistic precedents that are so intrinsic to Italy's—and Tuscany's—cultural status. Back in the studio, these precedents hover amongst constant sources of inspiration, for savouring, testing, interpreting. Of course another, simpler source of inspiration in Prato is the pleasurable act of walking along Via Pugliesi as a temporary 'local'.

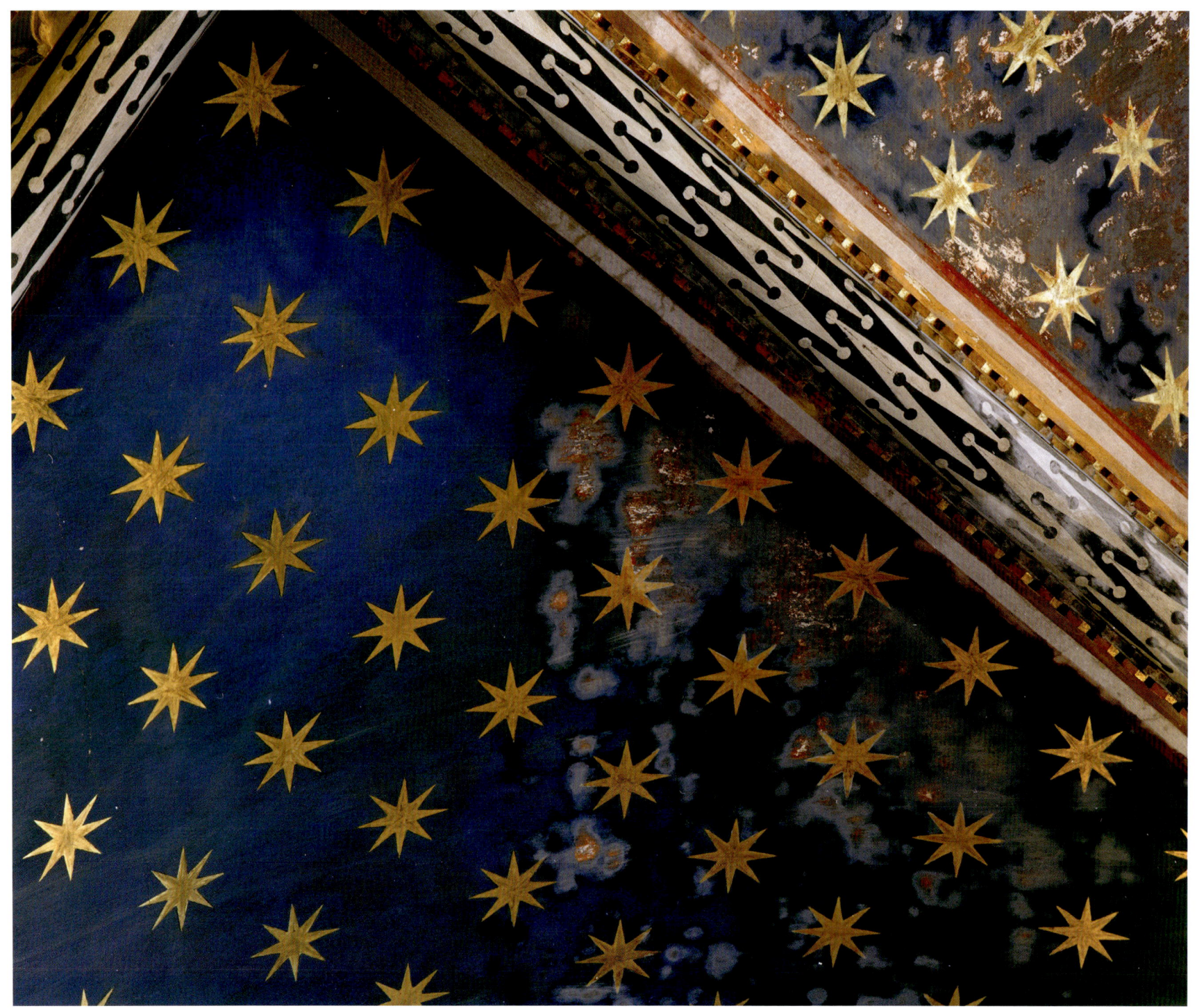

IMPOSSIBLE GAZE

Impossible Gaze #2, Room L—The Carrand Room, Museo Nazionale del Bargello, Florence

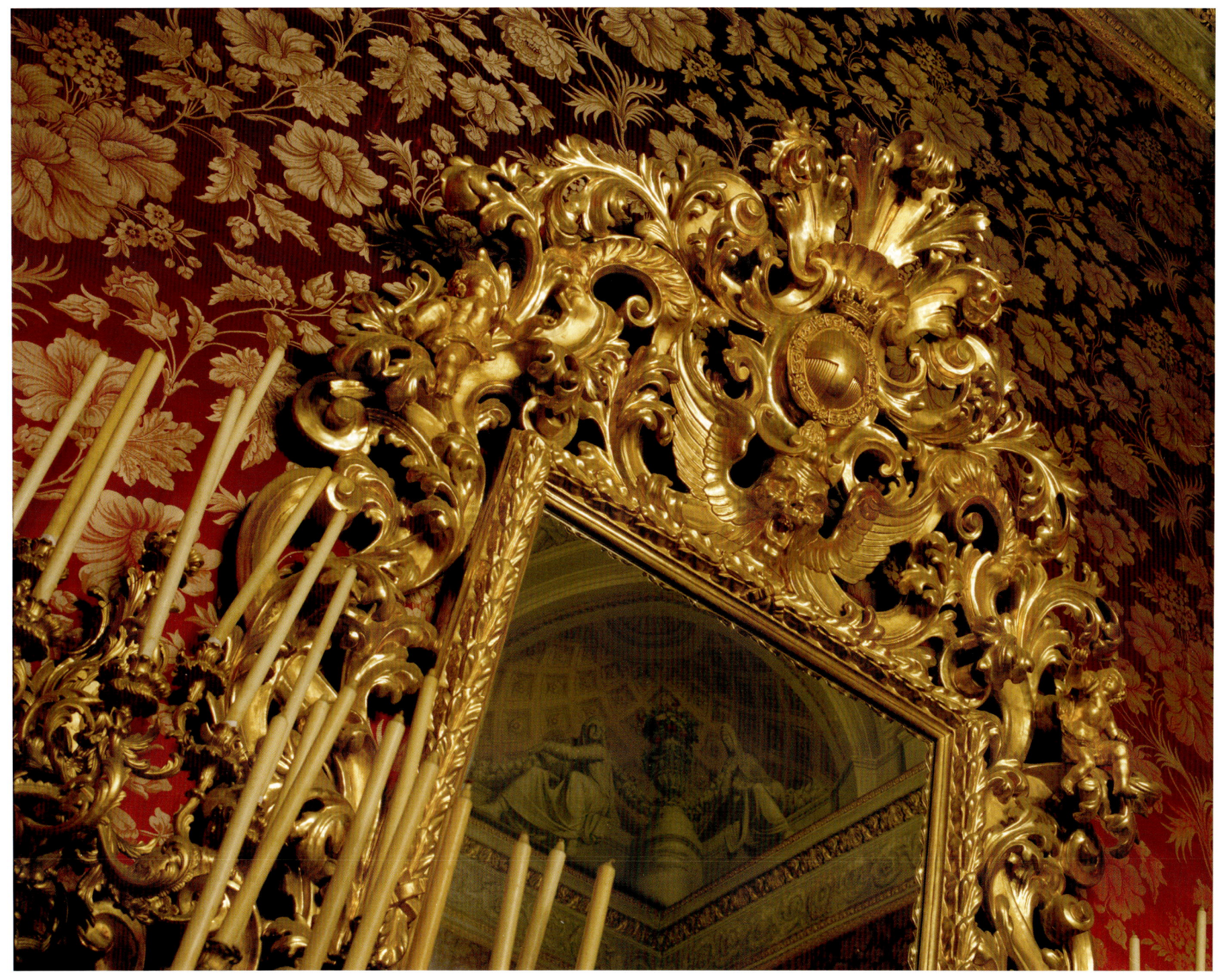

IMPOSSIBLE GAZE

Impossible Gaze #1, Room II—The Throne Room, Appartamenti Reali, Palazzo Pitti, Florence

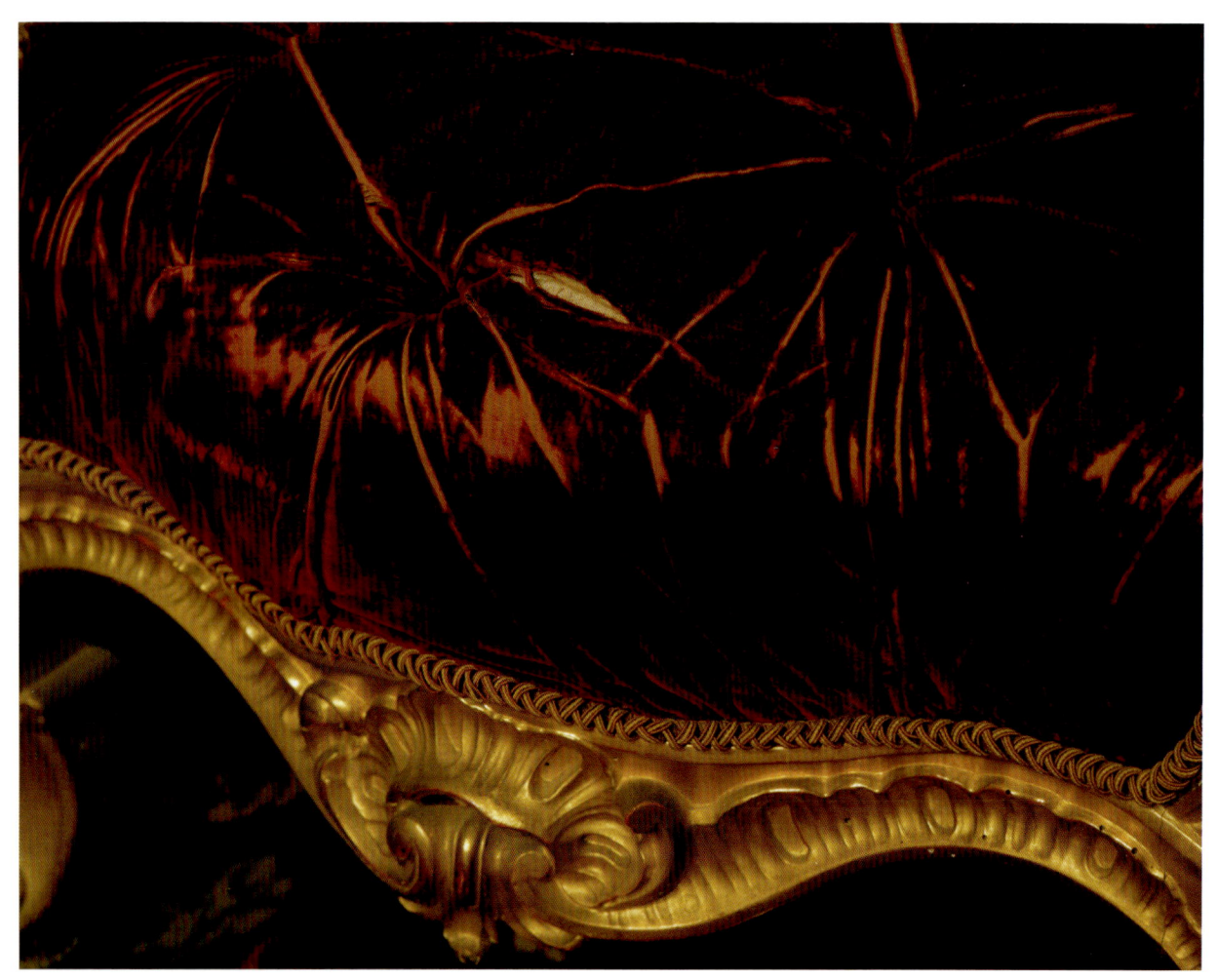

IMPOSSIBLE GAZE 1020mm x 1220mm chromogenic prints, 2002

Impossible Gaze #15, Room XII—The Red Room, Appartamento del Re, Palazzo Pitti, Florence

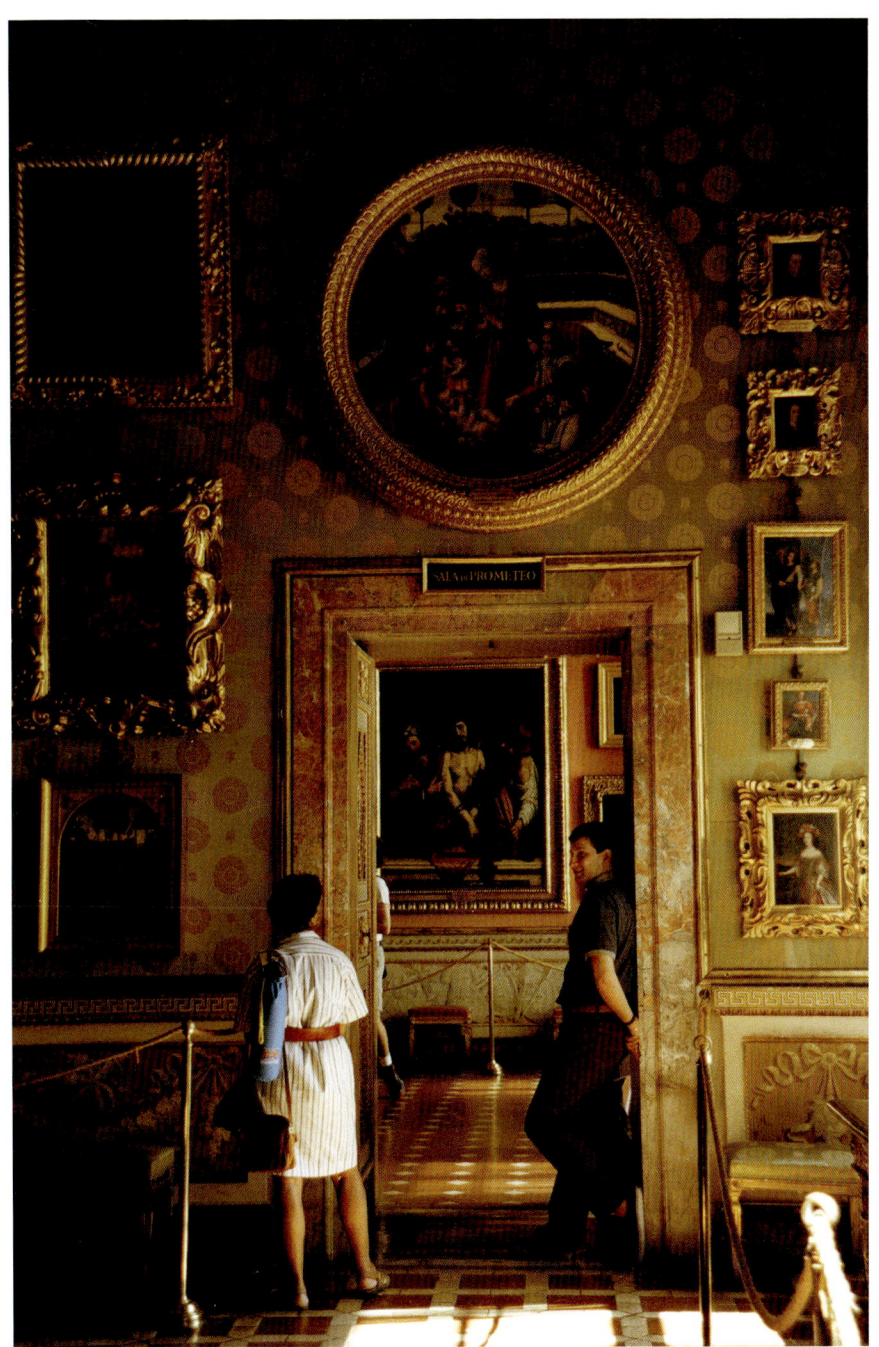 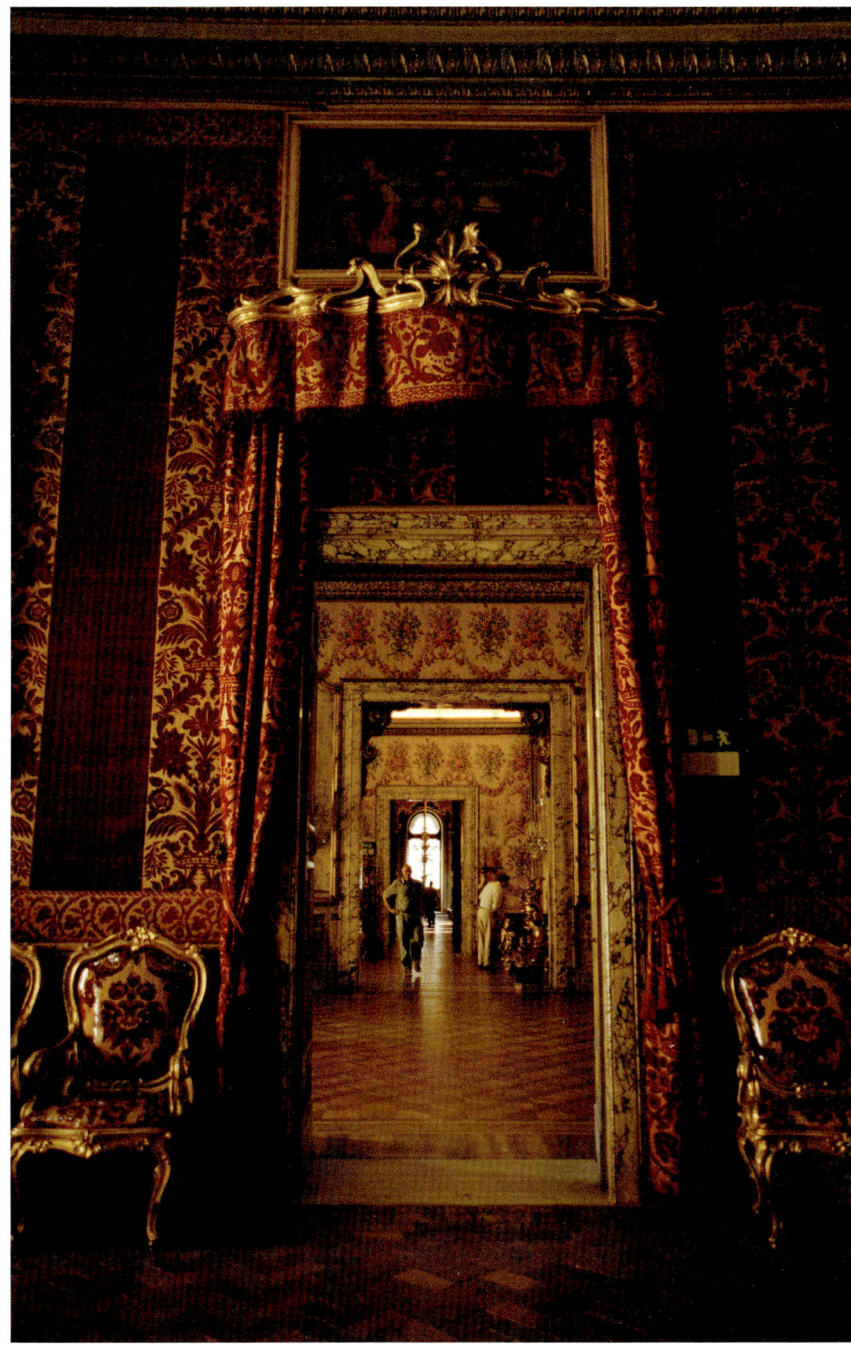

BEFORE THE MUSEUM   1500mm x 1000mm chromogenic prints, 2000

Before the Museum #1, Galleria Palatina, Palazzo Pitti, Florence

Before the Museum #3, Galleria Doria Pamphilj, Palazzo Doria Pamphilj, Rome

The images of *Before the Museum* foreground the insistent pattern of frames and framing devices found in some of the most widely recognised museological spaces in Florence and Rome: for example the Palazzo Pitti, the Palazzo Vecchio, and the San Marco Museum, in Florence, the Galleria Doria Pamphili and the Vatican Museums in Rome. Each image includes human figures, those of contemporary visitors, whose proximity to the Renaissance artworks highlights the aesthetic effect of surroundings dense with historical information, ornament, design. By their scale, the figures literally provide some 'measure' of these remarkable surroundings.

The first of my solo exhibitions seen in Italy, *Before the Museum* was shown at Florence's Studio Arts Centers International (SACI) Gallery in 2001, and in 2002 at Sydney's Casa d'Italia. For the project that followed, called *Impossible Gaze*, my practice concentrated on Florentine museums—once again as spaces evoked by art history textbooks, and by standard guidebooks and postcards for Italy. Yet the images of *Impossible Gaze* interrogate the photographic close-up for its capacity to abstract fine features of the museum interiors, while providing evidence of the material resilience—and instability—of the sumptuous decoration and furniture.

It was *Impossible Gaze* that travelled to the Western Australian Museum in Perth in 2003—and brought about my introduction to the Monash Prato Centre. With the benefit of hindsight, I can say that this introduction had an ineffable impact on my personal and professional development.

Later in 2003 I lived in Milan for three months, having been awarded a residency funded by the Australia Council for the Arts at Viafarini Contemporary Art Space. I first travelled to Prato at that time, to speak with Bill Kent and see the spaces that he had proposed for exhibiting *Impossible Gaze* at Palazzo Vaj. It was a thrill to visit Palazzo Vaj, and to note its bustling location so near the Piazza Duomo, the hub of the *centro storico*. I was also already aware of Prato's significant contemporary art scene, and of the well-deserved reputation of the Luigi Pecci Centre for Contemporary Art.

Impossible Gaze was shown at Palazzo Vaj from June 2004 to July 2005, and formally opened by the historian of medieval architecture Daniella Lamberini, Associate Professor of Architectural Restoration at the University of Florence. A catalogue was printed, making available my introductory essay in Italian and English. The work was hung along the corridors of the first floor, and in the panelled room known as the Sala Giochi.

As mentioned, *Impossible Gaze* addressed the observable residues of the past in palatial suites and chambers. Therefore I couldn't have wished for a better context for exhibition of this work in Italy. The sensitively renovated interiors of the Palazzo Vaj felt truly sympathetic to the images; to their conceptual basis, and to the 'grand' dimensions of the photographic prints. Moreover, Prato's ongoing dialogue with Florence as a destination for cultural tourism—its proximity to the famous museums in which the photographs had been taken—gave the exhibition an unplanned local relevance.

IMAGINATION AND THE IMMEDIACY OF HISTORY

Jo-Anne Duggan

In 2009 I was named the first artist in residence of the Monash Prato Centre by the current Centre Director, Loretta Baldassar. I took up the residency in 2010, and in countless ways it proved to be a timely and meaningful development from my past achievements and longstanding focus on Italian material culture and history. My practice as a photomedia artist—and the research and reflection that my image-making always involves—has been profoundly influenced by the heritage associated with Italian Renaissance painting. Since 1997, travel and residency in Italy have continued to deepen this influence. I had met Loretta in 2003, when the Australasian Centre for Italian Studies (ACIS) Conference coincided with an exhibition of my work at the Western Australian Museum in Perth. Since 2003, when I first visited the Monash Prato Centre, I have always been warmly welcomed into a dynamic community gathered at Palazzo Vaj; my connection with Centre has resulted in the growth of treasured friendships. For weeks or months at a time, these have had as their setting the prismatic grain of Prato's urban landscape and the vigour and diversity of Prato's cultural scene, a scene proud of continuities with town life in the city's past. My association with the Monash Centre has also generated audiences for my exhibitions of a range, size, and intensity of interest that I had not previously experienced. Working in Prato made it possible to refresh my fascination with persistent themes in my research. It transformed my self-confidence, such that in the project *Wondrous Possessions* I was able to create—and exhibit at Palazzo Vaj—images characterised by a new quietude and breadth of vision; a new integration of ideas.

Since the late 1990s I have studied the habitual ways in which museum or gallery environments structure our encounter with historic artworks: this might be described as the most sustained theme of my work. In Italy, the viewing experience is not an engagement with singular objects. Rather it is governed and enriched by the intricate conditions of place and culture, with historic backdrops that have been constructed over centuries; repeatedly rebuilt, restored, or left to the forces of ruin and decay. So many of the panel paintings, frescoes, sculptures and furnishings that remain *in situ* continue to belong to everyday rituals, kept in circulation through centuries of shared experience inside or outside the civic buildings, *piazze*, palaces, cathedrals and churches.

information and communication technologies. The painting, sculpture, photography, collage, film and installation works of *Stranger Geography* were presented in the first-floor studios of the Palazzo Vaj. An exhibition of student work on similar themes was presented in the Sala Toscana, and so the mood of the opening formalities—apertifs on the *terrazza*, speeches in Italian and English—was reportedly heightened by the students' exhilaration.

The foregoing account of visual art and music-related activity during Centre's first decade is necessarily a brief outline of particular highlights and continuities. Even so, it leaves no doubt that the presence of art and practising artists has remained integral to the pulse of daily life and planning at the Centre. Evidently, the Centre deserves its reputation as a place where creativity as directed into artistic disciplines is deeply valued. From this standpoint, the announcement of a formal Artist in Residence program on Open Day 2010 seems at once a logical development, and new evidence of a commitment to contemporary art as a facet of the Centre's unique identity and enterprise. Recounting details of the Open Day in the Prato press, Alessandra Petrelli noted Loretta Baldassar's announcement of the Artist in Residence program first amongst the Centre's 'substantial' and 'interesting new initiatives' sure to 'enrich firstly the university and therefore also the cultural life and "scene" ("*movida*") of the city' of Prato.

In 2004, describing the opening of Jo-Anne Duggan's exhibition *Impossible Gaze*, Bill Kent noted that Duggan 'was in effect an artist in residence for some six weeks in June and July'. Duggan's own account of this time bears out this observation. During Annamaria Pagliaro's directorship, a long paragraph on the *Mates* exhibition in the June 2007 Centre report stated, 'Mr Kevin Shaw was visiting artist at the centre for the [show's] duration'. Likewise, in May 2009, Loretta Baldassar designated Chinese artist Flora Fuljena as 'an informal artist in residence'. These remarks point up an awareness of the desirability of a formal Artist in Residence program at the Centre. Such a program defends and benefits the humanist tradition of welcoming the artist as a potent contributor to debate and exchange of ideas. As with visiting fellows, a resident artist can complement the recurrent, often strenuous bursts of activity occasioned by short-term visitors with a more sustained presence, particularly because the residency is site-specific: in addition to studio and exhibition spaces, the artist is offered a furnished apartment on the third floor of the Palazzo Vaj.

Documents outlining the program insist on the diversity of the artforms it can provide for: literature, performance, theatre, music, and curatorial practices, as well as the variform media of visual art. The aim to 'showcase Australian artists' is affirmed. Yet perhaps most excitingly, as conceptualised by Loretta Baldassar, the Artist in Residence program has scope beyond this aim. That is, in keeping with sensitivity to the processes of cultural globalisation and localisation in contemporary art practice, the program has potential to nurture relationships established through memoranda of understanding between Monash University and partner institutions—and bring to Prato artists from around the world. The prospect of the great diversity of their creative responses to the Centre, its setting, and issues of importance to the city and province, is compelling indeed.

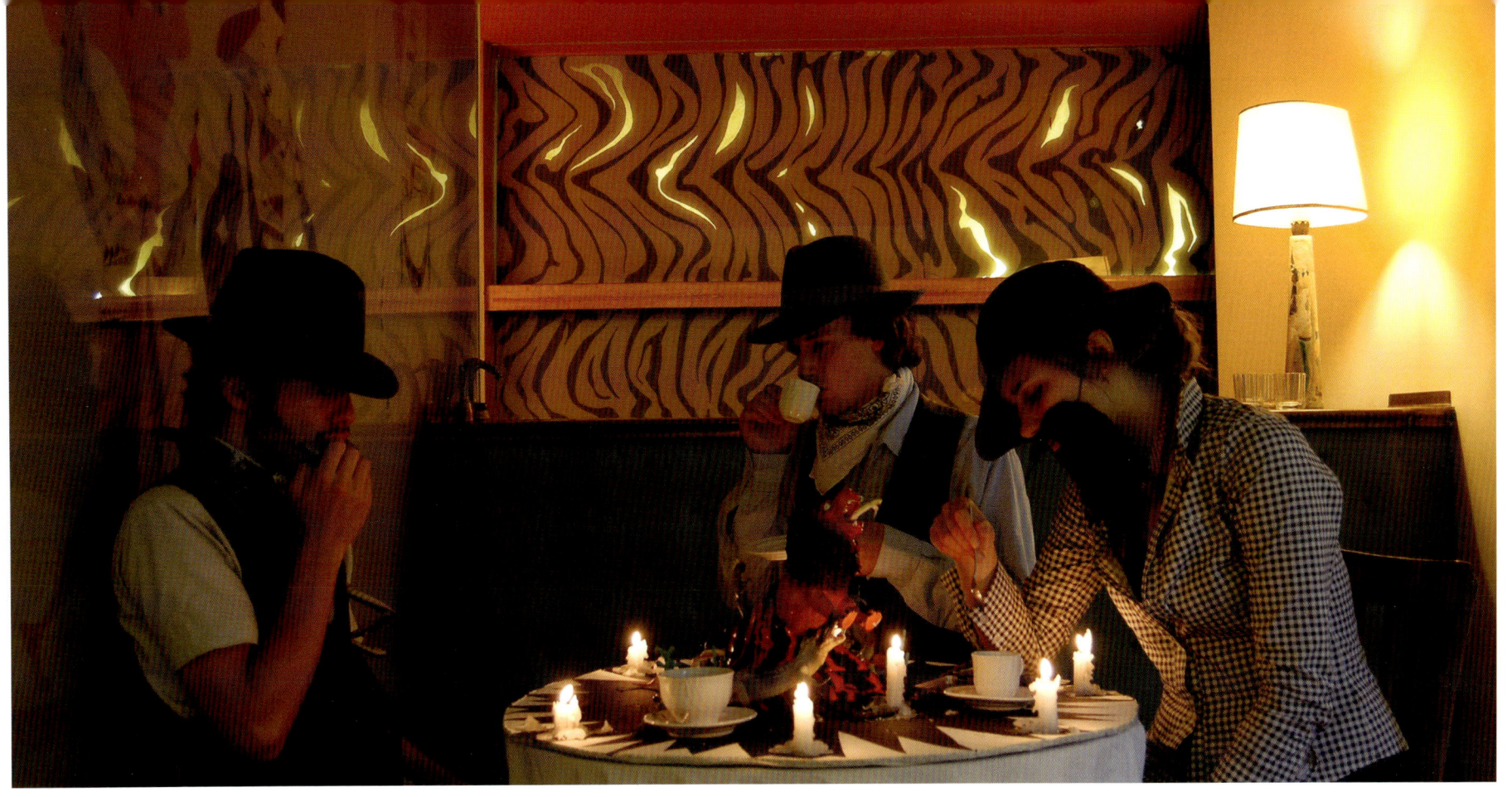

Still from *Molto Morte* 2006–07 created by Safari Team (Blaine Cooper, Jon Oldmeadow and Lillian O'Neil), filmed in Prato, Lake Mungo and Melbourne. © Safari Team

in Melbourne, Sydney and Montreal. *Molto Morte* merits mention here because, with the help of Nicola Pietroniro, the long-serving porter of the Palazzo Vaj, it was shot partly inside the Palazzo Vaj, in the Salone Grollo, the Piccolo Bar, and the cellar. Pietroniro also willingly provided the original voiceover in resonant Italian. *Molto Morte* represents one amongst now countless imaginative reactions to the design, aesthetic and location of the Palazzo Vaj observable in student artwork since 2001. If the exhibitions chronicled over the past decade create an impression of walls in a near constant state of transformation, the Art and Design students' interventions animate the spaces of the Centre's in memory and the mind's eye.

When feasible, a touring exhibition might be brought into coincidence with a studio subject in Art and Design, expanding the frame of reference for the students' work. This occurred, for example, in 2007, with *Stranger Geography*, a group show of 15 artists from Italy, UK, USA and Australia which was warmly received by Prato's art-going public, art associations and local government. The invitation to *Stranger Geography* described the Palazzo Vaj as 'an ideal venue or cross-roads for the presentation of new works by this group of international practitioners'. Curated by Kit Wise, the exhibition had been seen at Kingsgate Gallery in London earlier in 2007, under the title *Strange Geography*; it explored ideas of place with reference to a global context and the flourishing of

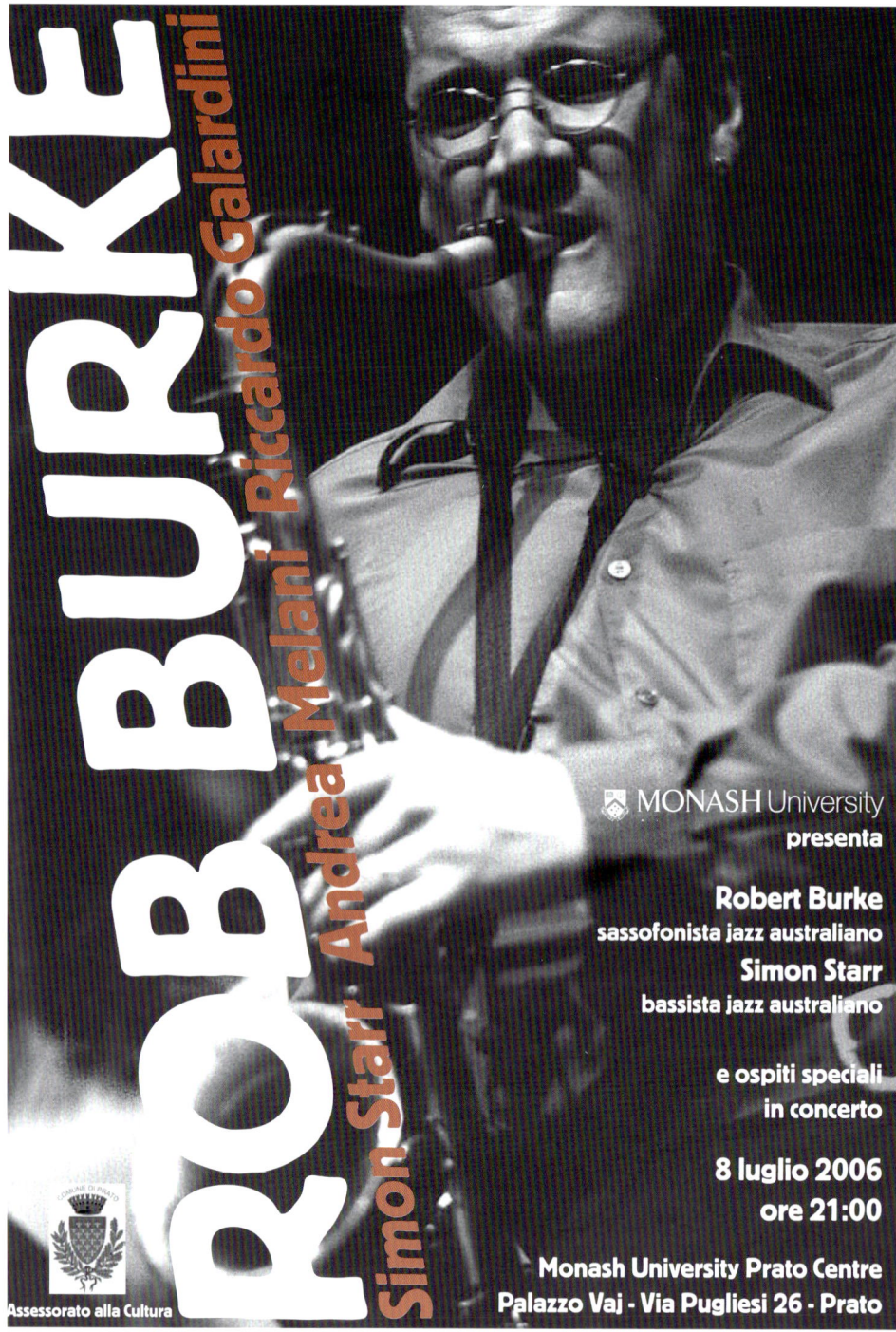

2006 jazz concert poster. Design © Robert Burke

In mid-2006, saxophonist Robert Burke, at that time Coordinator of Jazz and Popular Studies Monash's School of Music-Conservatorium, presented a free concert with Simon Starr on double bass, and other guest jazz musicians.

Burke returned to the Centre in 2007, with 26 Monash students of instrumental music, for the first 'Jazz at Prato' program. This biennial program now alternates with the classical 'Chamber Music at Prato' program, which similarly involves collaboration with the staff and students of the 'Giuseppe Verdi' Music School. In recent years, the Salone has served as a venue for the Metastasio Theatre's annual season of 'Metastasio Jazz' in February and March.

A regular counterpoint to the Centre's main schedule of performances and exhibitions is provided by the students and staff who visit the Centre in association with the academic programs of Monash's Faculty of Art and Design. With the benefit of the Centre's studio spaces, 'in the centre of Tuscany', as Bill Kent liked to say, they are 'by implication' artists in residence during their stay in Prato. Their studies usually entail a chance to exhibit new work, or work-in-progress, in the Palazzo Vaj. Kit Wise, Senior Lecturer in the Department of Fine Arts, has observed, 'contemporary art operates in an international, globalised realm. In Prato the [Faculty of Art and Design] students take that first step towards making work that speaks beyond their usual geographic and cultural boundaries. Study in Prato has always represented an opportunity for them to shapeshift'.

In 2006, for Blaine Cooper, Jon Oldmeadow and Lillian O'Neil (known as the 'Safari Team') such 'shapeshifting' involved creating the first version of *Molto Morte*, a witty short film inspired by the Italian legacy of the 'Spaghetti Western', which has since been shown at festivals

CONTEXT FOR THE ARTIST IN RESIDENCE PROGRAM

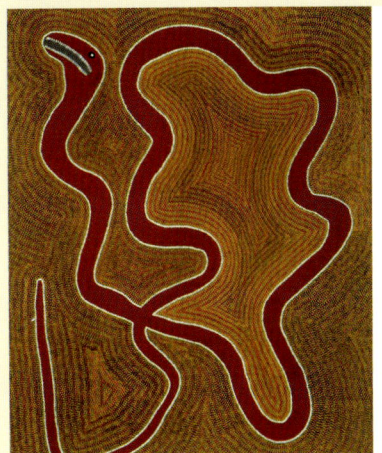

Invitation, *Aborigena* at the Antiche Stanze di Santa Caterina 2003, showing the painting by Mick Namarari Tjapaltjarri, *Water Serpent Dreaming at the Salt Lake Site of Piltartinya* 1986, 153cm x 122cm, part of the Gabrielle Pizzi Collection, Melbourne. Invitation © Gallery Gabrielle Pizzi; image © Estate of the artist 2011 licensed by Aboriginal Artists Agency Limited.

The photographs of the *Mates Collection* by Australian artist and anthropologist Kevin Shaw pay a deeply personal tribute to the indigenous people and landscape of Western Australia's Kimberley region. *Mates* was a feature of the international, interdisciplinary symposium 'Imagined Australia' hosted by the Centre; it was shown in the Palazzo Vaj and across the road at Dryphoto, generating opportunities for further exhibitions of the work in Turin and elsewhere in Europe. A selection from the *Mates Collection* was presented once more at the Palazzo Vaj on Open Day 2010, one of three exhibitions presented on that occasion.

Assisted through the patronage of the Prato Province and the Comune di Prato, larger touring exhibitions from Australia have continued to foster close cooperation with local organisations, in ways that extend the public reach of the artwork, and, in turn, pinpoint the Palazzo Vaj on any cultural itinerary through Prato's historical centre. A more recent example of such a show is *From Here To Eternity: Contemporary Tapestries from the Victorian Tapestry Workshop*—which opened in Prato in April 2008. In this case, two of the exhibition's 27 works were shown at the Museo del Tessuto, Prato's landmark Textile Museum, a means of correlating the long history of Prato's textile industries with the contemporary practice of the Victorian Tapestry Workshop's artists and weavers, and the European heritage of their techniques.

A related, though different, facet of the Centre's contribution to Prato's cultural calendar is the Centre's hosting of events initiated by local organisations, events that customarily take place in the Salone Grollo. Those organisations with the longest history of this kind with the Centre are the Metastasio Theatre (since 2001); the Associazione Pratese Amici dei Musei e dei Beni Ambientali, the Prato 'Friends of Museums' group (since 2002), as well as FareArte cultural association, Dryphoto, and the Scuola Comunale di Musica 'Giuseppe Verdi', the municipal school of music. As a space for performance, the Salone Grollo is highly reverberant, its acoustics nonetheless conducive to a surprisingly intimate atmosphere. Following the Centre's opening, the Salone has frequently served as the stately setting for public concerts of all types—keenly attended performances of Renaissance vocal music, folk music, operetta, orchestral and chamber music, and, latterly, jazz.

CONTEXT FOR THE ARTIST IN RESIDENCE PROGRAM

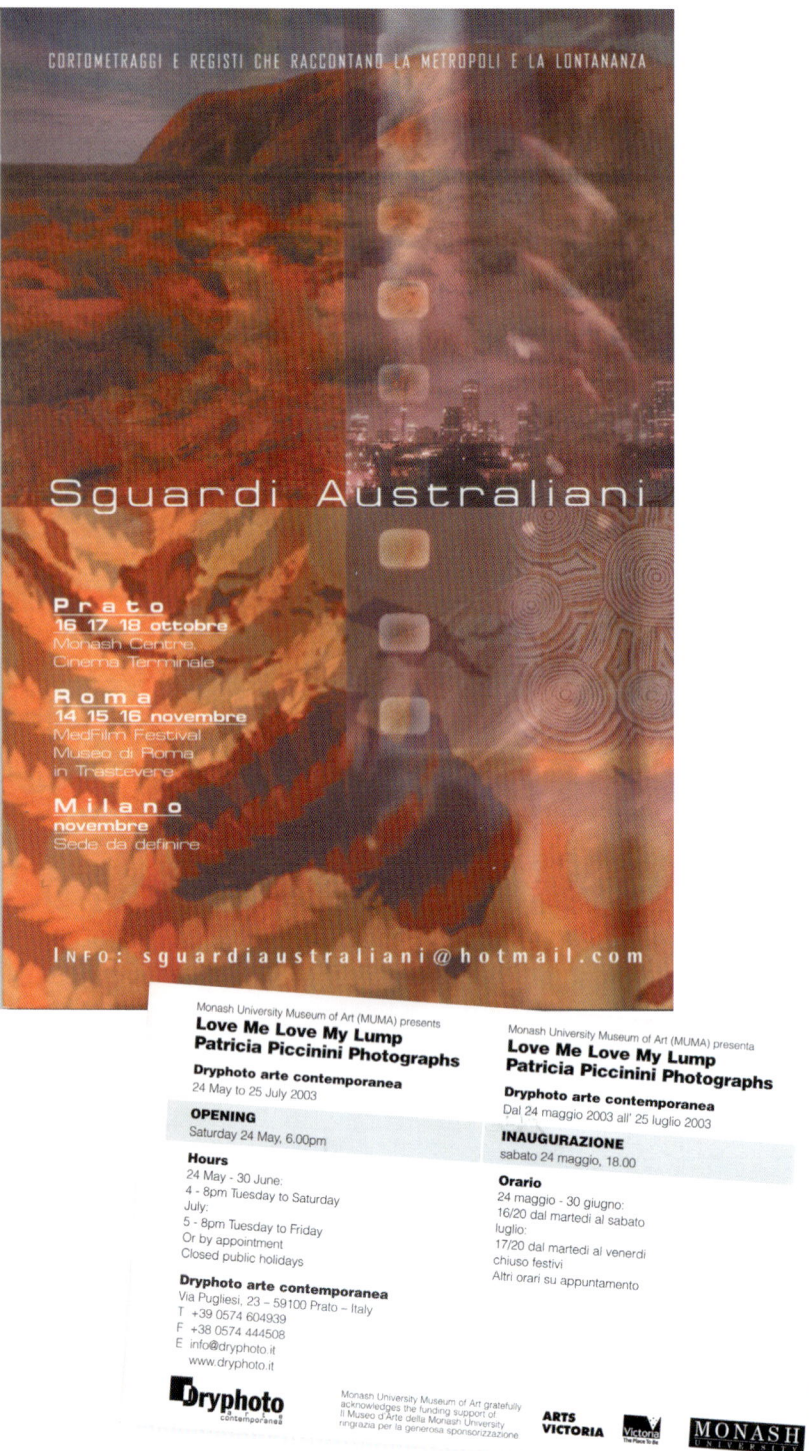

Poster for the 2002 tour of the first film festival titled *Squardi Australiani*, curated by Silvana Tuccio. Design by Harta Design, Roberto Rossini © Lacunae

Invitation, *Love Me Love My Lump: Patricia Piccinini Photographs* at Dryphoto Arte Contemporanea 2003. Design © Monash University Museum of Art

Palazzo. This close involvement with Dryphoto—both a gallery space and a local association dedicated to contemporary photography—led to the Centre's regular participation in 'Spread in Prato', an annual series of curated exhibitions in factory, office and commercial spaces throughout Prato. A collaborative relationship with Dryphoto remains indispensable to the Centre's exhibition planning.

2003 may prove to have been the Centre's most dazzling year for exhibitions, since the dates of *Love Me Love My Lump* overlapped with those of *Aborigena: Contemporary Australian Aboriginal Art from the Gabrielle Pizzi Collection*. A selection of works from Gabrielle Pizzi's extraordinary private collection had already toured to Turin and Utrecht under the name *Aborigena*. In Prato, 91 paintings were displayed to striking effect in the whitewashed surrounds of the Antiche Stanze di Santa Caterina, part of a former Dominican monastery belonging to the Comune di Prato, the city government—which gave the project its full support, also financing the publication of a bilingual catalogue. The opening drew over 100 guests. Bill Kent reported that the event received 'very favourable press coverage'; one news article mentioned the Prato Minister for Cultural Affairs emphasising 'the important contribution Monash University has made to the cultural enrichment of the city'. Within 22 months of the Centre's opening, such a statement was understandably felt to be highly significant. The opportunity to involve local dignitaries as well as the art-going public is part of the significant diplomatic role—and shared enjoyment—of such high-profile events. This said, Centre directors and staff invariably work hard to mark each new exhibition with a convivial sense of occasion.

In 2007 the exhibition *Mates: Images and Stories from the Kimberley* also attracted memorably large audiences and widespread interest.

CONTEXT FOR THE ARTIST IN RESIDENCE PROGRAM

but at the Monash Prato Centre … they will'. The 'dinosaurs' refers to the exhibition project *Dinosaurs of Darkness* curated by palaeontologist Professor Patricia Vickers-Rich, part of which was touring to Europe for the first time. Between the dinosaur bones and casts, the exhibition *Our Place*, and the Monash University Music Ensemble, the local press in Prato considered the dinosaurs the most 'photogenic' of the Centre's opening activities.

At the Palazzo Vaj, *Dinosaurs of Darkness* proved extremely popular with the Tuscan schoolchildren. By comparison, *Our Place* presented a more subtle and complex message about contested histories and multiculturalism in contemporary Australia, through 28 works made during the preceding decade by established and emerging Australian artists. The illustrated catalogue, in both English and Italian, outlined the selection as a basis for questioning 'universalising political narratives, as they mark the limits of certain nationalisms'—thus proposing the exhibition as a contribution to dialogues of global resonance and scale. By all accounts, *Our Place* drew steady and discriminating attention in Prato. It took an added topicality from the fact that it was drawn from the permanent collection of the Monash University Museum of Art (MUMA). Introducing the catalogue, Jenepher Duncan, museum director at that time, outlined the national importance of the collection, and its origins in the foundation of Monash University at Clayton in 1961. From this point of view, *Our Place* was a sophisticated means of identifying the opening of the Prato Centre with the University's 40 year history and innovative vision.

The Prato Centre presented two further major exhibitions sent by Jenepher Duncan as part of the MUMA international touring schedule. The distinguished indigenous artist Judy Watson had been represented in *Our Place*; in 2002 her stunning unstretched canvases soaked in natural pigments featured in the exhibition *Judy Watson*. Organised by MUMA, the show travelled to Prato in April of that year, and Watson gave a public lecture, and a tour of the exhibition at the Palazzo Vaj. Amongst the Centre's activities at the time was the research forum 'Imaging Aboriginality: Indigenous/European Entanglements in Culture and Representation', organised by Professor Lynette Russell, Director of the Centre for Australian Indigenous Studies at Monash, and Marcia Langton, Professor of Indigenous Studies at The University of Melbourne. Austrian colleagues from the University of Klagenfurt also attended. Whenever possible, such complementary programming in relation to an exhibition is always pursued.

Judy Watson was just one of six exhibitions seen at the Palazzo Vaj in 2002. The 2002 record of events approximates that of an art gallery, with a confident emphasis on artists with Australian connections; it lists shows by landscape painter Maurizio Bottarelli, who had been artist in residence at Monash Caulfield campus in 2000; master printmaker Patrick Aubert; Melbourne-based artist Judy Holding; a retrospective of paintings by Australian expatriate author and artist Russell Foreman, in addition to the festival of Australian films, *Squardi Australiani*, (the first of its kind) which had opened that summer in Genoa.

Love Me Love My Lump: Patricia Piccinini Photographs was the third MUMA exhibition seen in Prato. Patricia Piccinini represented Australia at the 2003 Venice Biennale, and the Prato exhibition was promoted as a Tuscan 'satellite' to the Australian Pavilion at Venice. Piccinini's glamourous and glamourising photographs of genetically engineered life-forms were displayed in the Palazzo Vaj, and also at Dryphoto Arte Contemporanea, located in Via Pugliesi opposite the

CONTEXT FOR THE ARTIST IN RESIDENCE PROGRAM

The scope of activities envisaged for the Monash Prato Centre has always explicitly embraced a role for creative artists and their work. In one sense, such a role reflects the conceptual prehistory of the Centre—its links to the tradition of the foreign 'national academy' for humanities, modelled, for example, on the British School at Rome. Yet it was easily translated into the more far-reaching concept of a study centre for 'the global Monash' that became the Monash Prato Centre at Palazzo Vaj. When in May 1998 Vice-Chancellor David Robinson wrote to the Tuscan President, Vannino Chiti, seeking support for Monash's intention to establish 'an international study centre in the Florence area', he stated, 'we have in mind a building which would enable the Monash Centre to hold international conferences and exhibitions of Australian art', as well as the necessary office space.

The most concise statement of a commitment to provide opportunities for artists appears in the one page 'Statement of Objectives' for the Centre which was submitted in December 2000 for consideration by the Monash University Council—part of the due process for establishing the Centre as a legal entity under Italian law. The dot points of this document include mention of 'the provision of studio space for Monash Art and Design Students', 'exhibitions of Australian art', and 'showcasing Australian performing arts'.

In the Centre's earliest days, the Salone Grollo proposed itself as a venue for musical performance, and free exhibitions were integral to attracting publicity and a wide variety of visitors up to the first floor of the Palazzo Vaj. The Centre's earliest exhibition was mounted in May 2001, a compact series titled *Works on Paper* by photorealist Donald Campbell, a long-term resident of Tuscany. This was also the first of the Centre's exhibitions of work by local artists. Founding Director Bill Kent remembered seeking 'to have something on the walls because I wanted people to come in. Very early we tried to have exhibitions of all sorts'. At the outset, this desire arose from the simple need to put the Centre 'on the map' in Prato and beyond, though of course it was inseparable from the mission of raising the Centre's intellectual profile.

The events programmed for the Centre's official opening in September 2001 duly announced the scope of the Centre's cultural and artistic purpose. As declared in the letter of invitation sent to Australian members of federal and state parliaments, 'it is not often that dinosaurs come together with contemporary Australian art and a music ensemble,

Donald Campbell

Opere su Carta

14 maggio - 17 giugno

aperto al pubblico
Venerdì dalle ore 17:00 alle ore 19:30
Sabato dalle ore 16:30 alle ore 19:30
Domenica dalle ore 10:00 alle ore 13:00
o con appuntamento

Ricevimento per l'artista, lunedi 14 maggio, 18:00-20:00

Monash University in Prato

Palazzo Vaj
Via Pugliesi, 26 Prato
Tel. 0574 484948 Fax 0574 445784

PART FOUR
A Centre for Art and Artists

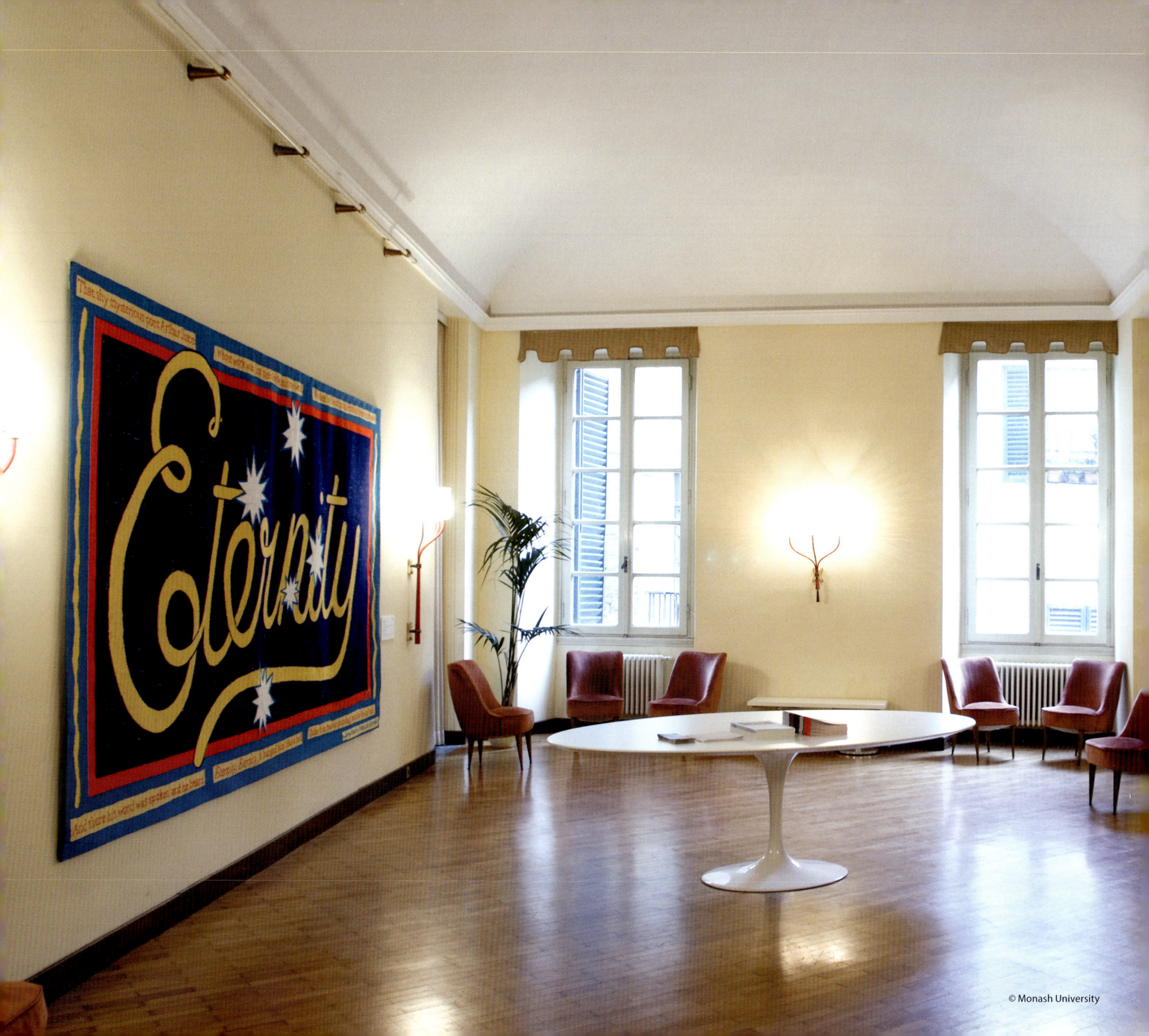

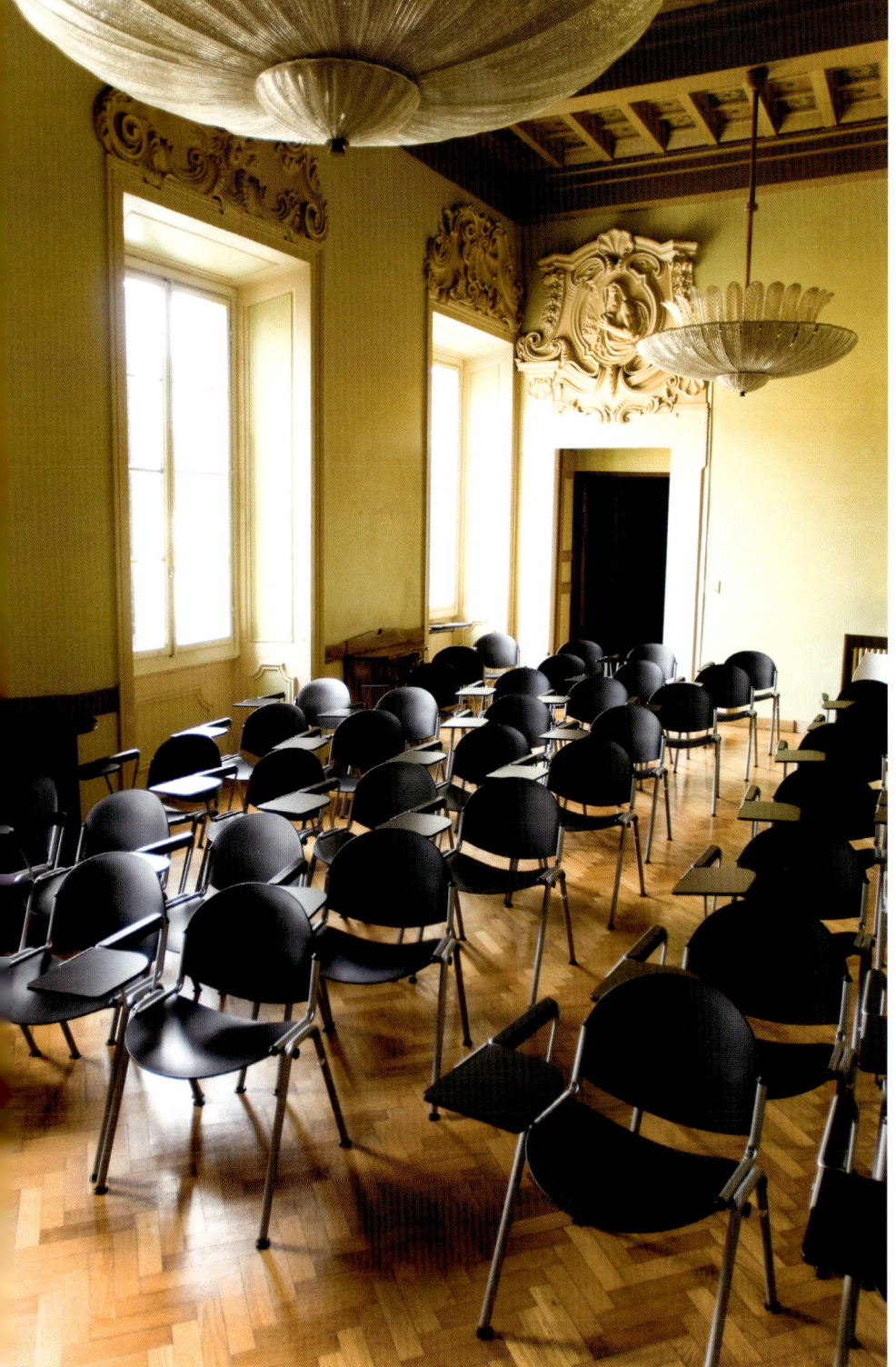
© Monash University

for lunch in the afternoon. That's part of the Italian culture, and an insightful experience when you can witness it first-hand.

Our tour included a study day at the Centre, with content custom-made for the Chisholm students. As with the teaching staff I had appreciated in 2006, the teachers Catia Santi and Antonietta Colotti were brilliant. The morning was devoted to classroom activities: grammar, linguistics, conversation. After lunch we were given an orientation tour of Prato. Then the students took part in *la caccia al tesoro*—a treasure hunt— which involved walking around the city and asking different questions in Italian. They really enjoyed this, especially because the people of Prato were so obliging.

My students were excited to attend a university centre. Walking into the Salone Grollo immediately gave them an impression of importance— so they felt important. Centre staff were wonderfully helpful, both before and after our arrival in Prato. I feel now I have a friendship with the Centre, which will help me plan future study tours from Perth!

From Perth to Prato: A Life-Changing Experience

Fiona Millimaci Head of Languages, Chisholm Catholic College, Perth

The Endeavour Language Teacher Fellowships (ELTF) is the name for a national program of immersive study offered in January every year to primary and secondary school language teachers from around Australia. It aims to extend cultural and linguistic knowledge. The fellowships are managed by Asia Education Foundation, and were first offered in 2004. From 2004 until 2010, the Monash Prato Centre organised and hosted two weeks of the program for teachers of Italian. I would never have travelled to Prato were it not for the presence of the Monash Centre there.

My participation in the 2006 Endeavour program was a life-changing experience, and the benefits continue. It was so useful for my professional development that my husband, Joseph Millimaci, also a teacher of Italian, applied for and received a fellowship for 2008.

I was one of three teachers from Western Australia selected for the 2006 ELTF Italian program; the group numbered 18. During the fortnight spent in Prato we were involved in highly intensive linguistic and cultural activities from 9 am until 5 pm. We were taught with great skill by Laura Brachi and Carla Giovannelli. Over two days we also had the opportunity to meet local teachers in their schools; the schools were mostly within walking distance of the Palazzo Vaj. A couple of us went to the Conservatorio San Niccolò di Prato, into a secondary level class, where we taught some of the lessons. On the second day we gave a lesson on Australian music.

The program as organised by the Centre gave me numerous teaching strategies, and so much exhilarating material. All in all, staying in Prato and studying at the Palazzo Vaj made it possible to live as part of the community, and to get to know many local people and businesses. Personally and professionally it was invaluable to be taken directly into that experience of Italian urban life. Prato is a beautiful jewel of a Tuscan city, and I loved being there. So much so that, in January 2011, I took 20 senior students from Perth's Chisholm Catholic College to Prato, as part of a study tour. We stayed for a week at the Hotel Giardino, a family-run hotel, where the Centre had arranged accommodation for the ELTF group in 2006.

In Prato, classroom lessons literally 'came to life' for my students. We sat on the steps in Piazza Duomo watching school children walk home

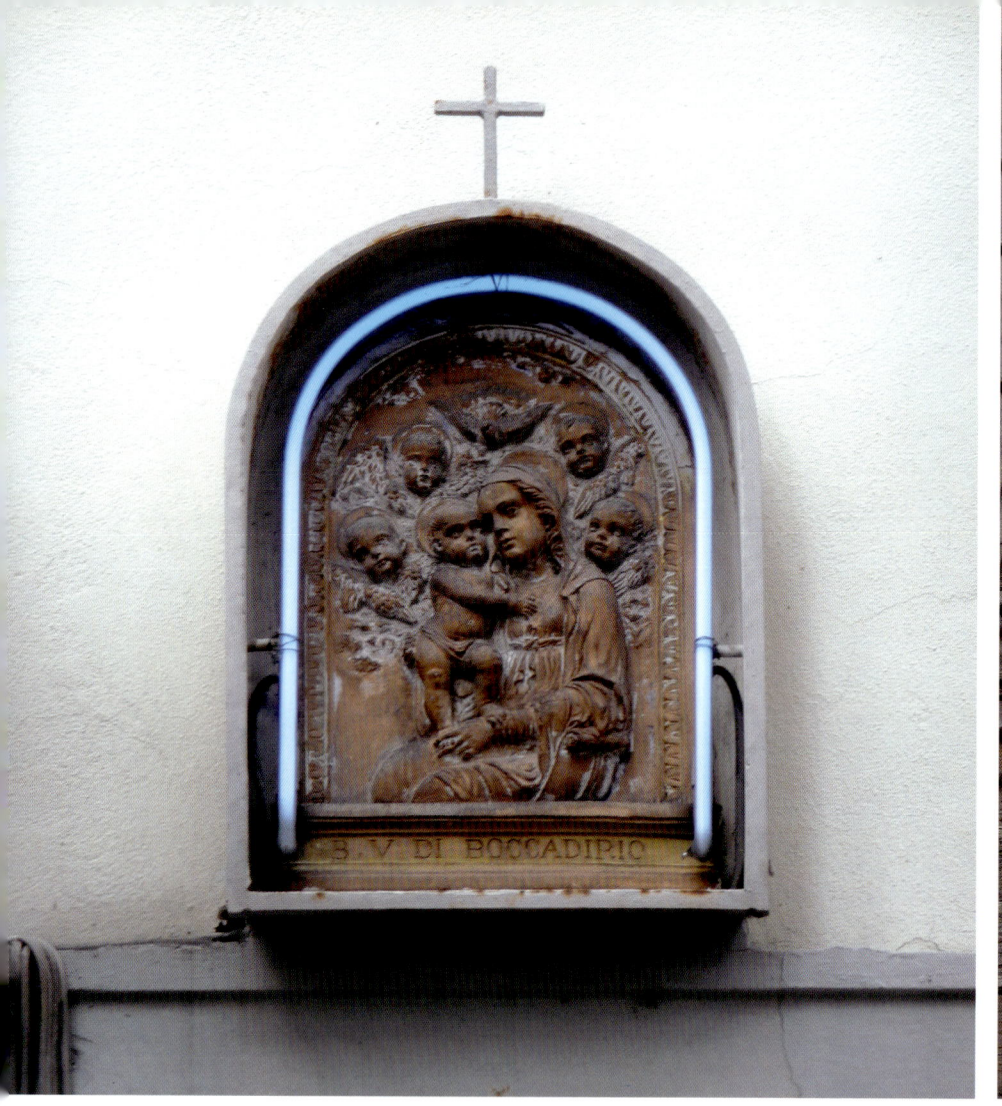 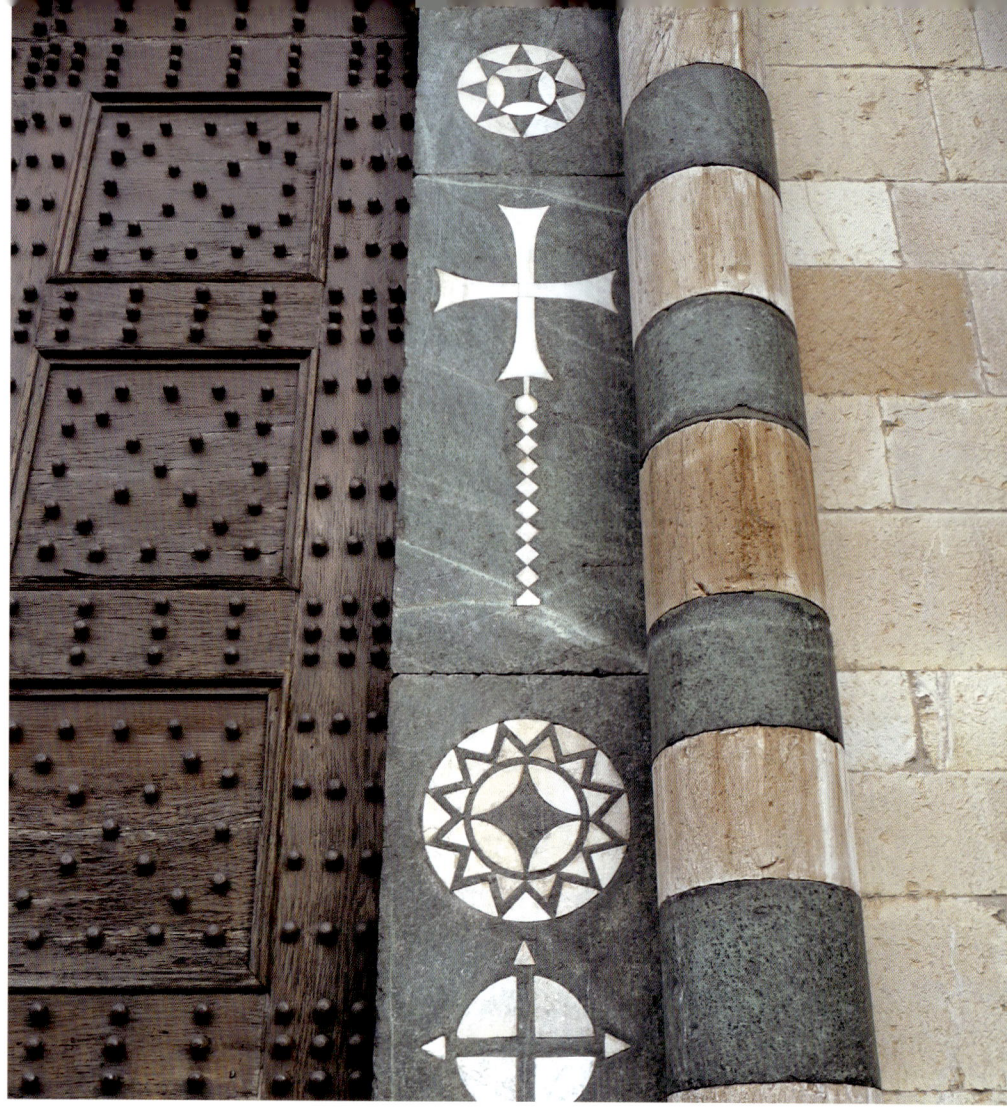

we realised later, a number of touristic clichés about an 'unchanging' Tuscan past. The Christmas pageant is not performed in Florence as a museum piece with actors. Of course it is alive with the realities of the twenty-first century.

During the month that followed, we reflected often on our encounter with the Epiphany day rituals. Fittingly for Dante, the metaphor of pilgrimage is apposite here. As a collective, we had been on a first pilgrimage to Florence, interested to experience the beginnings of some sort of intellectual and social transformation. In a suitably complicated way the encounter had served to introduce the theme of 'how things change and how they stay the same' far beyond the abstractions of the classroom, and highlighted the need for extreme sensitivity to assumptions about what is 'customary' in the globalised present. I like to think that studying Dante in Tuscany enables students to think equally deeply about Tuscany at the turn of the fourteenth century and about contemporary debates concerning the nature of European identity, national identity and the world stage. Prato is exactly the place from which to pursue and explore all of these subjects.

Teaching Dante from Contemporary Prato

Clare Monagle Lecturer in Historical Studies, Faculty of Arts, Monash University

In January 2010, Constant Mews, Hannah Fulton and I led a group of mainly third and fourth year students to Prato, to study a new unit in Historical Studies titled 'Dante's Medieval World'. Our task was to take Dante's *Divine Comedy* as a source through which to investigate the politics, society and religious life of medieval Tuscany. The *Divine Comedy* bristles with references to Tuscan towns; Dante tells the story of a world in which social identity was almost entirely bound up with birthplace. Taking for granted the location of the Monash Prato Centre, the structure of 'Dante's Medieval World' involves exploring the Tuscan region through trips to Pisa, Arezzo, Lucca, Siena, and San Gimignano as well as Florence, to seek out evidence for the geographical dimensions of life in the Middle Ages.

In every sense, perhaps most exhilarating about teaching a Prato-based course is the blurring of boundaries that occurs, producing a genuinely shared intellectual journey. Our arrival in Italy coincided with the traditional Christian feast of the Epiphany, 6 January. On that date each year a wonderful pageant takes place in Florence. From the late morning a nativity scene sits outside the cathedral, in which locals play Mary, Joseph and the infant Jesus; oxen and sheep brought in from the countryside complete the live tableau. In the afternoon a formal procession accompanies 'The Three Kings' through the city to the Duomo; the parade includes representatives of various Tuscan communes in late medieval or Renaissance costume, all bearing gifts for the newborn Jesus. As such, on that feast day in 2010, we were able to see historical power relationships being played out in the Tuscan capital. Through a ritual both pious and political, surrounding cities and towns were paying homage to Florentine might, as well as performing their own devotional display.

The students of 'Dante's Medieval World'—and likewise their teachers—were very stimulated by this display. It seemed to embody the enduring connection to the medieval and Renaissance history for which Florence is so famous, and to demonstrate the profound importance of the past to contemporary life in Tuscany. Many in our group were already well aware of Prato's significant Chinese community; nonetheless the Chinese appearance of one of the representatives from Prato drew particular attention, challenging,

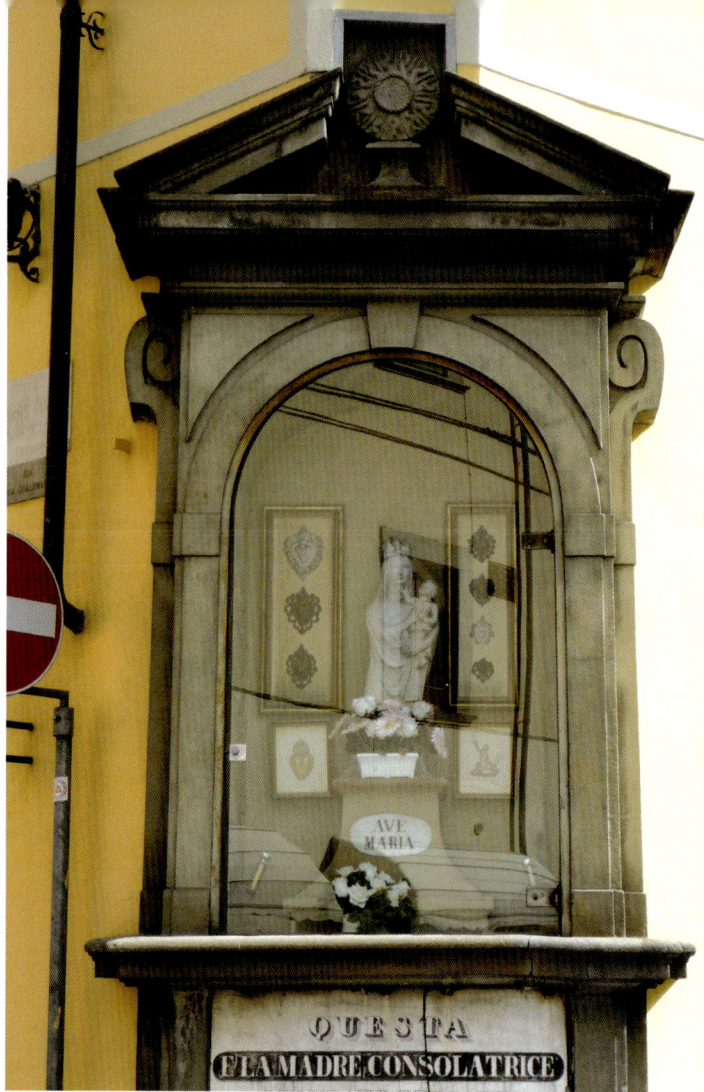

the backdrop to conference sessions on the uses of technology in memorialisation; the creation of community in an inner city housing development in Brisbane; the building of a unifying community in a divided Jerusalem; the creation of a virtual community by women on isolated farms; an online Maori archive; the digitisation of late medieval manuscripts in the Prato State Archives; and many other fascinating—often moving—explorations of communities in conjoined physical and technological spaces.

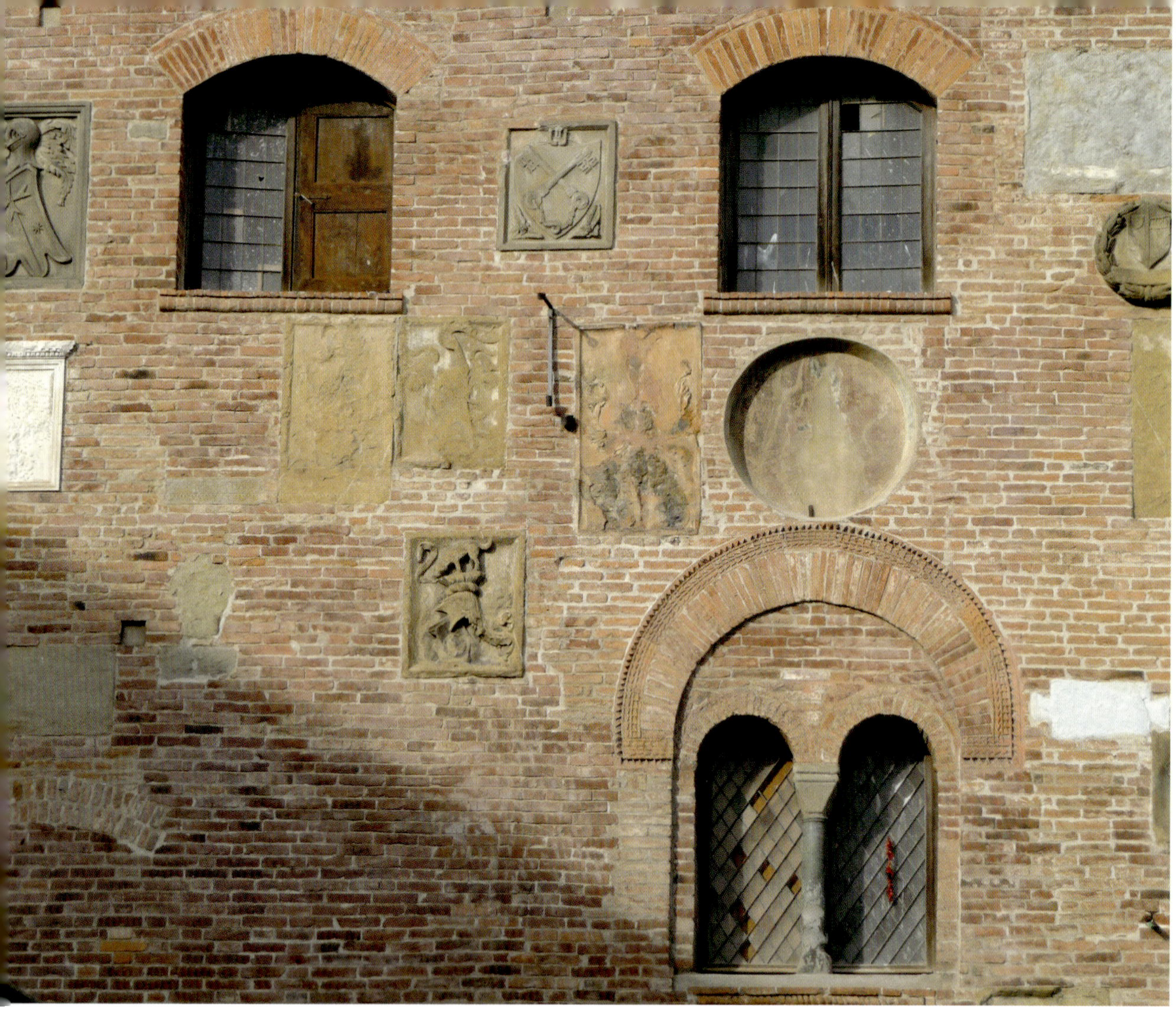

The 2006 conference at the Prato Centre was an intensely creative and productive meeting; it led to the formation of the current Centre for Organisational and Social Informatics (COSI) at Monash, as well as a number of ongoing research relationships, including with PROV. The intelligent, thought provoking papers and the many discussions I enjoyed with colleagues still stand out in my memory. I also well remember the conference catering, the wonderful food brought to Palazzo Vaj. Free of the usual dry conference sandwiches, the final lunch featured a whole *porchetta*, or pork roast, and chunks of parmesan cheese drizzled with local honey. And so the Prato Centre is forever associated in my mind with far-sighted thinking, stimulating conversation and delicious Tuscan food.

Memories and Communities in Prato

Justine Heazlewood Keeper of Public Records, Public Record Office Victoria

My journey to the Monash Prato Centre began with lunch in a Malaysian restaurant near the Monash Caulfield campus. I had been asked to lunch by Sue McKemmish and Don Schauder from the School of Information Management and Systems, with whom I had a professional association due to my work in archives. It was 2004, and the Prato Centre's Founding Director, Bill Kent, had recently retired from the directorship and was in Melbourne, continuing to encourage researchers to visit Prato and benefit from the presence of the Monash Centre there.

Along with Sue, Don and Bill, my fellow diners were Marian Quartly from Monash's School of Historical Studies, and Eric Ketelaar, Professor of Archivistics from the University of Amsterdam. Discussion at the lunch centred around the then new concept of e-Research—the application of advanced information and communication technologies to research practices, especially collaborative ventures. We were asking what e-Research meant for the humanities, and what kinds of subjects were appropriate to its disciplines.

From that lunch evolved a series of meetings held over the next two years, which culminated in a three day conference at the Prato Centre in October 2006, attended by 70 participants, including community representatives from Australia and New Zealand, the UK, Europe, South Africa, the USA and India. Under the rubric 'Memories, Communities, Technologies', the meetings investigated concepts such as 'communities of memory', particularly with reference to indigenous or immigrant communities; issues such as the impact of digital technologies on memory production and distribution—by archives, libraries and museums, for example. As the project grew, it drew in a larger number and wider array of partners. Eventually it involved contributors from a number of Australian universities as well as King's College London, the University of California, the University of Amsterdam, a delegation of Maori, Melbourne's Koorie Heritage Trust, and my own organisation, the Public Record Office Victoria (PROV).

Prato was a fantastic location for the project's closing meeting because the city retains that strong communal feel shared by many similar medieval cities, a sense of community naturally derived from a long-held sense of place and spatial integrity. This became

from Canada and Israel, and The Honorable George Hample AM QC ran the advocacy program; in 2009, staff at Prato also included United States District Court Judge Nancy Gertner.

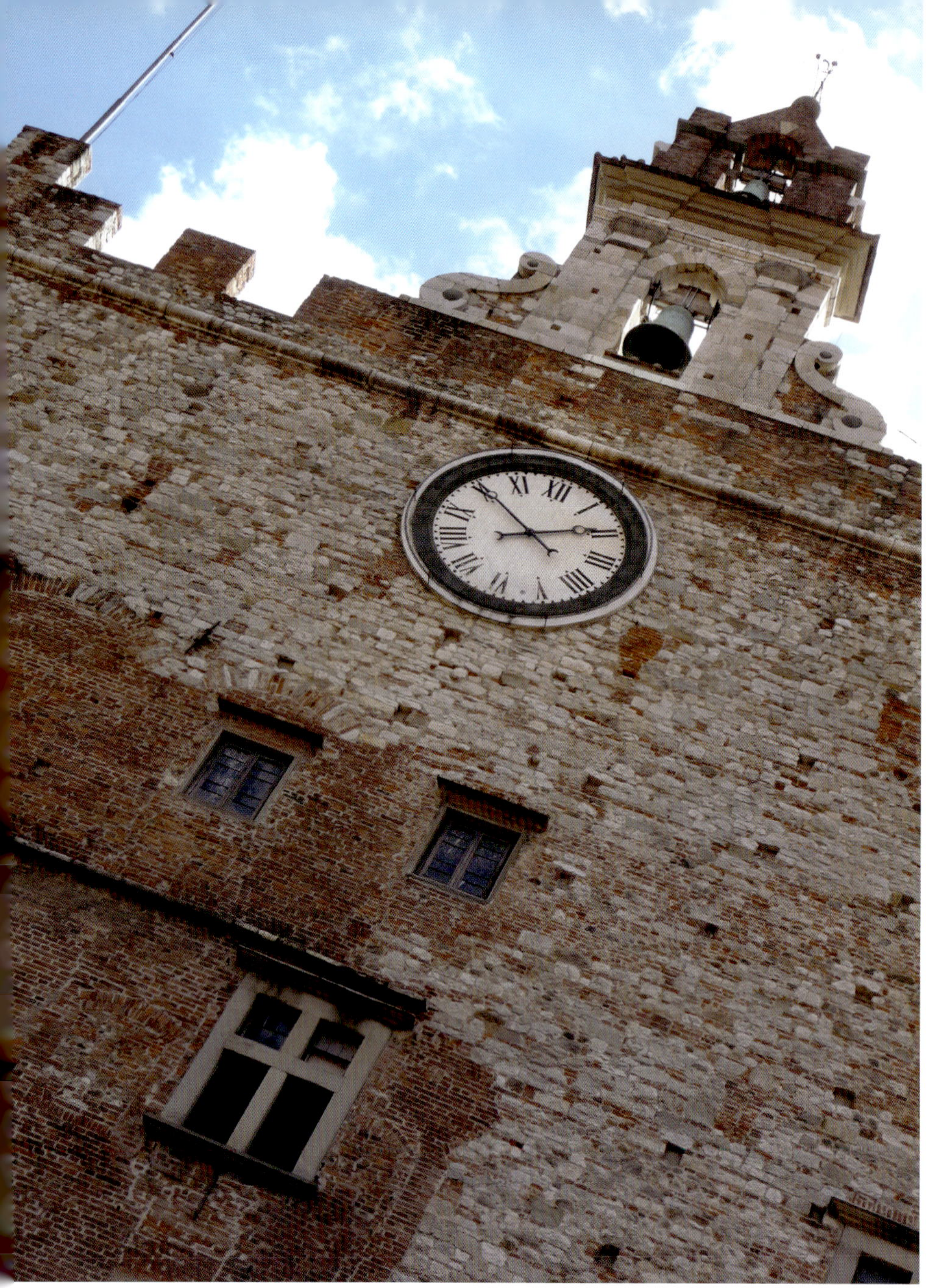

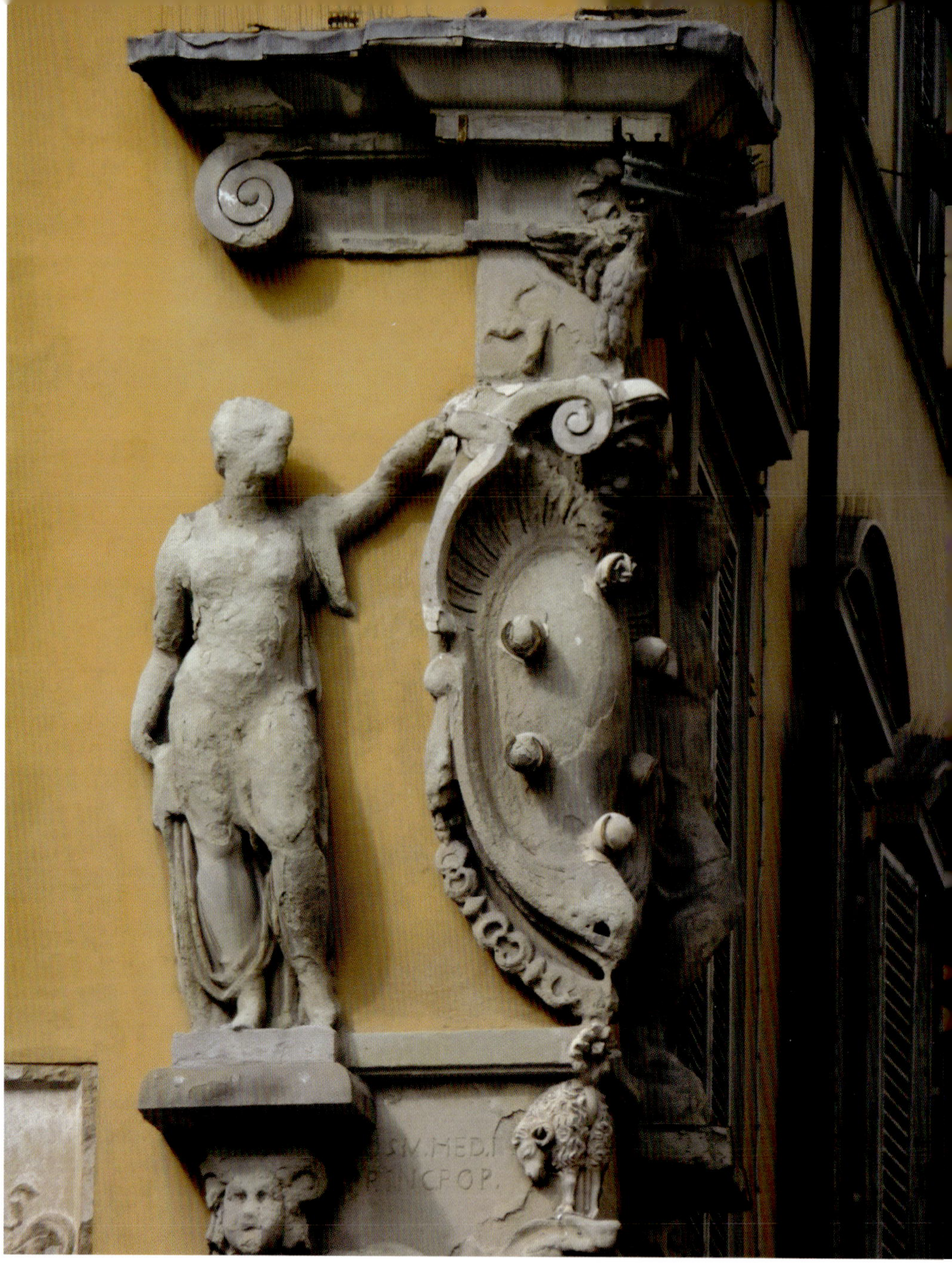

My final elective in 2009 was 'Representation of Law in Film', and this proved an interesting way to conclude my degree. The subject was taught by Shulamit Almog from the Faculty of Law at the University of Haifa, at that time a visiting professor at Prato—and it was quite different, an example of a subject that the Prato program makes possible. We watched films in the Palazzo Vaj, and afterwards we would walk downstairs for a coffee in a *pasticceria* nearby while the discussion kept flowing.

Global Context for a Law Degree

Marianna Linnik Arts/Law Alumna, Monash University

Before I travelled to the Prato Centre as a law student, I had heard about the Monash Law international study program; I saw it as a great opportunity to study in Europe and to gain experience of the global context for my undergraduate degree. Professionally and personally the experience proved of so much benefit, and was definitely helpful when I applied to join the 2011 Graduate Program at AusAID in Canberra, where I now work.

In 2006, I took part in the Willem C. Vis International Commercial Arbitration Moot in Hong Kong and Vienna, and from there travelled straight to Prato. Palazzo Vaj was astonishing; I was amazed that I could study in such beautiful surroundings, and I enjoyed the fact that the classes were quite small. I found I could really take part in debates and discussions. My 2006 semester at Prato included a compulsory subject and three electives, one on 'International Human Rights'. Studying international human rights law was truly inspiring, and the Palazzo Vaj and the city of Prato made it a holistically wonderful experience.

For a month in 2006 I stayed in Florence, in the Santo Spirito area which is quite bohemian. I then moved to stay in Prato which I also really liked; it was good to be part of the Monash student community there. I'm still friends with the people I met that way.

After Semester 1 of 2006, I was an exchange student at the University of Copenhagen, where I wasn't identified with Monash—living in a foreign country was challenging, but made easier by already having lived and studied in a European country, while at Prato. I returned to Prato in April 2009, after an internship with the Australian delegation to the United Nations Human Rights Council in Geneva, which was made possible through the Castan Centre Global Internship Program.

Overall, the lecturers were excited to be teaching at the Prato Centre. In 2009 I studied 'International Commercial Arbitration' with Judd Epstein, and classes were held at the University of Florence, mainly with Italian students. So that subject involved real intercultural exchange of ideas. Judd Epstein was a central figure of the Monash Law program at Prato. I remember him organising activities such as visits to a vineyard, and to a Prato church to see some beautiful frescoes. He involved teaching staff from universities around the world, as well as distinguished law practitioners: in both 2006 and 2009 there were students and academics

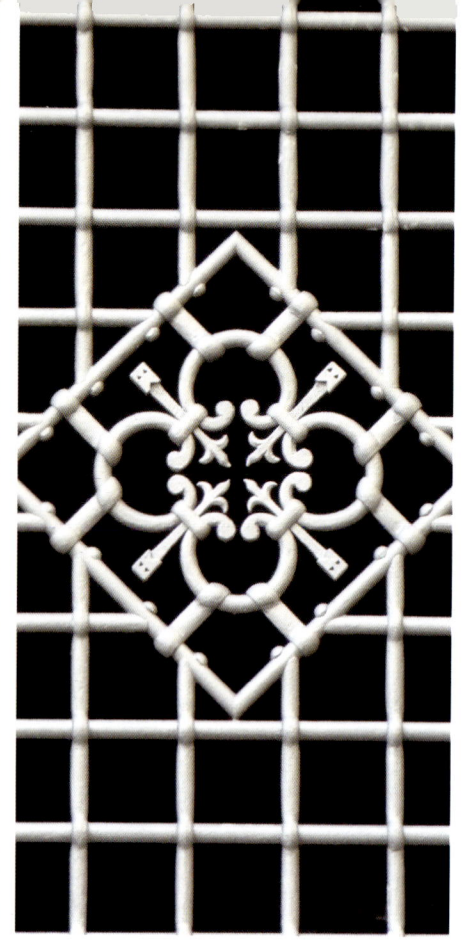

of Medicine and the University of Florence. If possible, at the GP conferences we like to teach applied skills. In 2007 for a dermatology skills program, the Salone Grollo was converted into something that resembled a dissection room, with doctors working in small groups to dissect and suture oranges and chicken skin!

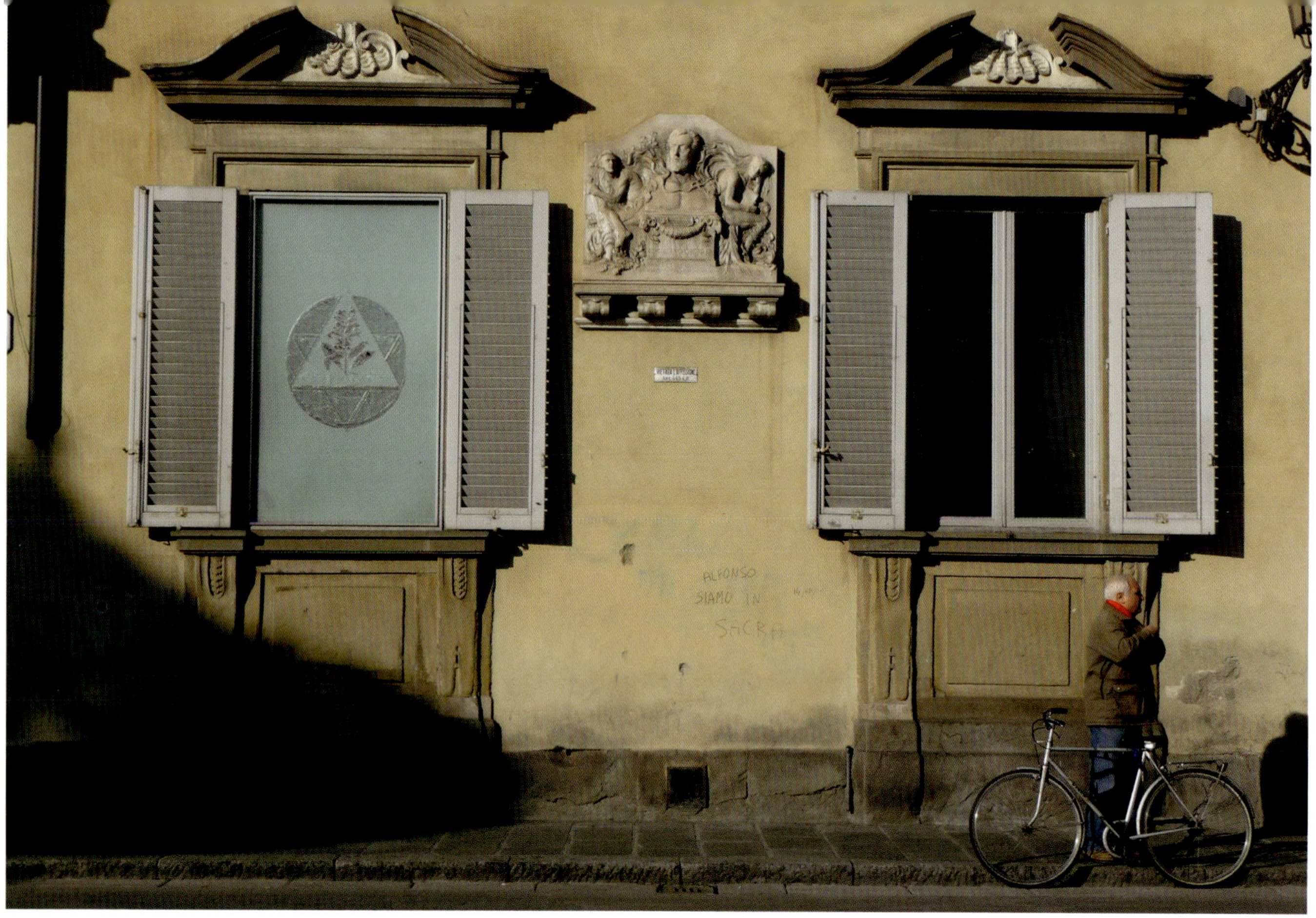

Monash's Faculty of Medicine, Nursing and Health Sciences has been involved with an international conference or research workshop at the Centre every year since 2003, collaborating particularly with counterparts at King's College London, and other UK-based networks and colleagues. In 2005, the 'First International Clinical Skills Conference' was hosted in Prato: these have been held there every two years, most recently in 2011, and always filling the Centre to capacity.

Mental health is one of my areas of interest. Australia is quite advanced in terms of primary care mental health; beyondblue, the national depression initiative, and other organisations have greatly assisted progress in this area. Through the Monash Prato Centre, very fruitful international connections have been established in the field; for example, I worked with Domenico Berardi, Professor of Psychiatry at the University of Bologna, and we took part in an international forum on Community Psychological Medicine in Hong Kong. When the collection *General Practice Psychiatry* was published by McGraw-Hill in 2006 (edited by Grant Blashki, Fiona Judd, and Leon Piterman), it was rapidly translated into Italian, the only translation so far. One Italian reviewer described the volume as 'an extraordinary work of collaboration'.

'The New World of Medicine' and Beyond

Leon Piterman AM Professor of General Practice, Faculty of Medicine, Nursing and Health Sciences, Monash University

The Monash Prato Centre is a meeting place, an incubator of ideas, and one of Australia's great international success stories. In 2001, I was deputy dean of the medical faculty at Monash—responsible for international engagement—and head of the Department of General Practice in the School of Primary Health Care. Wearing both 'hats', and touched by the beauty of Palazzo Vaj, it was clear to me that we should run a conference at the new Prato Centre as soon as practicable.

For years I have been organising conferences for general practitioners (GPs) in various locations outside Victoria. Monash has a history of providing continuing professional development for GPs, as well as teaching undergraduates. These conferences help to build strong relationships between medical researchers and the GP community, and academic capacity within the discipline on national and international bases. For the first GP conference at Prato, which took place in 2003, the aim was to attract a large, international audience. Called 'The New World of Medicine', the conference included many speakers who had made major contributions to knowledge at Monash. These were mostly clinician scientists of enormous importance in a global sense: people like Alan Trounson, at the time transitioning from work in in vitro fertilisation (IVF) to stem cell research, and really breaking new ground; and like David de Kretzer, a world leader for his work in male infertility, who was already working on male reproductive health with Gianni Forti, Professor of Endocrinology at the University of Florence.

We had planned to hold the conference in the Centre's Salone Grollo. However, the Datini Institute's conference on 'The Real Estate Market in Ancien Regime Europe' was also taking place, and involved simultaneous translation into five languages—so we were moved to the adjoining Metastasio Theatre. Nonetheless our delegates were overawed by the superb quality of the speakers, the atmosphere at the Palazzo Vaj, and the town of Prato. A second GP conference was held at the Centre in 2007, and along the way the School of Primary Health Care established ties with the medical community in Tuscany, and with the University of Florence. These are continuing—for instance, through an undergraduate student exchange program between Monash Faculty

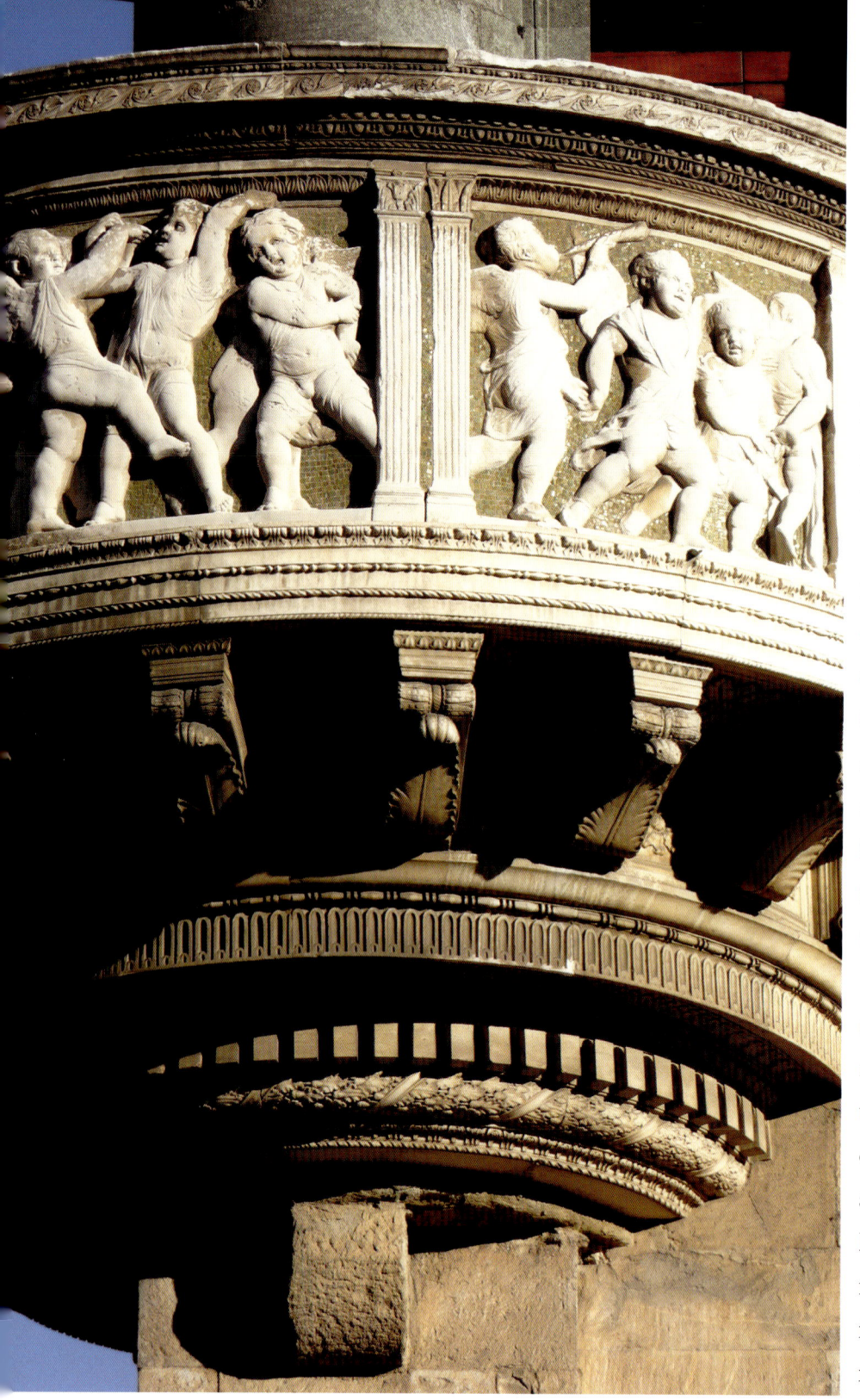

him, with 'she's right, it was Michelozzo'. The argument went for some minutes, giving the students a fascinating example of the way local art history continues to live in the conversation of the *piazza*.

The cathedral interior offers an exceptionally rich experience of medieval and Renaissance art. From 2001 until 2007, the famous cycle of frescoes by Filippo Lippi behind the high altar were the focus of an ambitious restoration project. Helped by the staff of the Prato Centre, I arranged special viewings of these images from the restorers' scaffolding, viewings which became a highlight for all involved. Such a rare opportunity enabled unique insight into the creation of the figurative scenes; into the artist's use of certain 'tricks' of perspective, form and colour—and the methods by which the frescoes have been restored for twenty-first century viewers.

Teaching on-site is difficult but immensely enjoyable; my enjoyment of Prato-based teaching has been continually reflected in students' responses to their environment. Throughout 'Concept and Creativity', they are constantly encouraged to reflect on themes common to their own preoccupations, and to contemporary art practice more widely, such as perspective and perception, narrative, ritual, the body, and space. Especially for those students who have only studied historic artworks in reproduction, or as examples dislocated from their original settings, the impact of such a wealth of visual and cultural material could not be more exciting.

VIGNETTE • ART HISTORY IN PRATO

Art History in Prato

Bronwyn Stocks Formerly Senior Lecturer in Theory of Art and Design, and Deputy Associate Dean, External Affairs, Faculty of Art and Design, Monash University

The subject 'Concept and Creativity, The Development of Italian Art and Design' has been offered annually at the Monash Prato Centre since 2001—it forms part of the Monash Faculty of Art and Design semester program for Fine Arts students. Although taught for just a fortnight of the eight weeks spent in Prato, this subject manifestly influences much of the studio teaching, as well as the students' individual art practice. Every year, between 20 and 24 undergraduates from the Faculty of Art and Design are selected for the program. Since 2003, students from the prestigious Glasgow School of Art (GSA), selected by the GSA Wider Access Development Officer, have also taken part.

The curriculum for 'Concept and Creativity' includes visits to well-known artworks in nearby cities and towns such as Florence, Siena, Arezzo, Lucca and Pisa; and exposure to the treasures in Florence's Uffizi Gallery, and to artists' preparatory drawings that can be studied in the Museo delle Sinopie at Pisa. Prato itself boasts a remarkable, if lesser-known collection of civic monuments of great historical significance. Each student gains first-hand experience of extraordinary paintings, sculpture and architecture in their original contexts.

The subject begins in Prato's main square, before St Stephen's Cathedral, the Duomo. Here the students learn how the passing of time can be observed in stylistic changes layered into the facade of the church and surrounding buildings. Such sites allow, too, for observation of social rituals that have long histories in ancient customs; rituals such as women greeting one another at the church entrance, and men nearby commenting on the world around them. In such on-site teaching, interruptions and the unexpected can be turned to advantage. The ringing of church bells, for example, alerts students to the notion of 'belonging' to the space of that sound—this concept of *campanilismo* is fundamental to a wide range of medieval and Renaissance buildings and artworks, and to traditions that remain part of contemporary Italian life. The memory of one particular interruption stands out: discussing the history of the Duomo's highly unusual, exterior pulpit, I noted its creation by the Florentine sculptor Donatello and his assistant, Michelozzo. Immediately, a vigorous argument erupted at the adjacent news-stand, with one man announcing that I didn't know what I was talking about—'the assistant was Michelangelo!' Others challenged

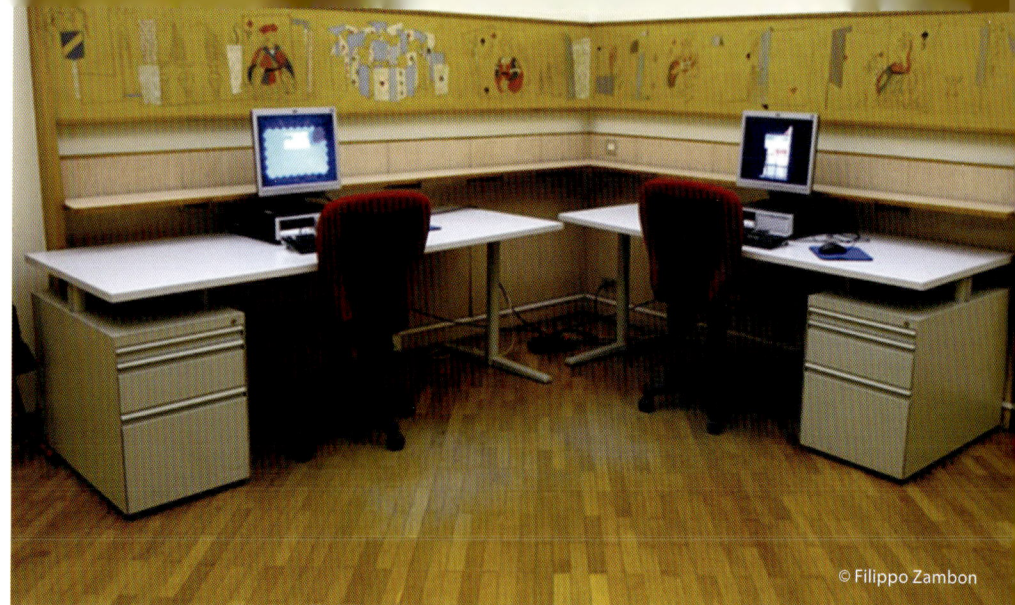

electronic funds transfers in Italian Lire, and then, from 2002 onwards, in Euro. Simultaneously these transactions had to be converted, recorded and reported in the Monash University financial system at Clayton. Looking back I'm pleased to say that within a few months the procedures and systems were in place.

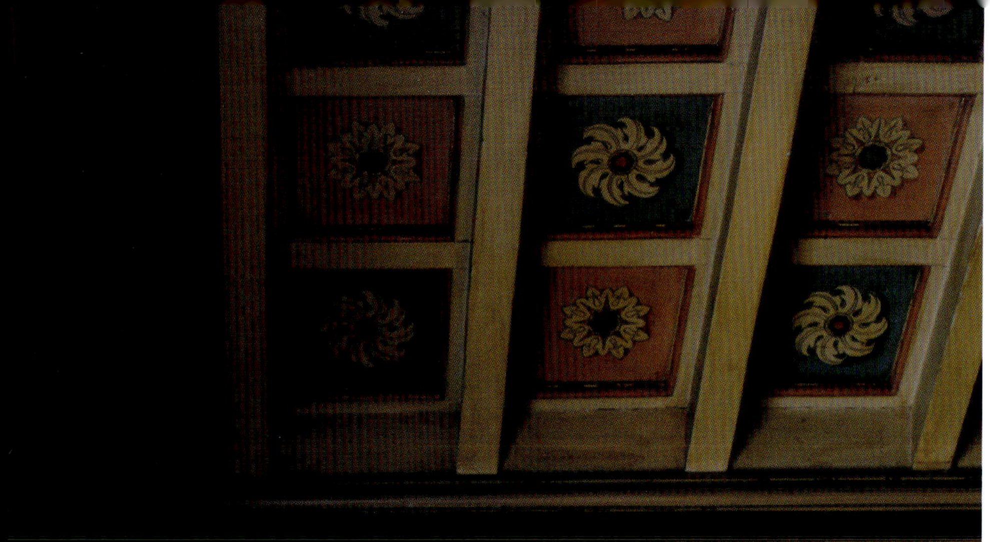

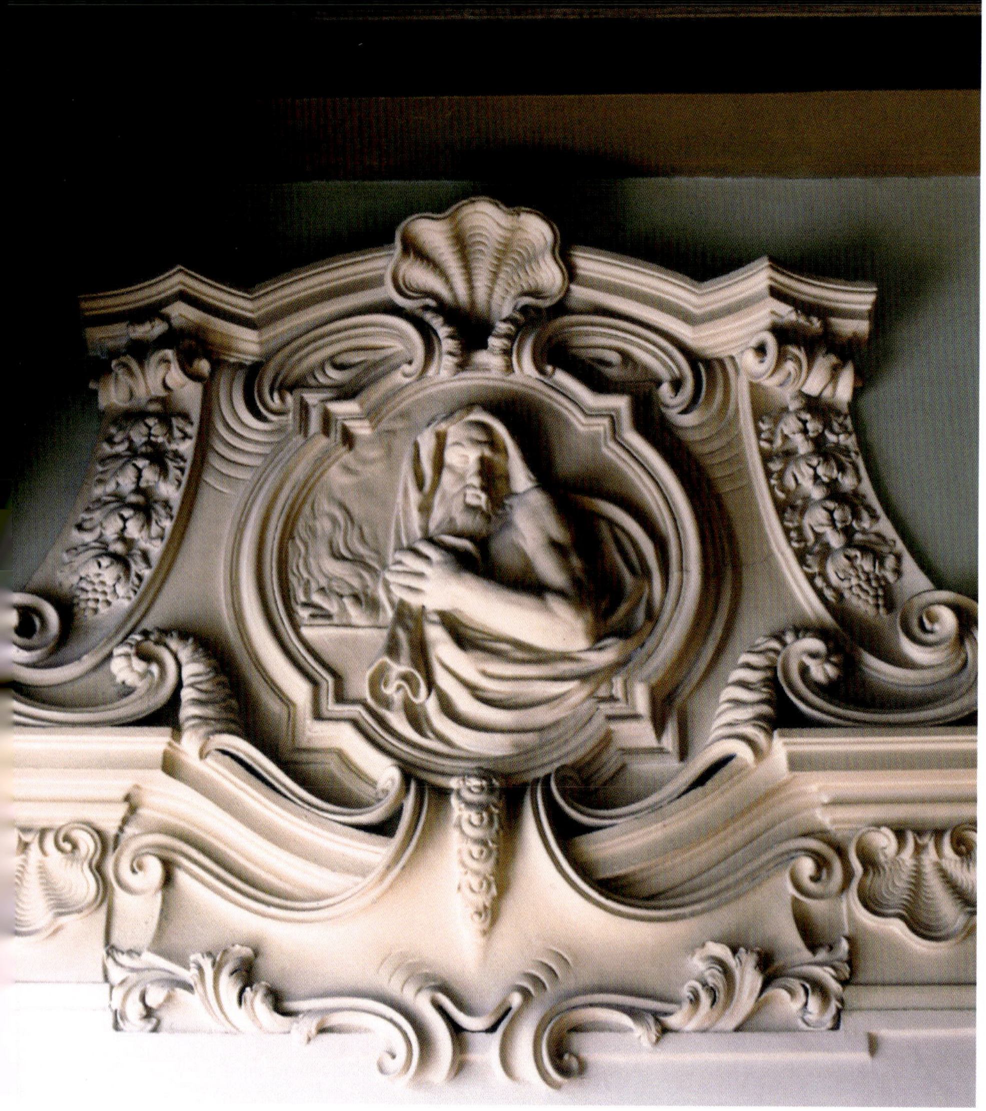

I was fortunate to visit Prato in October 2001, shortly after the Centre's official opening. When I entered the Palazzo Vaj for the first time, I was immediately impressed by the building's architecture, the formal entry staircase, the marble floors, the artworks scattered throughout the Centre, the majestic Salone Grollo and the decorations and style of the last century. I knew straightaway that our efforts were entirely worthwhile.

Together with Bill and Cecilia, I met key Prato contacts from the Wool Guild, the bank, Studio Borio and other service providers to the Centre. Following these meetings I was able to finalise and confirm details of the financial procedures for the Centre—procedures which in terms of format and design are essentially still in place to this day.

Budgeting for a Remarkable Pace

Terry Masocco Financial Resources Management Division, Monash University

In early 2000 a basic one page budget had been prepared to support the University's decision to establish the Monash Prato Centre. The expected cost was AUD $736,000. My task during late 2000 and into 2001 was to facilitate the establishment of the Centre from the University's financial point of view; this included devising the accounting procedures for Italy, reporting to Monash in Australia and the transfer of operating funds to Prato. Very soon the one page budget had expanded to four pages, and the expected cost had grown to approximately AUD $1.4 million.

Looking back now, the contrast between that first budget and the indicative operating and capital budget created in May 2001 offers some measure, from the fiscal standpoint, of the remarkable pace at which our understanding of the scope of the project developed over just a few months.

The May 2001 budget included the lease charges for Palazzo Vaj, estimated staffing costs, as well as expected costs for water, power, and heating and cleaning the Centre; photocopiers, printing and stationery supplies; a car lease, local travel costs and expenses related to legal and accounting services in Italy. A separate budget related to the costs of fitting out the Centre with a computer system, network hardware and a telephone system. A plan was also drawn up to purchase desks, chairs, workstations and other office furniture.

Those first months of 2001 felt like we were on a rollercoaster. While we were still establishing and fitting out the Centre, Bill Kent's confidence in its success was evidenced by the fact that, between February and December of that year, he had programmed 12 major events, including conferences, visiting school groups and other cultural activities.

With Cecilia Hewlett's direction and local knowledge, the purchasing and renovations at Palazzo Vaj proceeded apace, and our budget planning was further expanded to include the development of the 2002 and 2003 budget forecasts.

The Italian legal requirements, in combination with Monash University's own management requirements, called for unique accounting procedures to cope with the differing currencies, the geographical separation and the daily operations of the Centre at a local level in Italy. Practical methods were devised to open a Centre bank account in Prato, to provide petty cash, pay invoices and arrange

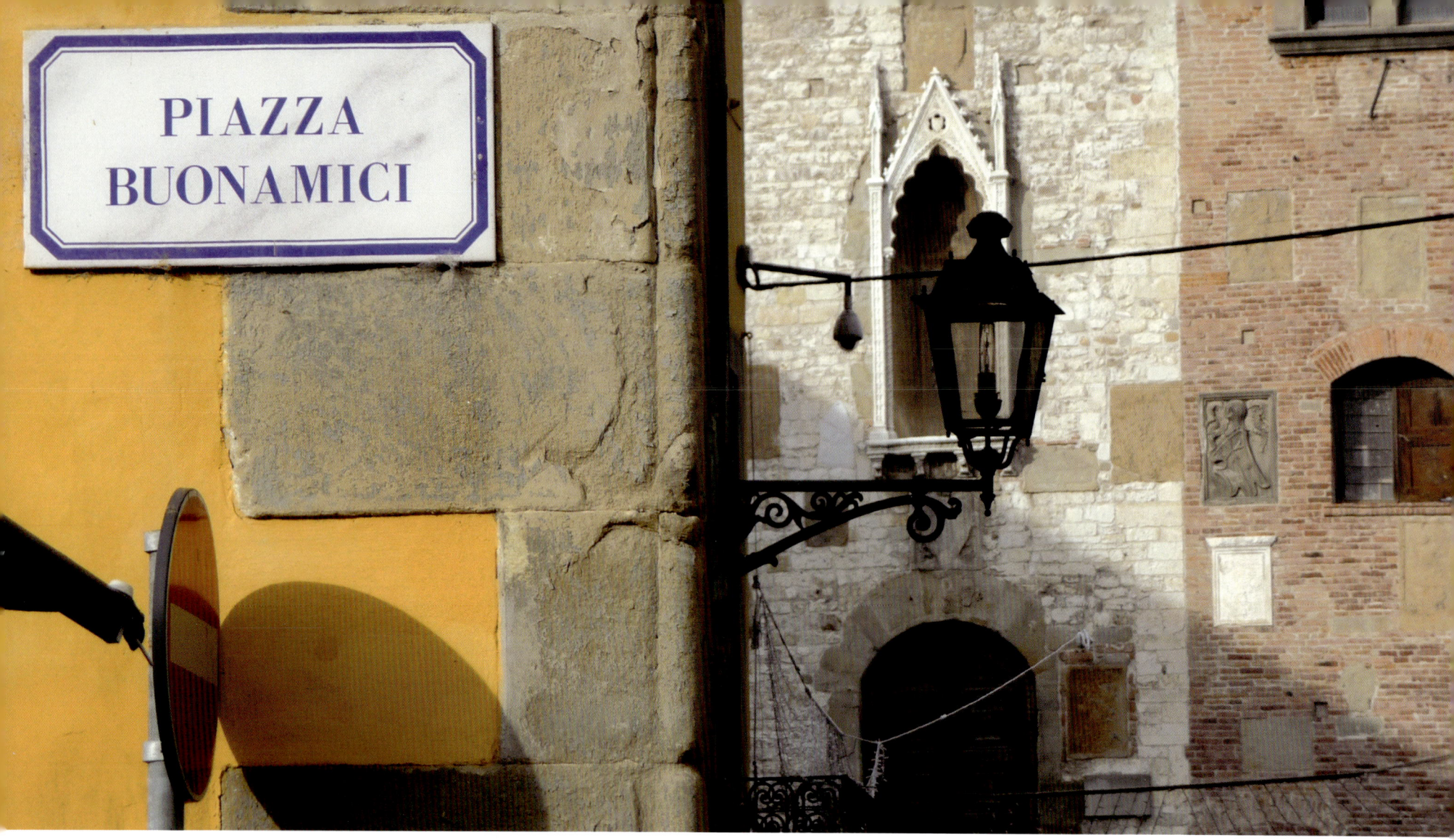

2000, it was not until April 2003 that I finally received—again by fax—notification from the Italian authorities of the registration of the Prato Centre in the most formal sense. To achieve the long awaited registration the authorities required that Monash, amongst other things, provide key documents authenticated by Apostille, and secure a *codice fiscale*, an Italian fiscal code used for taxation purposes. Moreover Monash had to commission a full translation into Italian of some 60 pages of its founding document, the 1958 Monash University Act. During the three years it took to complete the legal processes, enormous goodwill and optimism on all sides carried us through.

When, in May 2006, I finally made my first trip to Prato, it felt wonderful to be 'on the spot', to see the Centre in three dimensions. By that stage, with an intimate knowledge of the floor plans from the lease documents, I could probably have walked through the Palazzo Vaj with my eyes closed, but its spaciousness was a surprise—none of the legal paperwork had imparted a sense of the noble scale and proportions of the building.

A Pioneering Project

Renn Wortley *University Solicitor 1983–2007, Monash University*

Reflecting on the establishment of the Monash Prato Centre I am reminded of stories I had heard about the founding days of Monash Clayton in the early 1960s; so many able people enthusiastically 'pitched in' to cooperate freely on what was felt to be a pioneering project. The Centre also represented a conjunction of interests in Prato: as centuries of prosperity based on fine wool and textiles were ending, the Prato city government was working energetically to attract new and different activity to the city and the region, and so enliven its community and economy.

As the University Solicitor, I was necessarily involved in negotiations concerning the original lease for the first floor of Palazzo Vaj, and the legal, financial and fiscal matters related to securing authorisation for the Centre's operations from the Italian Ministry of Universities. On 12 June 2000, in a memo regarding the 'Prato Leasing Proposal', John Trembath, then divisional director of Facilities and Services, mentioned attempting 'to finalise the lease for one floor' of the Palazzo Vaj from the Wool Guild. Annamaria Pagliaro, at that time lecturer in Italian Studies at Monash, very kindly provided me with elegant English translations of successive drafts of the lease document, and ensured my comments in reply were received by the Guild in fluent and unambiguous Italian. I particularly remember visiting Annamaria on the evening of 13 October 2000—we had arranged to telephone the legal and accounting firm of Studio Borio in Florence from Annamaria's home—so that she might raise in Italian my questions concerning the lease proposal. This phone call effectively marked the beginning of an indispensable relationship with the Studio Borio, drawing on its long experience in helping foreign universities register and operate in Italy. From then on, as we followed the long and sometimes tortuous path leading to the Centre's registration and full legal status in Italy, I took the role of the intermediary between Monash University in Australia and the Studio Borio.

In a fax dated 16 October 2000, and marked 'urgent', Bill Kent asked whether I had 'any idea' how long it would take 'to clinch' the signing of the lease. While that first lease was finalised by the end of October

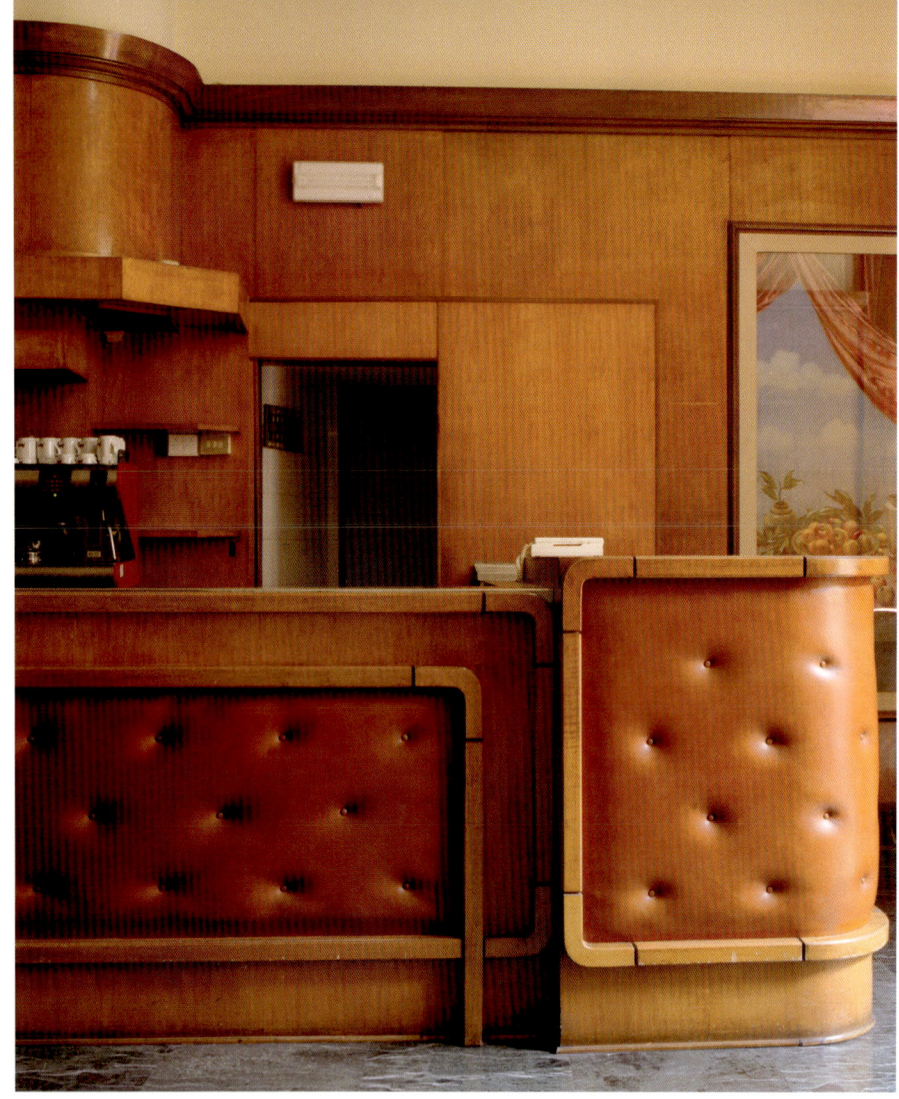

dialogue. For researchers involved in international partnerships, this is a place where differences of time zones, seasons, workflows or teaching semesters become at least temporarily immaterial. As with 'Memories and Communities at Prato' by Justine Heazlewood, '"The New World of Medicine" and Beyond' illustrates something of the exceptional momentum with which new opportunities for ongoing collaboration emerge from face-to-face meetings at the Palazzo Vaj. Ideally, in turn, results from these collaborations are applied to their best purpose in the wider public domain.

The annual Law in Prato program commenced in 2002, under the inimitable leadership of Judd Epstein. It is now taught with experts from 10 partner universities, and offers 13 intensive study units in international and comparative law, from April to July. Interviewed about the program for *Monash Memo* in 2007, Associate Professor Epstein stated, 'we aim to sensitize students to the different thinking they will encounter when dealing globally—thinking that's shaped by different traditions, legal systems and procedures'. Marianna Linnik completed her Law degree at Prato in 2009, the year in which the Law in Prato program gained an ALTC award for 'Internationalising Law in Action', on the basis of its breadth and inclusiveness, quality and flexibility.

Commencing in 2001, with 'The Renaissance in Florence', Monash Faculty of Arts has regularly offered undergraduate subjects at the Centre. In many ways 'The Renaissance in Florence' was an antecedent to the genesis of the international forum for research and teaching known as the Prato Consortium for Medieval and Renaissance Studies. The consortium, in turn, provided the logic for developing 'Dante's Medieval World', which was first taught in 2010, taking young academic Clare Monagle to Prato for the first time. Fiona Millimaci presents an extremely personable view of the Centre's schools-related programming, which began in April 2001 when 20 students from Methodist Ladies College in Melbourne took part in workshops with master printmaker Patrick Aubert. Vignettes 'Teaching Dante from Contemporary Prato' and 'From Perth to Prato: A Life-Changing Experience' both resonate with the energising effects of encounter promoted by the Centre's location and collegial atmosphere.

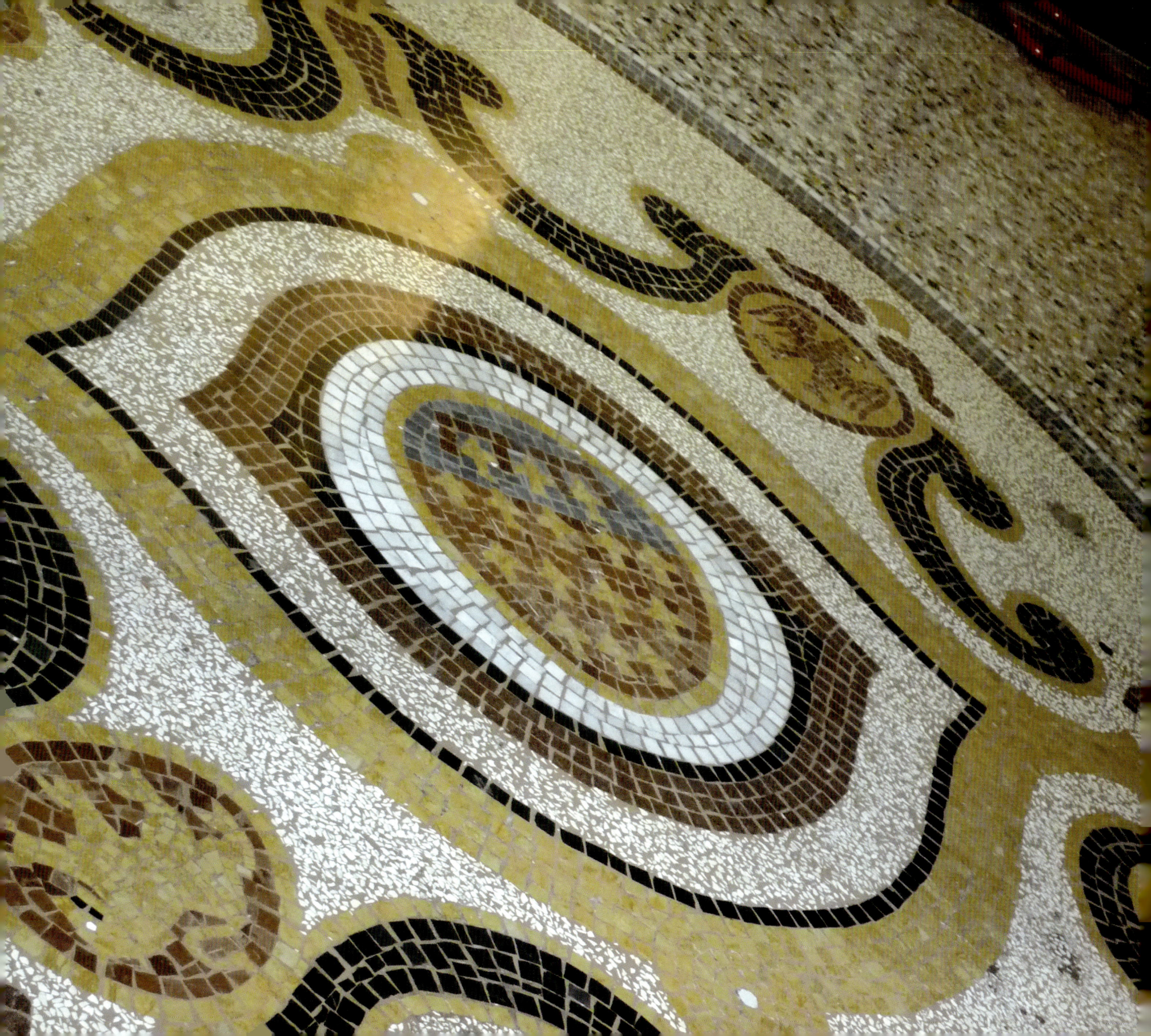

CAMARADERIE AND COLLABORATION

The following vignettes attest to the Monash Prato Centre as a stimulus to creativity in the contributors' professional lives. They witness exuberant responses to the idea of the Centre in Prato—and lived experiences of wholehearted participation in some aspect of the Centre's development or activities. At Monash Clayton both Renn Wortley and Terry Masocco played indispensable roles in the Centre's prehistory from the year 2000, when Bill Kent was named Founding Director—and when, from November of that year, he began living and working in Prato in this capacity. Also at Clayton, Wendy Perkins provided part-time administrative support, and Helen Fletcher-Kennedy acted as Executive Officer, Monash International. These were the early days of Monash's bold 'leap of faith' in the venture: hectic months of refurbishing the first floor of the Palazzo Vaj; seeking to register the Centre in accordance with Italian law; devising methods for financial planning and reporting; constructing the Centre's preliminary schedule of activities. For those at Clayton who were responding to such challenges 'as needed' across the hemispheres, this was a project requiring particular resourcefulness, and a memorable time of camaraderie and optimism.

Together with the Monash Faculty of Law, the Faculty of Art and Design was the first to express interest in developing an academic program based at the Centre. Its multidisciplinary curriculum has evolved to take every advantage of the resources that are local to the Palazzo Vaj and to the city of Prato, including the Luigi Pecci Contemporary Art Centre, with which the Centre enjoys excellent collaborative relations. Based on student feedback, study at the Centre—living in and looking at its surrounds—has especially helped to foster a thirst for knowledge of art history. In 2006, Bronwyn Stocks was cited for an 'Outstanding Contribution to Student Learning' by the Carrick Institute (now the Australian Learning and Teaching Council, or ALTC) on account of her imaginative approach to developing the Fine Arts full semester program at Prato.

'If we are going to connect with other cultures', Leon Piterman has observed, 'we need to understand their cultural perceptions of communication'. An implicit theme of Professor Piterman's vignette is the fundamental importance of 'the human element' to medical communication of every kind—and the value of the Centre for productive

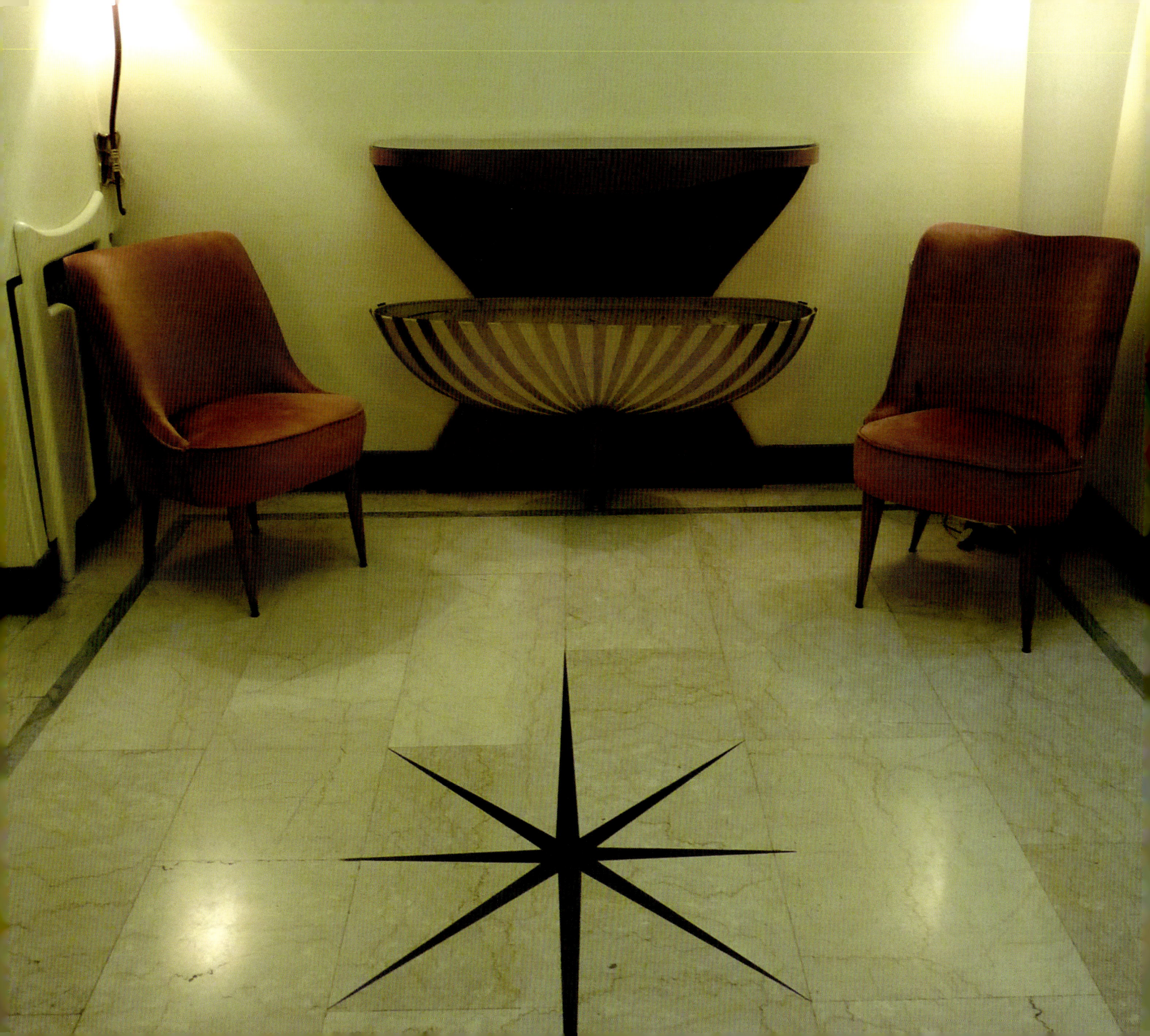

PART THREE

Multiple Perspectives

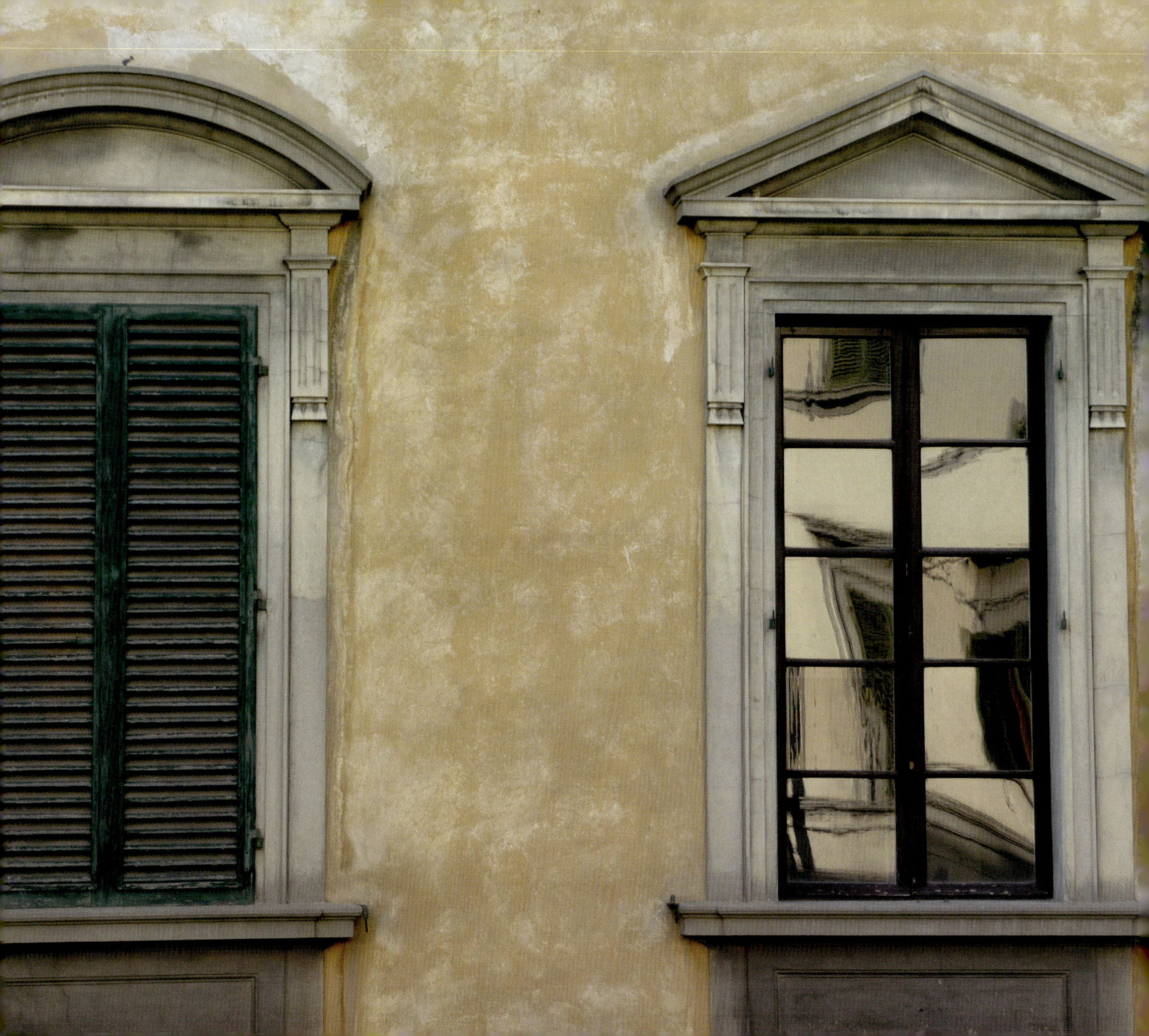

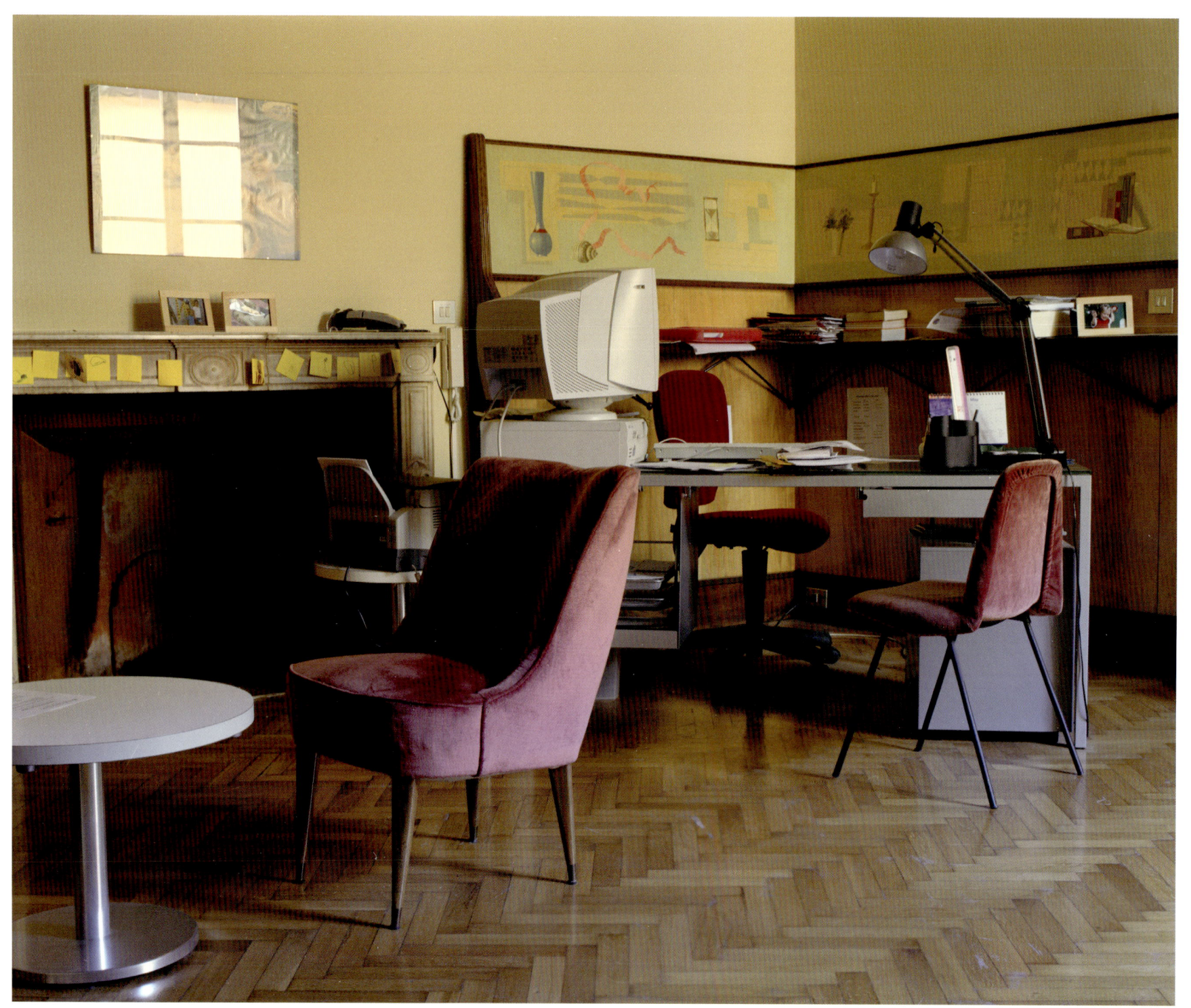

PIANO NOBILE, PALAZZO VAJ

Ufficio

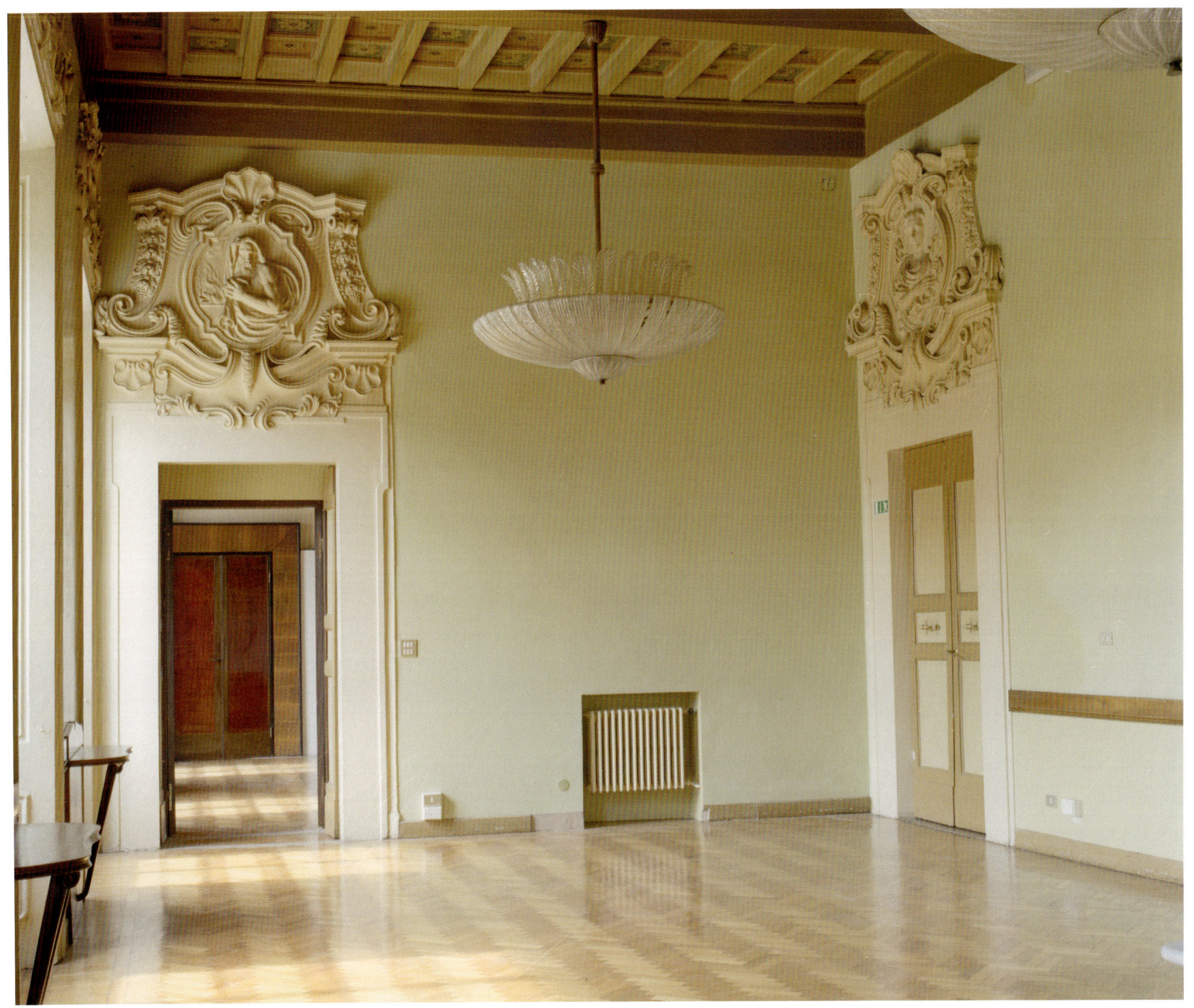

PIANO NOBILE, PALAZZO VAJ

Sala Toscana

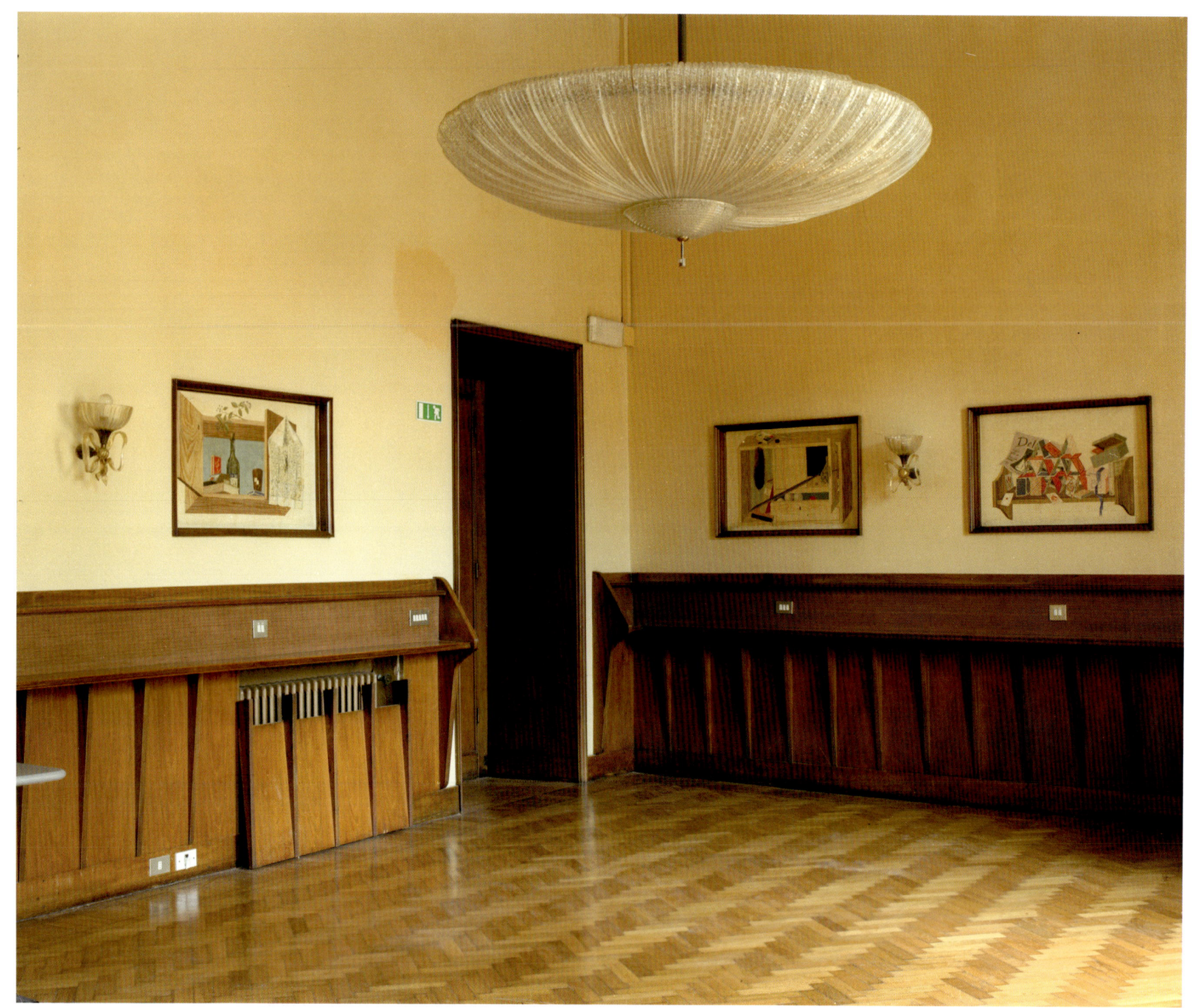

PIANO NOBILE, PALAZZO VAJ

Sala Giochi

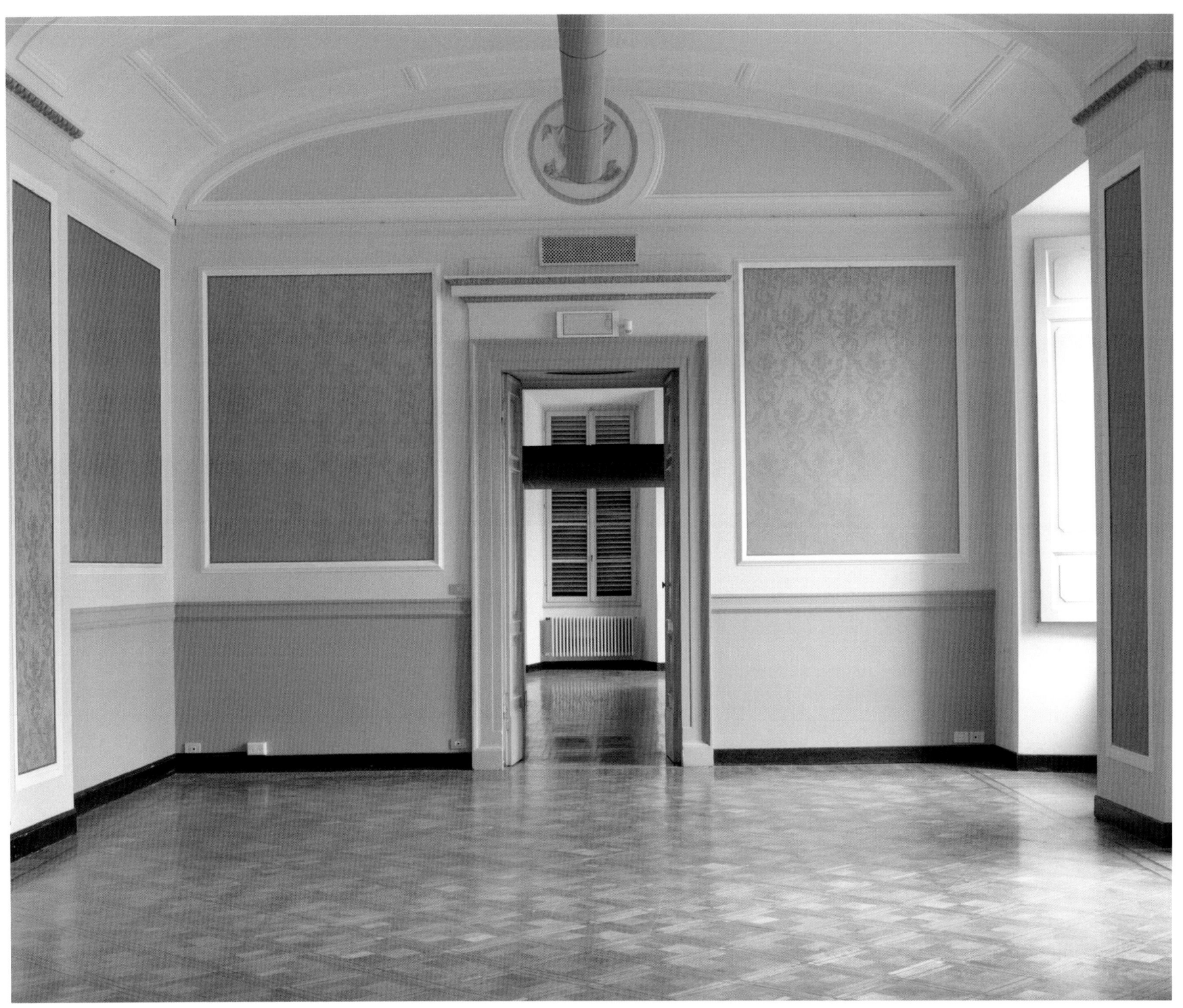

PIANO NOBILE, PALAZZO VAJ

Sala Veneziana

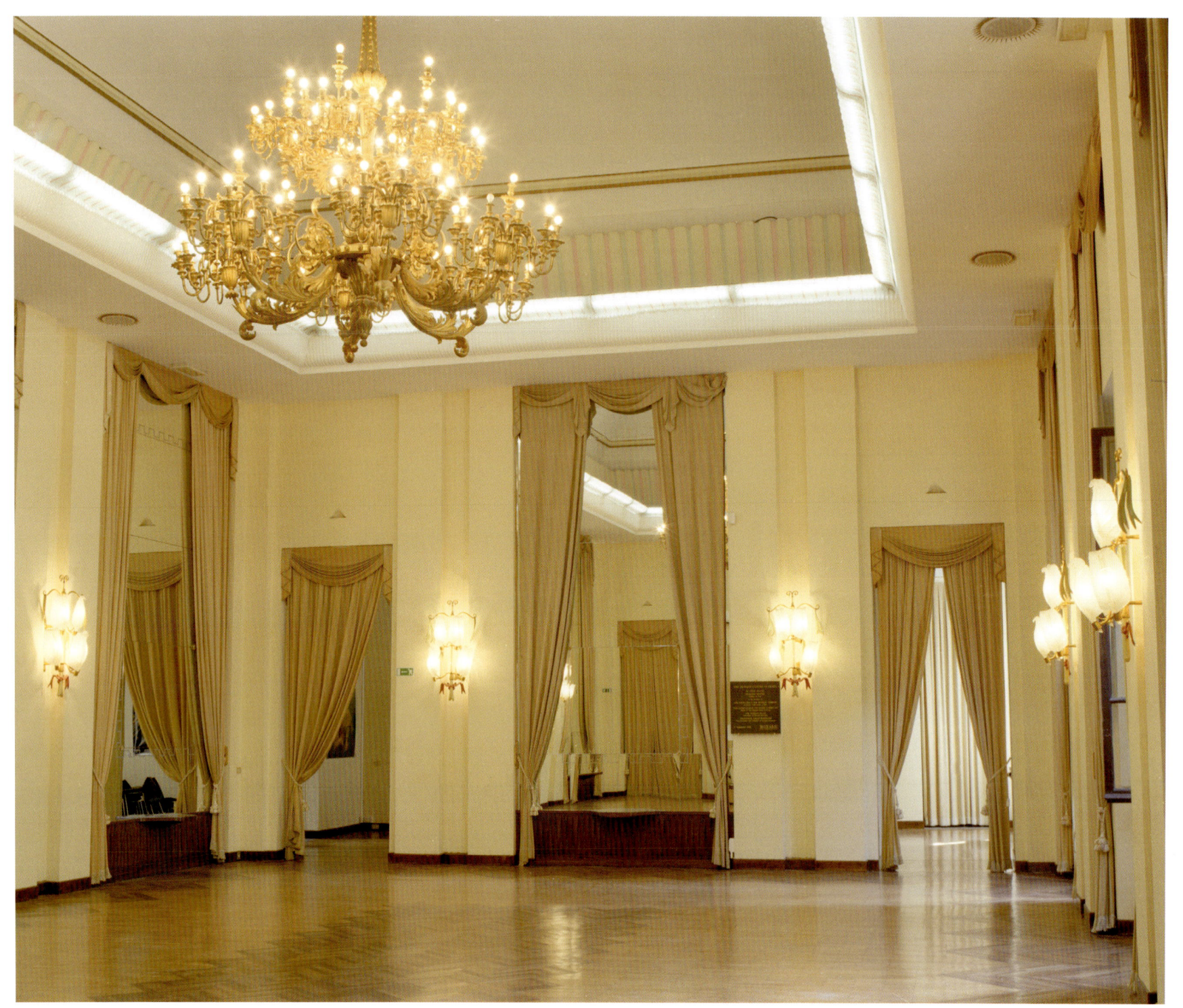

PIANO NOBILE, PALAZZO VAJ

Salone Grollo

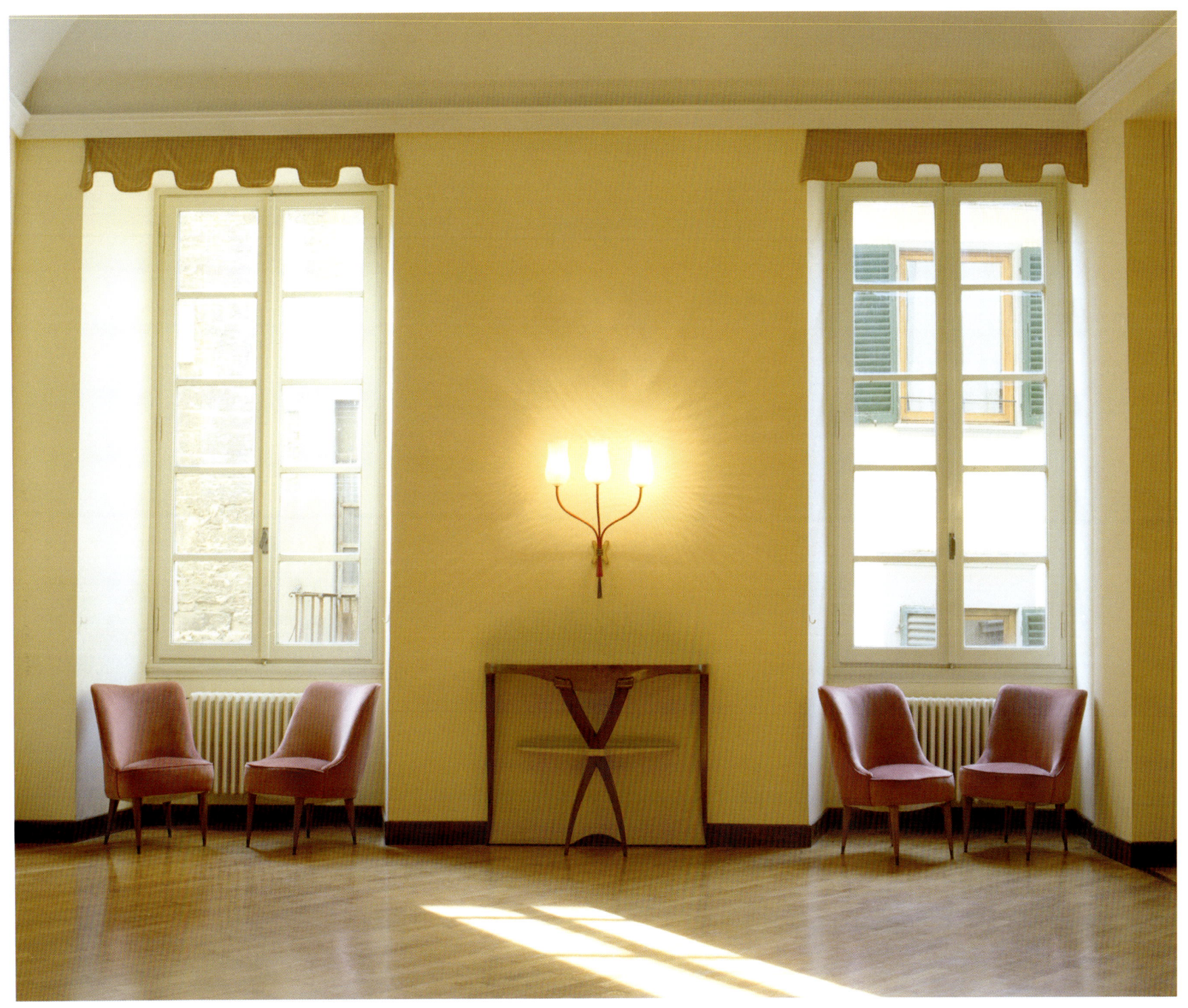

PIANO NOBILE, PALAZZO VAJ   Chromogenic prints, 2004

Sala del Caminetto

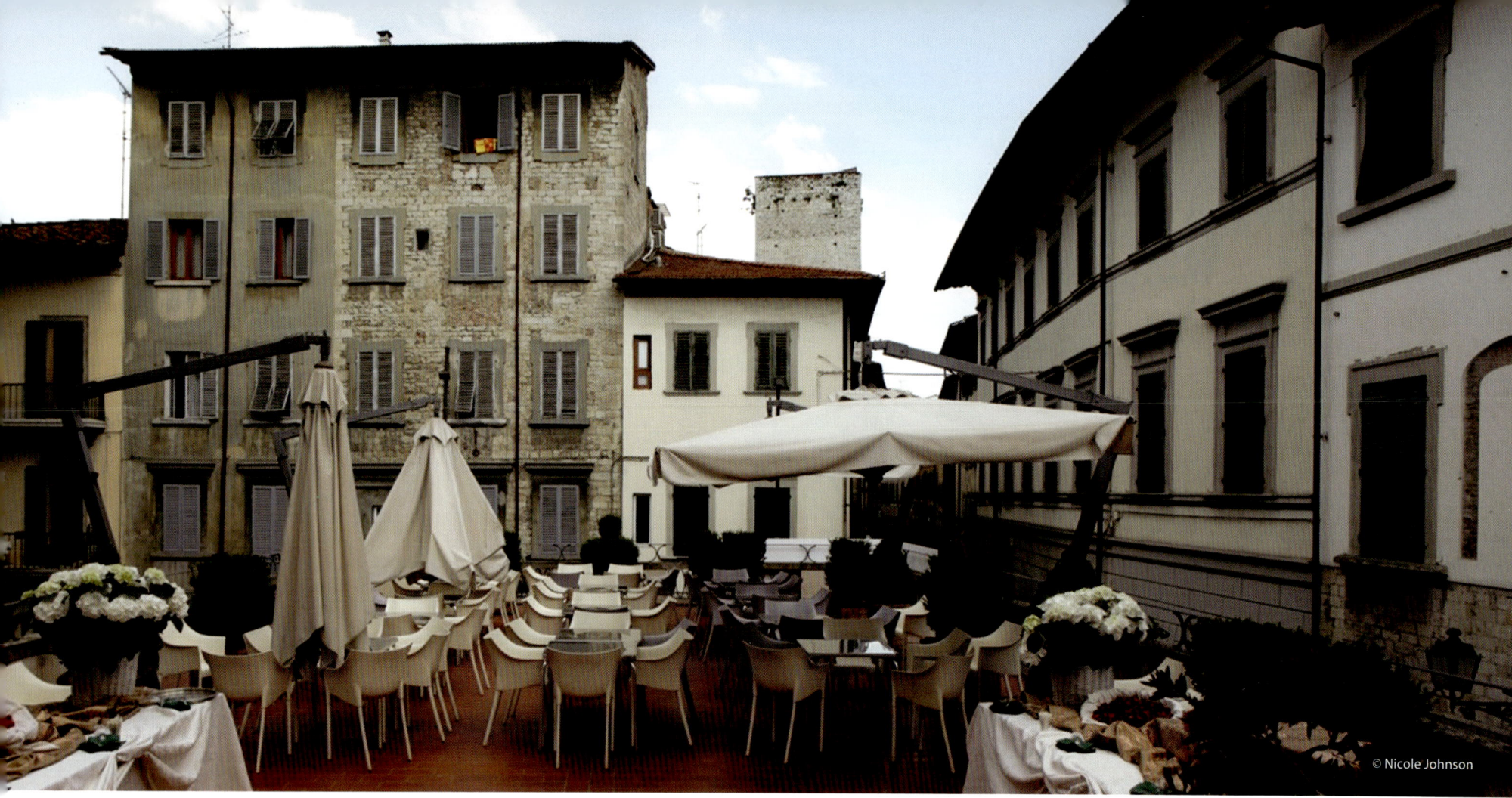
© Nicole Johnson

Earlier in 2010, Bill Kent had reminisced about 'keeping house, this extraordinary house', and in particular, the 'marvellous terrace that opens out into old Prato'. 'On a summer's morning', he recounted, 'I would be at the office by 7.10 am, and go and water the plants on the terrace [… for which] Cecilia and I had bought the soil. […] One of my great pleasures was the building itself, and the use of the building'.

While teaching at the Centre in January 2011, Annamaria Pagliaro also enthused about the Palazzo Vaj:

when I walk in, I take a deep breath and enjoy every aspect. Monash offers up-to-date facilities in an elegant European setting. Because it was a gentlemen's club, there are areas designed to welcome visitors, [… there are] luxurious spaces like the Salone Grollo, and so many corners where you can hide away with your laptop, and connect to email in private, but also sit and talk. It works so well, helping to create amicable relationships. I have always invited students to use the Palazzo Vaj fully—they absolutely love the spaces. Likewise, the academics have great praise for the Centre's home.

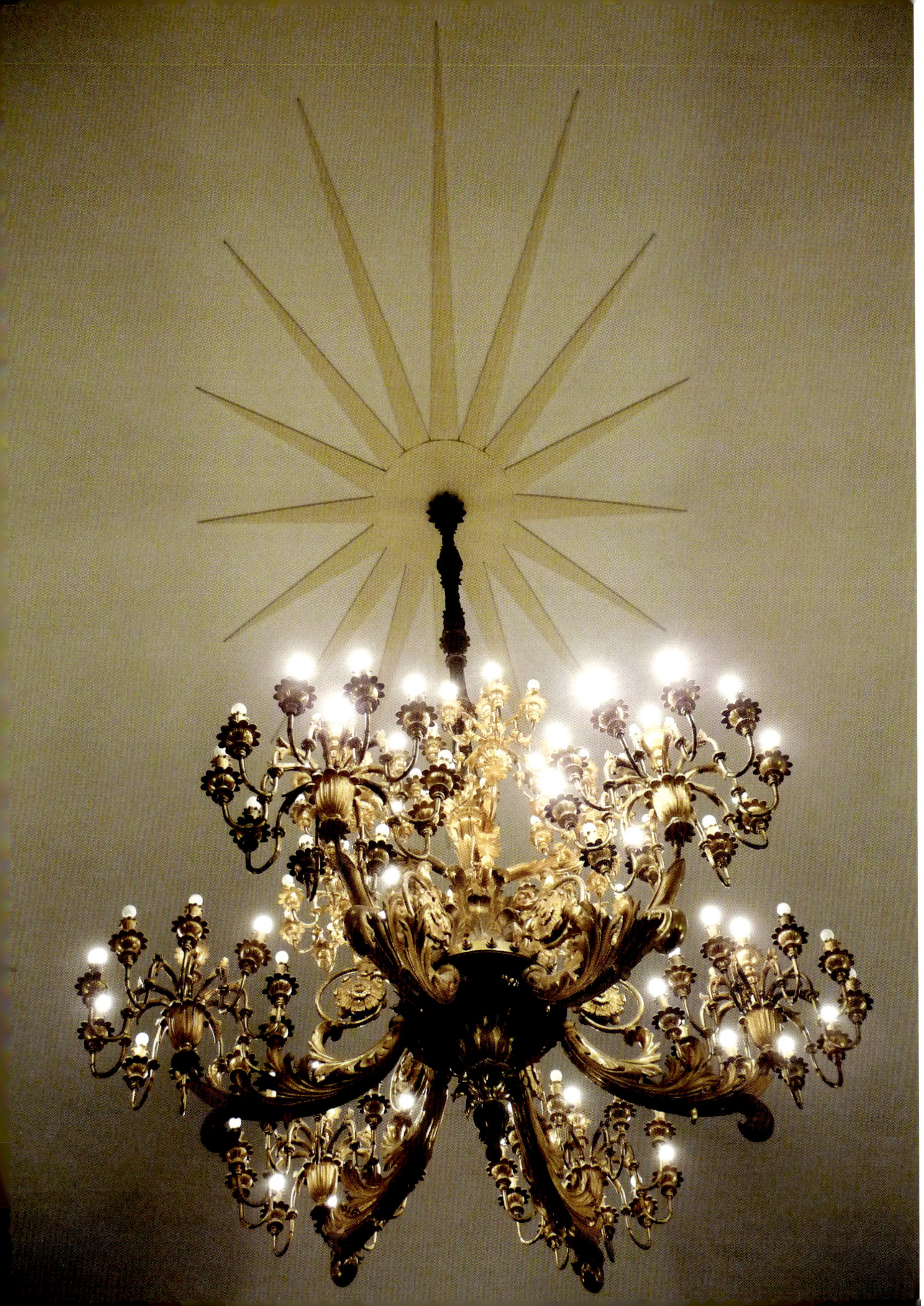

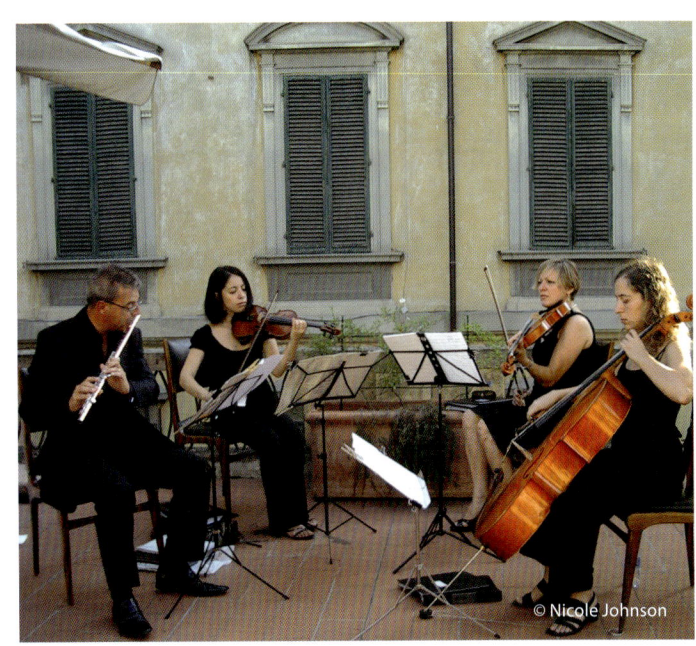
© Nicole Johnson

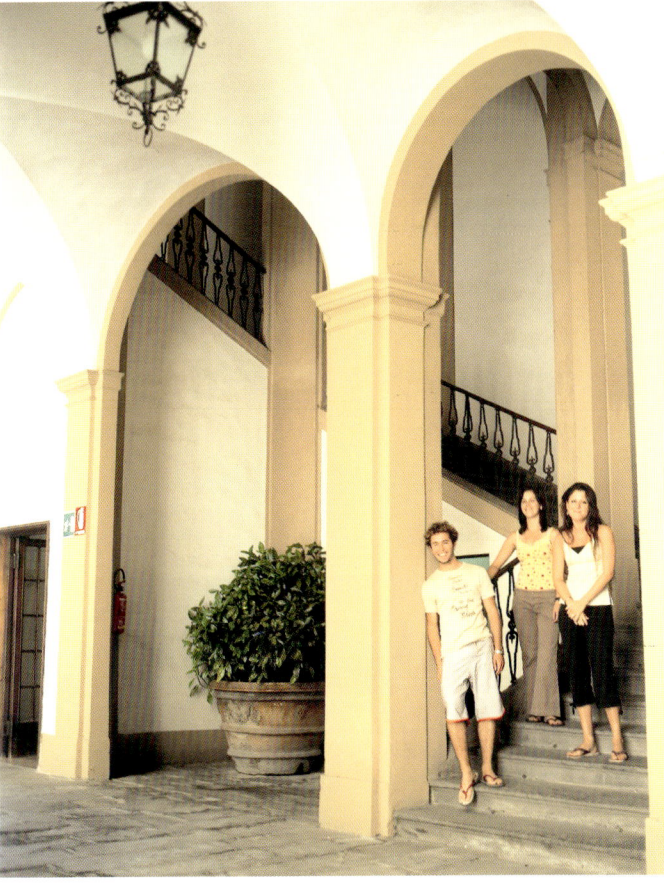

spaces; recreational areas. In consultation with the firm International Design, furnishings were purchased accordingly. Monash staff concerned with the project have recalled the first nine months of 2001 as a period when 'things moved very, very quickly'. At the Palazzo Vaj, this was due in good part to the extremely willing, energetic assistance of Anna Mazzoni, the building administrator, and, to quote Bill Kent, 'workmen and local artisans who knew the building backwards'. While enough of the necessary refurbishments were concluded for the official opening on 17 September 2001, it was six months later, in April 2002, that the Centre director's report declared:

> while finishing touches remain, the fit out of the Centre is rapidly approaching completion. We have now acquired the majority of the audio visual equipment required for teaching and conference purposes. The new offices in the ex-restaurant have been completed apart from some minor electrical wiring […] .

Terracotta pots for the terrace were amongst the long-awaited 'finishing touches'. These eventually 'arrived in time to be planted for the European Access Network conference' in June 2002.

Particularly during the Centre's first five years, in a spirit of demonstrating awareness of the Palazzo Vaj's importance to Prato and the *pratesi*, Centre premises were made available as often as possible to local organisations for their own events. A wide range of people entered the building then; many older *pratesi* returned, women mentioning with nostalgia the balls and festivities held there, when they were guests of the Società dei Misoduli.

From at least 2004, the flourishing and growth of Centre activities occasioned repeated discussion of a need for additional space. Consequently, by 2006, *la Monash* had gained three large seminar rooms, four smaller classrooms and two offices on the ground floor of the Palazzo Vaj—a major development in the Centre's architectural footprint, which was supported by the municipal and provincial governments, and the Prato Chamber of Commerce. Strengthening the Centre's identification with the Palazzo Vaj, the expansion was celebrated on 16 January 2006. The evening's formalities were attended by local dignitaries and a crowd of over 120, amongst them Marco Romagnoli, the mayor of Prato; academics from the University of Florence, the University of Hartford, and Melbourne's La Trobe University; Australian and other visiting students. Professor Graeme Davison, then director of the Monash London Centre, gave the closing address. Intensive press coverage of the event in Prato involved local and regional television stations, as well as radio and newspapers.

As evidenced by the vignettes in the third part of this volume, it is typical for Centre visitors of all kinds to express appreciation of the Palazzo Vaj's dignity and aesthetic qualities. Similarly, each of the Centre directors to date has freely expressed a love of the Palazzo Vaj, notwithstanding the demands posed by tenancy of such an esteemed heritage building. Determining the most suitable purpose, adaptation and refurbishment of the ground and first floor spaces continues to be an evolving process. In 2010, current Centre Director Loretta Baldassar commended further developments downstairs: two stylish new computer laboratories—sponsored by the Prato Chamber of Commerce—and the creation of the Bill Kent Library. 'With its high, vaulted ceiling, and its substantial core collection of books on the shelves, the Bill Kent Library really is a beautiful place', she said.

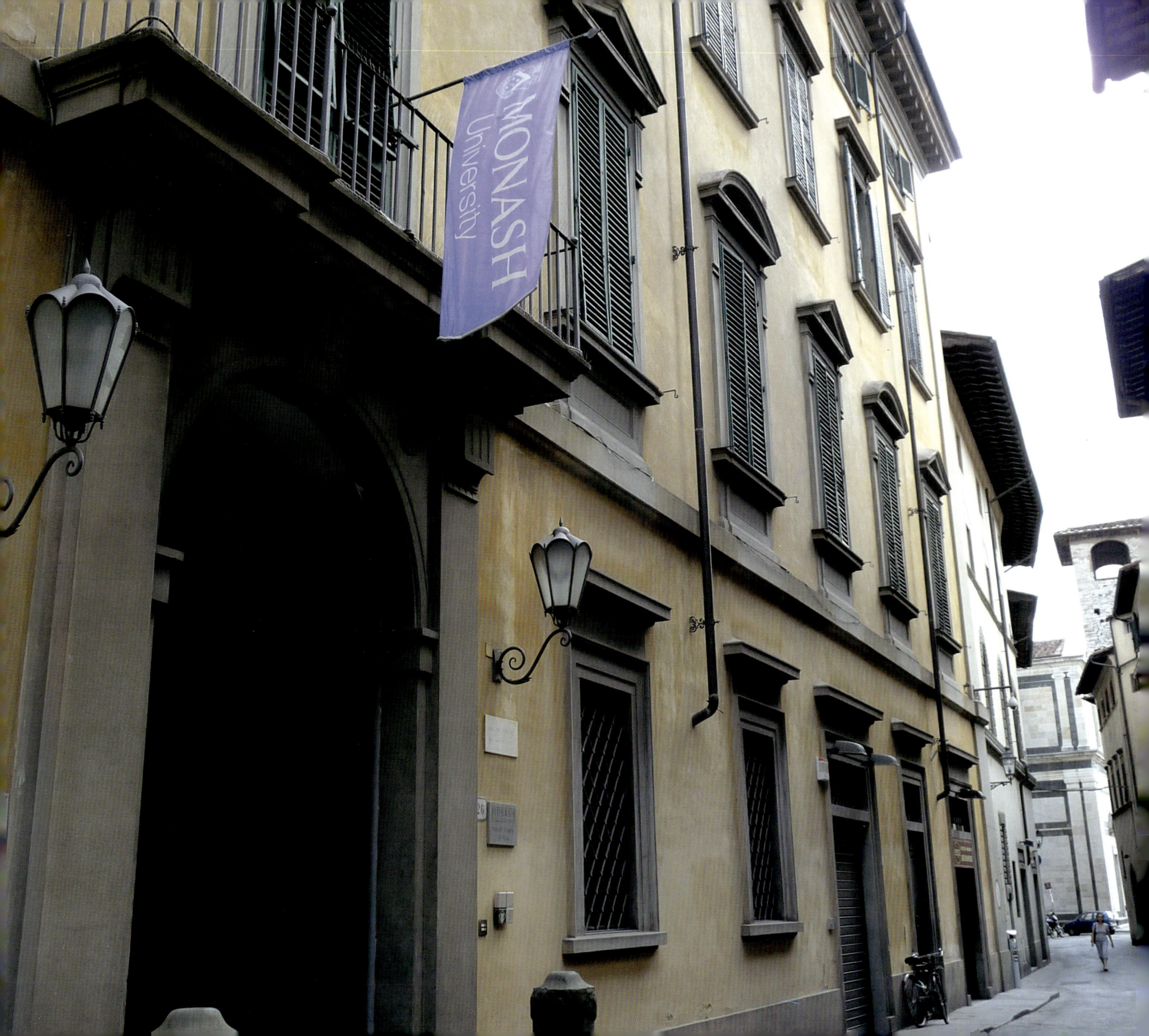

'KEEPING HOUSE' AT THE PALAZZO VAJ

The Palazzo Vaj has long been regarded by the *pratesi*, the people of Prato, with pride and admiration. Especially when heralding plans for the Monash Centre in 1998 and 1999, the local press reflected these feelings; in an article for *Il Tirreno*, Fabio Berni, for example, described the building as 'glorious'. At that time, the Palazzo Vaj featured in the civic memory as the historic headquarters of the Società dei Misoduli, a gentlemen's social club. Cecilia Hewlett began working with Bill Kent soon after he had arrived in Prato as the Monash Centre's first director; she managed the countless practical decisions through which the first floor was transformed to serve the vision of the new institution. Speaking about the immediate significance of the building for the Centre's atmosphere, she has observed, 'the Palazzo Vaj is an incredibly romantic building, not just as a grand mansion, but because of what it had become, as the home of the Misoduli'. That is, it had become a famously elitist establishment, which in its mid-twentieth century heyday hosted events on an impressive scale.

In his essay 'Gaining a Foothold: Australian Cultural Institutions in Italy', Bill Kent outlined the exigencies that followed from Monash's lease of the *piano nobile*:

Early in November 2000 I arrived in Prato as founding director to take possession of the cold and empty first floor of Palazzo Vaj, 1,500 square metres of former gentlemen's club requiring every sort of repair and renovation, not to mention furnishing and outfitting, as well as complete rewiring to serve the needs of a university in the electronic age.

While seeming cavernous, the first floor spaces evoked some of the building's past repute in the debris that lay about, and in remnants of the club members' gaming activities: for a while, old gambling chips kept surfacing in various cupboards. The bespoke art deco style furniture and fittings had been stripped from the rooms, but much of it was still piled in a dusty storeroom downstairs. Cecilia Hewlett remembers the satisfaction of being able to rescue 'some key pieces' from obscurity: a fireplace moulding, for instance; a number of chairs, card tables and light fittings.

The renovation program included mending floors, repainting, and network wiring for information technology. It evolved to include allocating rooms to particular uses: offices; teaching, conference and reception rooms; computer laboratories; art studio and exhibition

Il Tirreno — Mercoledì 24 gennaio 2001

Prato

Palazzo Vaj, arrivano gli australiani

Imminente l'apertura della Monash University nella vecchia sede dei Misoduli in via Pugliesi

di Camilla Bernacchioni

PRATO. Dopo il congresso nel novembre scorso, Bill Kent non vede l'ora di aprire le porte di palazzo Vaj agli studenti australiani che frequenteranno la Monash University. Il direttore non si sbilancia nel precisare la data ma spera di far coincidere l'inaugurazione con un evento che vede protagonista la sede pratese dell'università australiana: un convegno a maggio sulla multicultura in collaborazione con la Regione Toscana in cui saranno coinvolte anche le istituzioni locali. «Sarebbe perfetto - afferma Kent entusiasta - e speriamo di farcela».

Al congresso parteciperanno, oltre al presidente Claudio Martini, 4 relatori australiani e 4 italiani. «E' un modo per condividere le esperienze - prosegue Kent - che è poi quello che vogliamo fare con l'università». Non stupisce l'entusiasmo con cui Kent parla di tutto quello che riguarda l'Italia, visto che è docente di italianistica, specializzato in storia del Medioevo e Rinascimento fiorentino ed ha già pubblicato vari studi sull'argomento. Oltre a dirigere la sede pratese della più importante università australiana, infatti, Kent continua i suoi studi ed ha appena concluso un libro su Lorenzo de' Medici per la University of California press che sarà tradotto anche in italiano. Mostra orgoglioso il risultato dei lavori nel palazzo di via Pugliesi, a buon punto ma non conclusi, tessendo le lodi di chi ha dato la possibilità di realizzare questo ambizioso progetto, alla città e ai pratesi. «Ci tengo a precisare che quello di Prato non è un campus. La Monash è

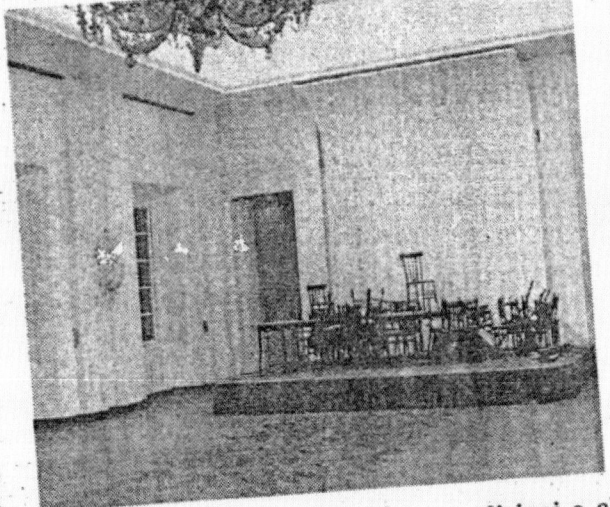

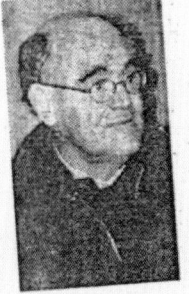

Il professor Kent e due immagini della nuova sede

un'università statale con uno sponsor, anonimo - sorride - qui abbiamo trovato molta disponibilità da parte di tutti. Gli stessi lavori di imbiancatura sono stati svolti in un solo mese. Credo che questa sia una città molto vivace, molto europea. Noi australiani siamo isolati e in questo modo possiamo aprire nuovi contatti con l'Europa, conoscerne la storia e le tradizioni e allo stesso tempo far conoscere l'Australia». Il palazzo, vecchia sede dei Misoduli, ospiterà ogni volta 100 studenti che potranno studiare tra le varie discipline, non solo italiano «anche se il mio invito è quello di arrivare in Italia già con la padronanza della lingua», ma anche legge, design, architettura, storia dell'arte e le dinamiche del mercato globale. «Ci saranno tutte le discipline - spiega il direttore - l'idea è quella di fare corsi modulari brevi ma su tutti gli argomenti, sempre in base alle richieste. In questi giorni, per esempio, ho preso contatti con Margherita Ciacci, che conosco da tempo, della facoltà di Economia a Firenze con cui dovremmo collaborare».

A disposizione degli studenti negli ampi spazi del palazzo, biblioteca, reception, sale con computer, di lettura e consultazione, un bar e una grande terrazza. I primi trenta studenti arriveranno a giugno per studiare legge mentre a luglio ne sbarcheranno altri venti per un corso di arte e design. progetto è ambizioso per c sto preferisco fare le cose calma. Le lezioni saranno gli studenti australiani presto vorremmo attivare che dei corsi per gli italian prattutto di inglese. L'uni sità sarà comunque uno sp aperto anche ai pratesi p organizzeremo periodica te mostre di artisti austra magari il collaborazione Pecci e concerti». La prim stra è in programma per gresso sulla multicultur nedi, intanto, Kent vol nuovo in Australia con famiglia per definire gli dettagli.

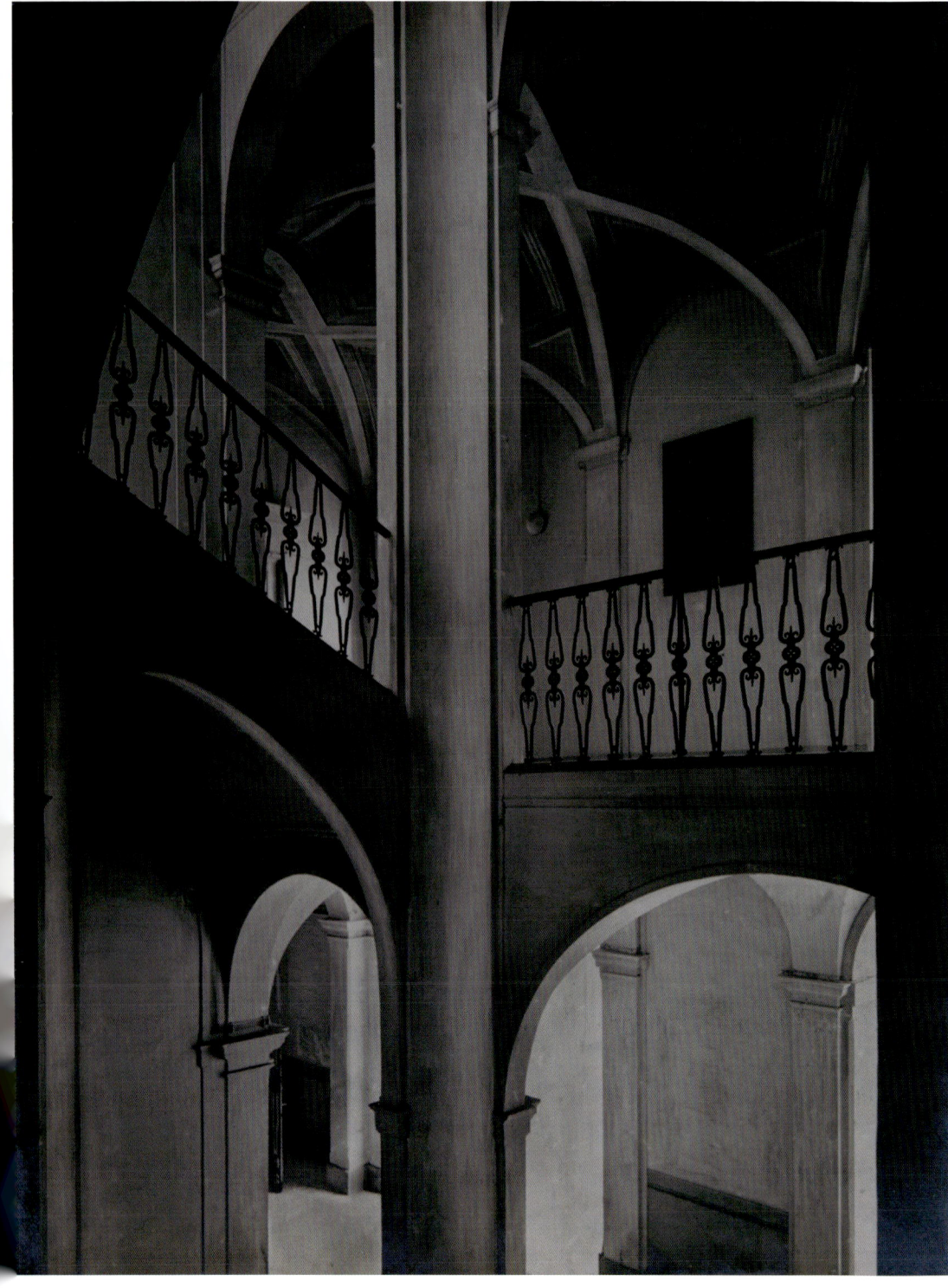

Staircase designed by Valentini, Palazzo Vaj. Photograph by Domenico Coppi (1920s), reproduced by Andrea Abati
© Associazione Industriale e Commerciale dell'Arte della Lana Prato

to mind card and parlour games; the creation of drawing rooms, and the bar room. Other rooms were decorated with still life imagery. Overall, not many of the older decorations are still visible: a few fireplaces and overdoors in stucco from the eighteenth century. On the recently renovated second floor, eighteenth century wall paintings and stucco ornamentation on fireplaces and doors have been brought to light.

A second courtyard leads to the chapel built on part of the demolished church of Saint George. Valentini designed its simple, neoclassical facade crowned by a triangular tympanum. The chapel interior is accentuated by columns, pilasters and friezes in *scagliola* (imitation marble); the elliptical dome was painted by Luigi Catani in 1797–98 with the *Virgin Assumed into Heaven and Angels*, and four saints in the pendentives below.

Palazzo Vaj is now owned by the Associazione Industriale e Commerciale dell'Arte della Lana (the Industrial and Commercial Association of the Wool Guild), which purchased the mansion complex from the Vaj family in 1920. One of the largest and most fascinating buildings in Prato's historic centre, today it hosts the Monash University Prato Centre on the ground and first floors, and, on the second floor, the headquarters of the Palazzo delle Professioni di Prato, an alliance of eight of the city's professional associations.

Translated by **Narelle McAuliffe**

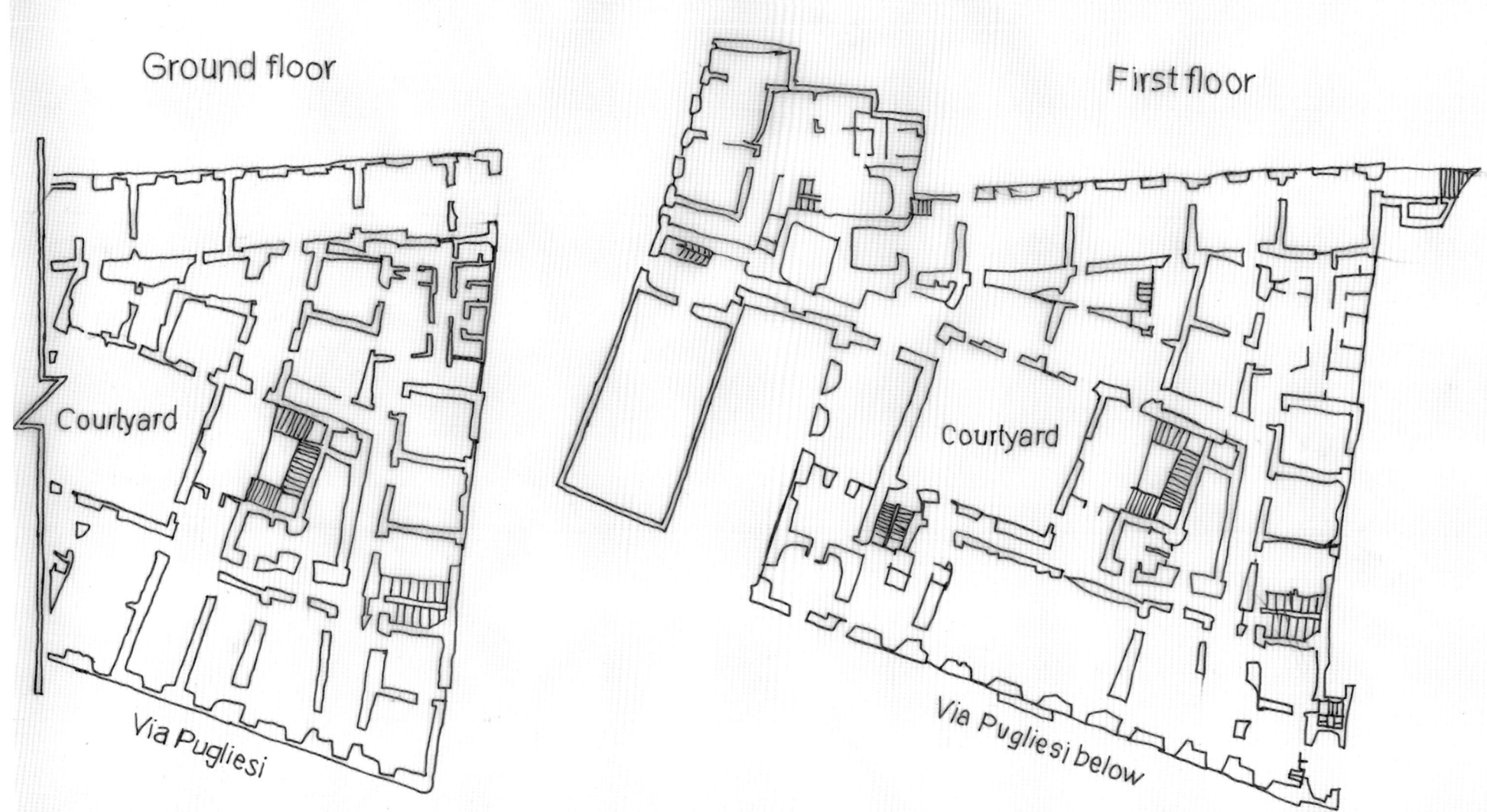

Palazzo Vaj, hand-drawn floor plan by Donata Batisti, 2011.

Palazzo Vaj: A Brief Historical Sketch

Rossella Foggi *Art Historian and Co-founder of FareArte Association, Prato*

Palazzo Vaj stands in the heart of the medieval centre of Prato, in the old Via delle Torri (Street of Towers), now Via Pugliesi. On the streetscape, the imposing edifice still presents the late eighteenth century appearance bestowed by the wealthy Vaj family.

In the Middle Ages, in this part of Prato—adjacent to a section of the twelfth century city walls—there rose numerous towers, as well as the parish church of Saint George. Subsequently a mansion was built with a garden, its boundary walls decorated with elegant, late fifteenth century *graffiti* (paintings in white on black). Depicting scenes of court life and May Day celebrations, the *graffiti* are now preserved in Prato's Museo di Pittura Murale (Museum of Wall Painting). In the early eighteenth century, a few of these buildings were purchased by the Vaj family who, around 1785, also bought the ancient church of Saint George with its presbytery. The Vaj commissioned the Florentine Luca Ristorini to design a building incorporating the various earlier structures, unified by a monumental facade. Ristorini's design was modified by the Prato architect Giuseppe Valentini, who worked on the mansion from 1796 to 1800. In 1825 Valentini also designed the open terrace on the first floor above Via Garibaldi, which was used for parties and receptions.

From Via Pugliesi, the main portal of the Palazzo Vaj opens into a courtyard and covered atrium, from where one reaches the first floor—the *piano nobile*—by way of the neoclassical grand staircase designed by Valentini. On the vault of the staircase is a 1796 painting by Luigi Catani depicting Apollo and *putti* holding the Vaj coat of arms.

From 1876 the building became the meeting place of the prestigious Società dei Misoduli—the mid-nineteenth century name for the Accademia degli Infecondi, a society created in 1712 with literary aims, and then transformed into a cultural and recreational club frequented by the manufacturing bourgeoisie of Prato. (*Misoduli* is a word derived from the Greek 'haters of slavery'.) In the mid-1950s, the Florentine architect Italo Gamberini was commissioned to transform the spaces of the first floor for the use of the Società dei Misoduli. Gamberini worked principally in Tuscany, and would later design the Luigi Pecci Contemporary Art Centre in Prato. His designs for the renovation included distinctive wall panels, false ceilings, modern furnishings, tapestries, mirrors and floorings. The focus of these works was the grand hall for parties (today's Salone Grollo); also the creation of games rooms—including today's Sala Giochi—decorated with motifs that call

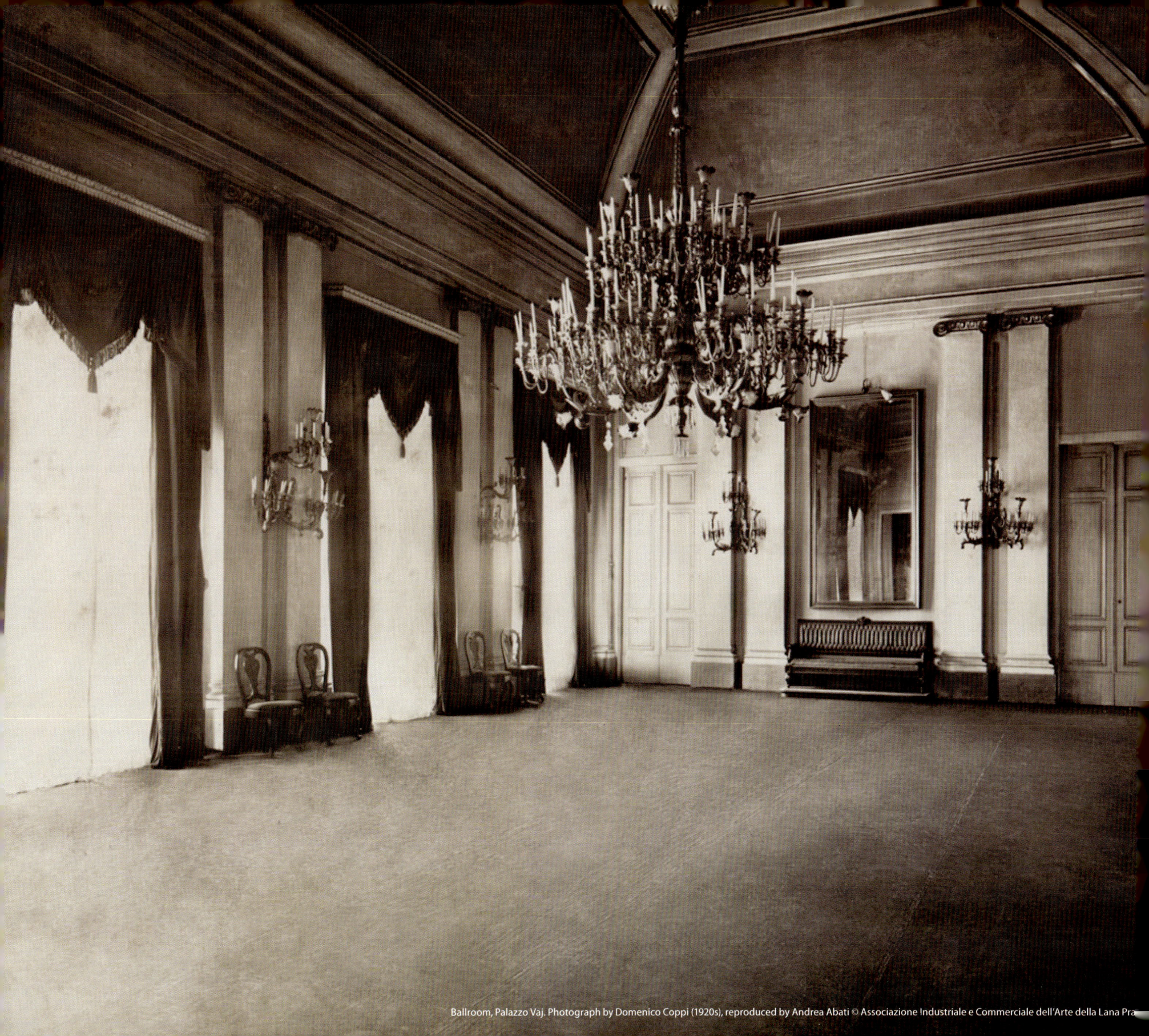

Ballroom, Palazzo Vaj. Photograph by Domenico Coppi (1920s), reproduced by Andrea Abati © Associazione Industriale e Commerciale dell'Arte della Lana Pra

the profoundly constructive ways in which the Centre has come to serve as a resource for the unique demographic circumstances of its locality.

In November 2008, the Centre gained a sophisticated and far-reaching avenue for engagement with industry. The president of the Tuscan Region Claudio Martini launched the Monash University Accident Research Centre Europe at the Palazzo Vaj. MUARC Europe (as it tends to be known), is dedicated to collaborative research, training and education concerned with vehicle and road safety—involving the European automotive industry and government institutions, also public organisations such as the Automobile Club d'Italia (the ACI). The Monash University Accident Research Centre originated at Monash Clayton in 1987, and was designated in 2005 one of only 23 World Health Organization Collaborating Centres on Violence, Injuries and Disabilities. The 'Europe node' has furthered the Accident Research Centre's international standing and developed projects of immense comparative scope. The Multi-National Database Study, for example, is evaluating the benefits of road safety technology using data from the Netherlands, Finland, Sweden, Spain, France, Germany, UK and Italy, as well as Australia and New Zealand. Where MUARC Europe began with one staff member, founding director Brian Fildes, there are currently four adjunct research fellows permanently based in Europe.

In 2009, the Prato Consortium for Medieval and Renaissance Studies became a fourth avenue through which to intensify the Centre's dynamic identification with Prato and Europe. This forum for cooperative research and teaching was generated through memoranda of understanding between Monash and the Universities of Arizona, Durham, Edinburgh, Toronto, and Warwick, and the State Archives of Prato, all institutions prominent in the field of Medieval and Renaissance studies. The consortium is premised on the Centre's location in Europe, Tuscany and Prato's *centro storico*—not simply because of its convenience as meeting place for the scholars and students, but because material for their field-work is found literally 'at the doorstep' of the Palazzo Vaj. In the story of the Centre, the consortium can be considered a formal structure for furthering Bill Kent's undisguised delight in Prato's medieval and Renaissance patrimony. Therefore, when launched at Open Day in 2010, the Centre's specialist library was named the Bill Kent Library; its nucleus of nearly 2000 volumes came from the private collection of Nicolai and Ruth Rubinstein. Nicolai Rubinstein, Professor at the University of London, was a renowned historian of Renaissance Florence and a mentor to Australian scholars in this field; Ruth Olitsky Rubinstein was a historian of Renaissance art. The Bill Kent library is housed in an airy room on the ground floor of the Palazzo Vaj. A precondition for its growth is the growth of the consortium's activities in Prato. Meanwhile, as every palace-builder of the Italian Renaissance knew, the founding of a library, however small, is an explicit statement about the pertinence of humanist values to the progress of fresh ideas and opportunities.

Monash's School of Historical Studies offered the first two undergraduate subjects associated with the consortium over November–December 2009 and January 2010. In the latter month, the weekly newspaper *Metropoli Prato* ran a full page interview with Centre Director Loretta Baldassar, preceded by a photo of a class-in-progress at the Palazzo Vaj. Fabrizio Nucci introduced the interview with reflections on 'a marriage between Monash University and Prato which is becoming more fruitful each year [...]'. The article headline was, 'Monash, The Good Side of Globalisation'.

the Study of Global Movements and its cooperative endeavours. More specifically, the topic of the Chinese community in Prato has become another main avenue of enquiry and activity for the Centre's future directions.

It was in November 2007 that the first research workshop on relations between the Chinese and Italian populations in Prato took place at the Centre. Titled 'Building Communities: The Chinese in Prato', and conducted in English, Italian and Chinese, the workshop presented perspectives of local residents and businesses; those of municipal, provincial and national governments, and Italian, Chinese and Australian academics. The 60 attendees were welcomed to the Palazzo Vaj by Amanda Vanstone, Australian ambassador to Italy; prefect of Prato, Eleonora Maffei; the president of the Prato Province, Massimo Logli; and the Chinese consul in Florence, Gu Honglin.

The 2007 workshop, and a second held at the Centre in 2008, became the basis for the collection *Living Outside the Walls: The Chinese in Prato*, edited by Graeme Johanson and Rebecca French, of Monash's Faculty of Information Technology, and Russell Smyth, of the Faculty of Business and Economics. Published by Cambridge Scholars Publishing in 2009, this volume is the first wide-ranging study of its kind in English. The preface by Professor John Nieuwenhuysen AM, founding director of the Monash Institute for the Study of Global Movements, describes the Centre as 'an ideal venue for European based activities of the University', and the publication's timeliness for Europe as well as Prato.

> A specially valuable feature of the volume and the Prato conferences themselves, is the interest shown in the project by Wenzhou University, a large delegation of whose members, including its Deputy Vice President, participated in the discussions leading up to the emergence of the manuscript, and two of whose scholars provided research inputs in an important chapter on remittances.

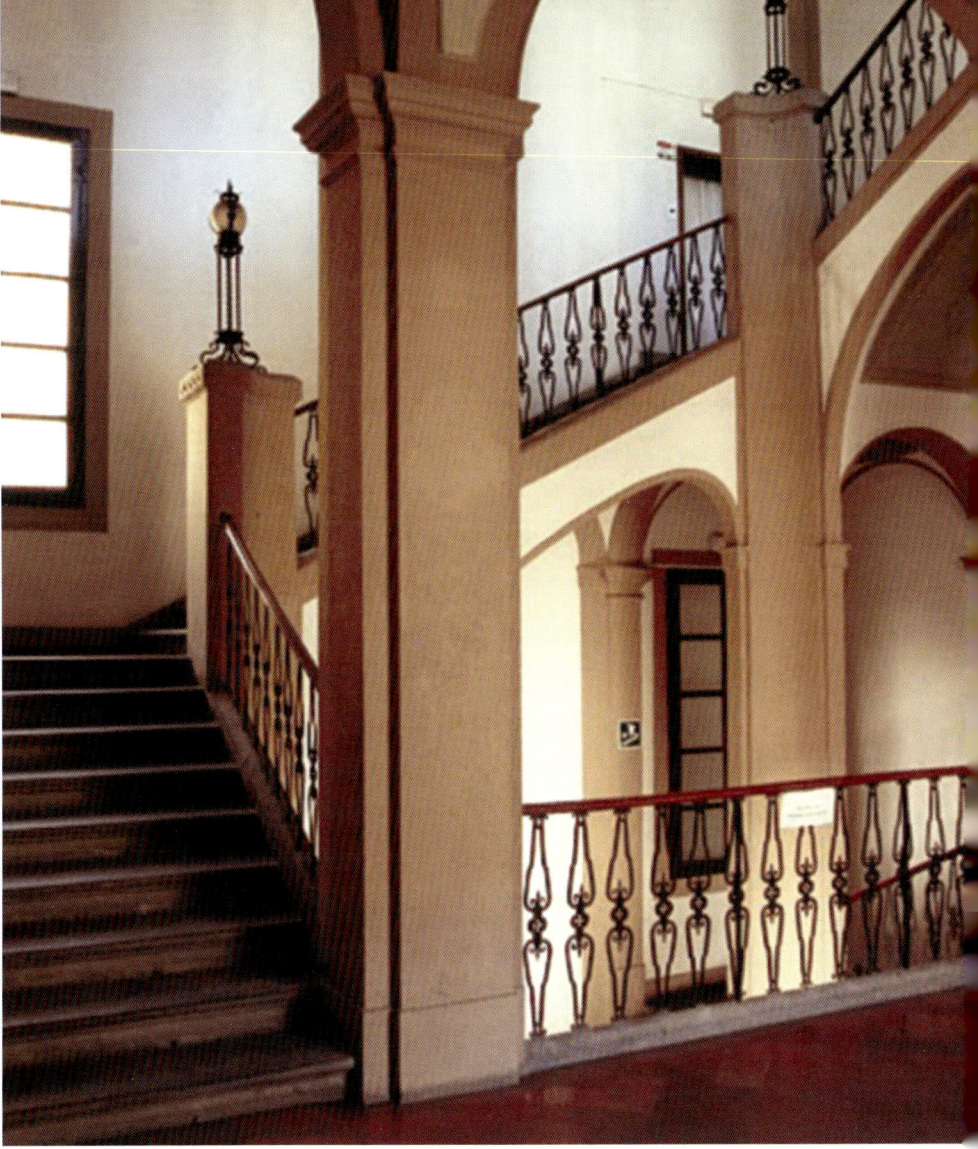

The Prato Province and the Centre jointly funded the translation of the collection into Italian, which was published in 2009 by Pacini Editore—and launched during the Centre's 2010 Open Day. Also in 2010, a four party memorandum of understanding was created between Monash University, Wenzhou University, PIN S.c.r.l., and the Prato Province administration, to facilitate research focused on Prato's Chinese community. Signing took place in the Palazzo Buonamici, headquarters of the Prato Province. Both of these recent achievements demonstrate

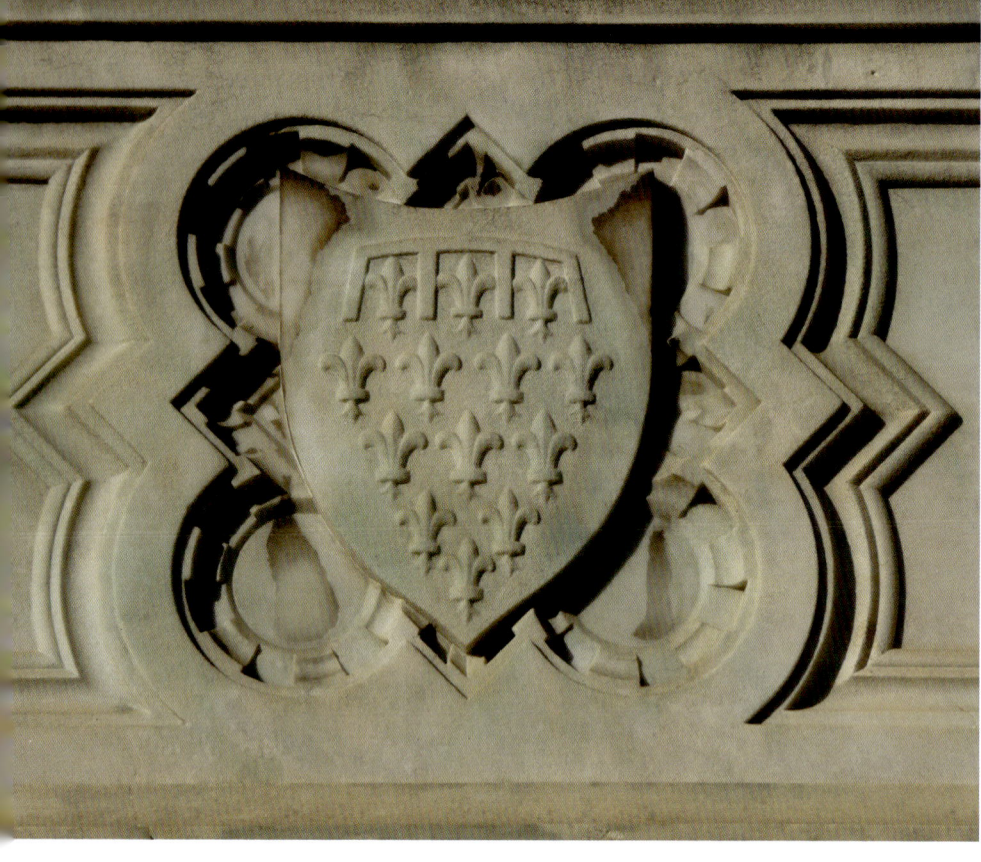

centre for teaching, research and outreach activities concerned with Europe and the EU. The Prato Centre's ability to provide students and researchers with an immersive experience of Europe contributed significantly to this development. Annamaria Pagliaro, Centre director at the time, was a member of the working party that prepared the successful bid. Recollecting the process in 2011, she enthused, 'by then, because of the opportunities and connections we had in Europe—as the only Australian Centre there of its kind—we had ample means to fulfil the objectives set out in the tender. At some level we were already doing much of what the European Commission had in mind. The funding for the EU Centre became an external recognition of the importance of the Prato Centre's EU orientation'. Closely involving the Faculties of Arts, Business and Economics, and Law, the EU Centre has since provided a firm multidisciplinary framework for expanding the teaching, higher degree and research programs offered by these faculties at Prato.

increased during the Centre's first five years, a key challenge for those leading and guiding operations became that of managing expectations in Prato, and in Australia—while staying amenable to those 'many other possibilities'. It follows that gradually, over the past decade, there has emerged greater clarity about the more pertinent and sustainable means of concentrating resources. And during that time there developed four particular avenues through which to deepen Monash's relationship with Prato and the wider European setting. Naturally in practice these avenues can and do converge, through the interests if not the expertise of Centre clients or visitors.

The first of these avenues to become established was the Monash European and EU Centre, based at Monash's Caulfield Campus. In January 2006, Monash University was named one of three Australian recipients of grants from the European Commission to host such a

Before 2000, initial discussions with the Tuscan Region and then the Comune di Prato referred to the mutual aspiration that the Monash Centre contribute positively to discourse on immigration at the local level. In May 2001, David Rosenthal wrote a feature article about Monash University's 'embryonic institution' at Prato, published in *The Australian* newspaper. Rosenthal took his theme from the Centre's 'first significant event', which had just taken place, the international conference 'Multiculturalism and Migration: Italy and Australia, Two Experiences Compared'. He quoted Claudio Martini, president of the Tuscan Region, saying that Italy stood 'at a crossroads' regarding attitudes to multiculturalism. The Centre's response to local issues of contention in this area has become carefully more confident in succeeding years, assisted since 2004 by the Monash Institute for

MONASH IN PRATO – MONASH IN EUROPE

During the 33 months prior to the Centre's official opening, the ample press it received in Prato repeatedly cited Prato's credentials as an industrial city—the traditions and reach of its textile industry on the one hand, and, on the other, the size and prestige of Monash, and the multicultural formation of Monash students. This said, in 2010 Bill Kent once again underlined that right 'from the start' Monash enjoyed the formal and active support of the Tuscan Region and the Comune di Prato, and very soon that of the owners of the Palazzo Vaj, the Associazione Industriale e Commerciale dell'Arte della Lana,

> and receptivity that went beyond a mere sense of the economic advantages for the city of Prato. ... There was an openness to our being there ... appreciation of our mission in the wider sense, and this has grown right through. [...] So now we're *la Monash*, and if you get into a taxi and say, *la Monash*, not a problem. [...] It was said to me early on in a number of places—though in one sense we were doing it by instinct—'you are founding an institution which is obviously not just about economic and trade advantages, it is about cultural exchange'.

The Centre, Kent remarked during the same interview, 'actually became an Australian institutional presence that goes far beyond the solely the educational, in Italy, but also in Europe'.

As envisioned in *Leading the Way: Monash 2020*, the internationalisation of Monash presupposed a network of collaborative relationships spanning the globe: partnerships with other universities, and arrangements with a variety of organisations, to advance a wide range of learning experiences, academic pursuits, sources of research funding. Thus the task for the directors of the Centre in Prato has been to cultivate such relationships, and thereby seek to ensure that the Centre serve in the long term as a vibrant context for Monash's commitment to Europe. With this in mind, even the most cursory glance through the directors' reports from the past 10 years will ascertain how assiduously each director has worked to build on the advantages of the Centre's location for research and teaching, business, industry and governments.

Cooperative relations with several of Prato's cultural institutions began very early in the Centre's history—with the Metastasio Theatre, for instance, and with the Datini Institute. Sharing the Centre for events with such neighbours could concurrently signify engagement with the local community and with the European scene. This has continued to be the case. Conference planning with Monash staff also swiftly vouched for the Centre's value as a site for international dialogue relevant to contemporary Europe. A summary of the Centre's activities presented to the Monash Academic Board in August 2002 makes this clear. The paragraph opens with an expression of receptivity, 'Monash has already learned to use [the Centre] in a number of ways, which is not to say there are not many other possibilities ...'.

> There have been a number of Monash-sponsored academic conferences, seminars and workshops—too many to detail here—on themes ranging from automobile accident research to forensic studies, from Asian security to Mediterranean health issues. The law conference, organised by the International Academy of Forensic Studies, brought together in Prato well over 100 Australian lawyers and other researchers, including distinguished judges and barristers. The Centre also hosted in June the annual conference of the European [Higher Education] Access Network, to which came some 180 delegates from universities and research institutions all over the world.

Diversity and intensity had almost straightaway become trademarks of the Centre's programming. Accordingly, as the volume of activity

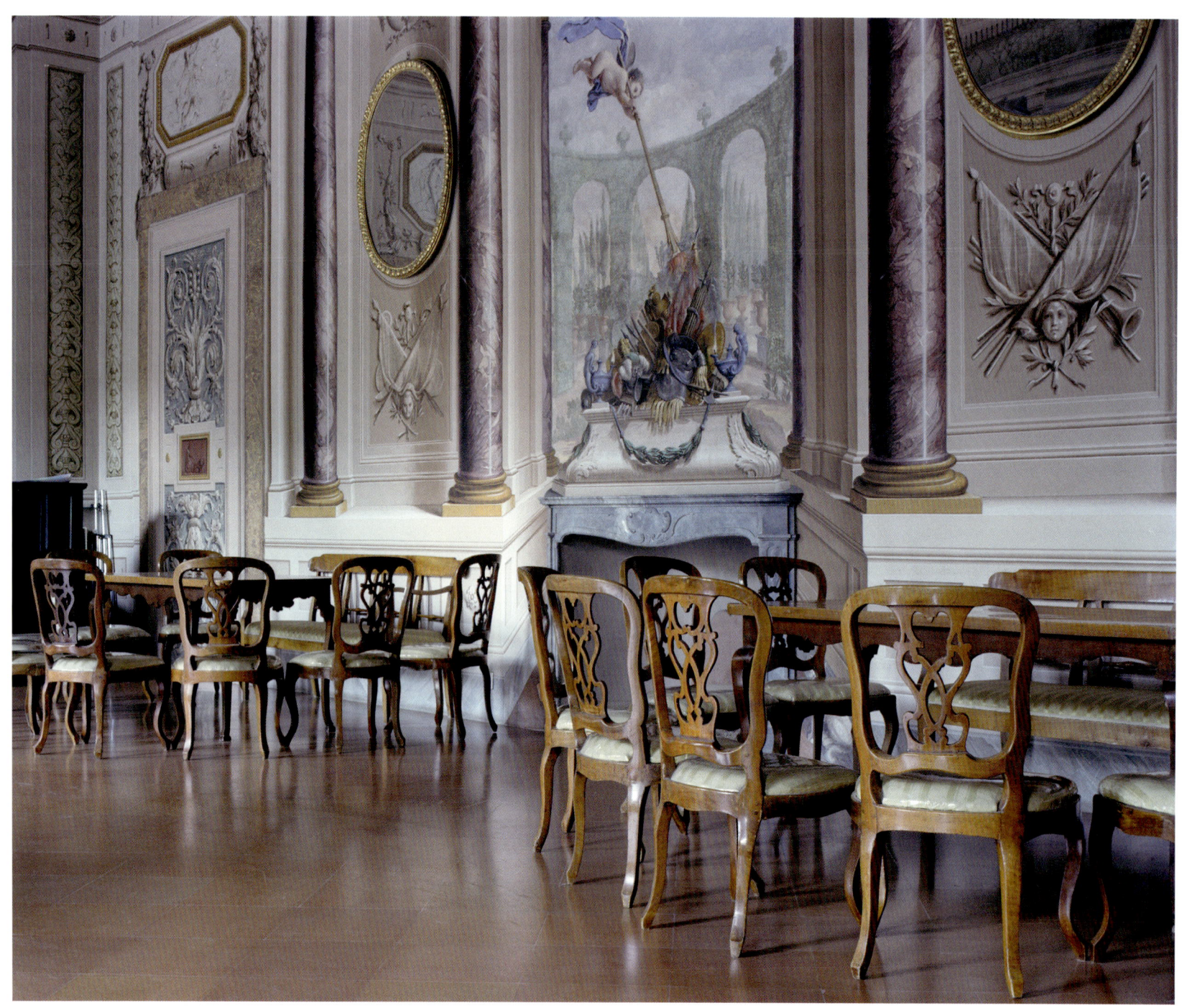

SITES OF CONVERGENCE

Amusement #1: Monastery of St. Niccolò, Prato, Italy

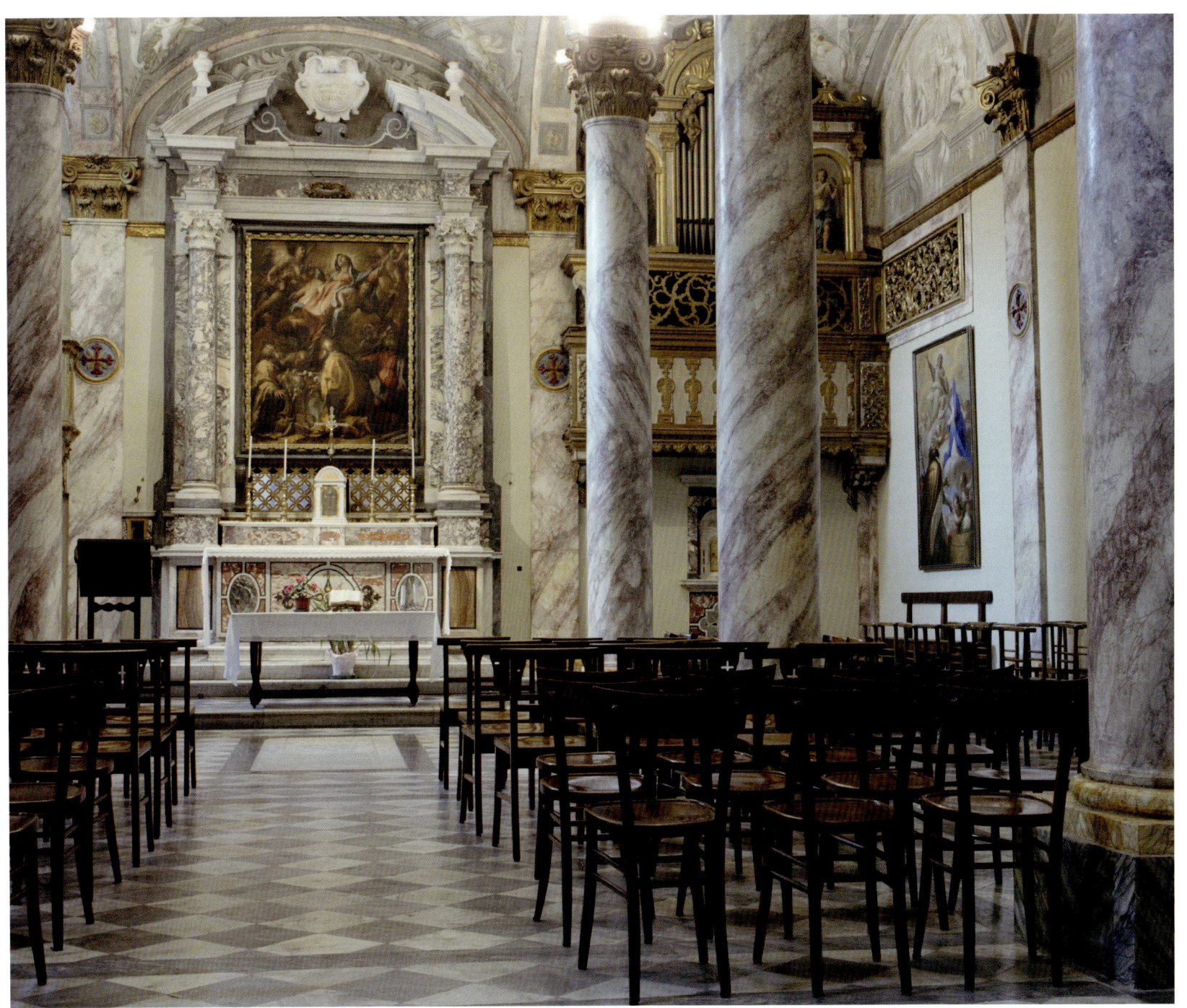

SITES OF CONVERGENCE

Reverence #1: Monastery of St. Niccolò, Prato, Italy

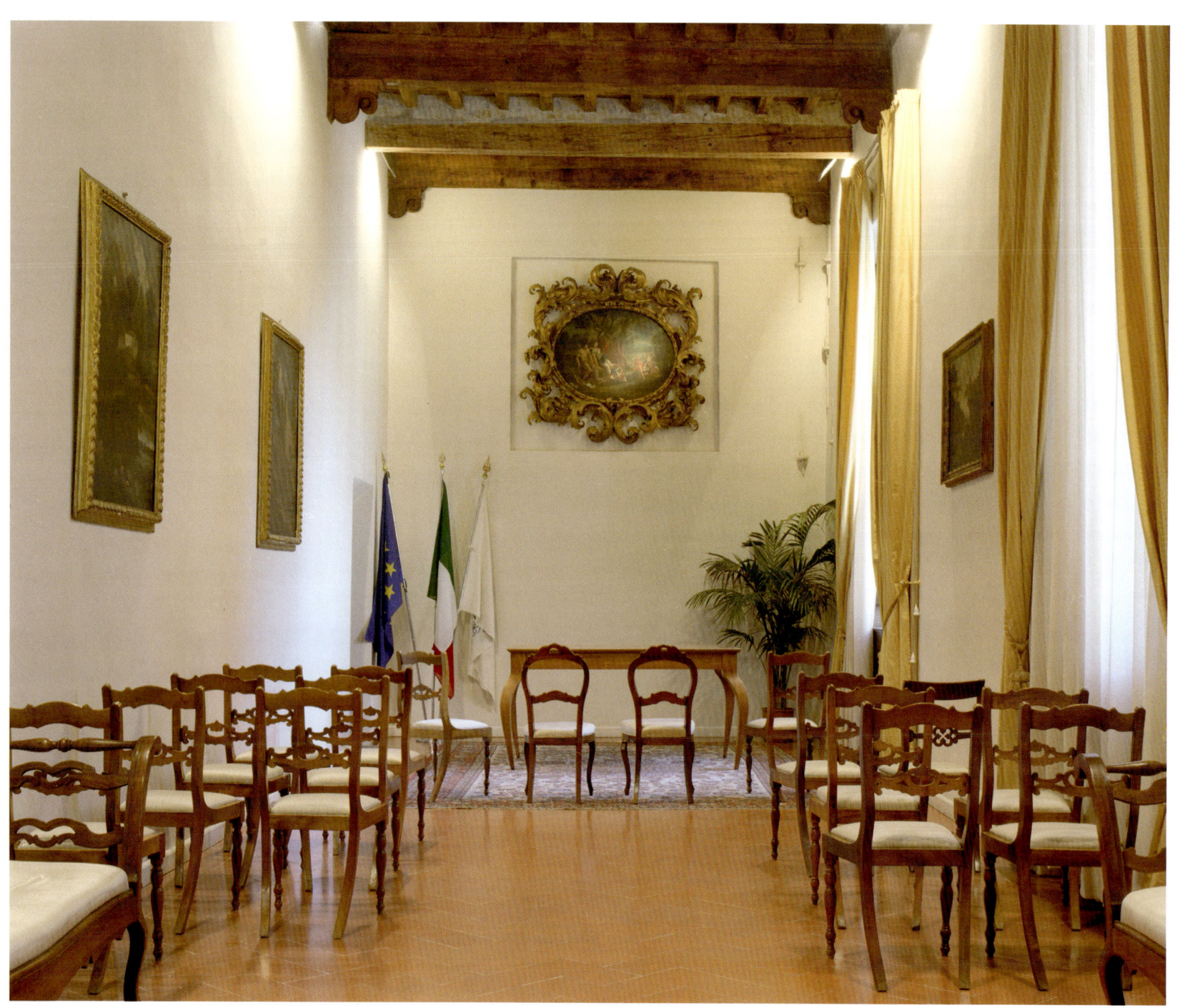

SITES OF CONVERGENCE

Ceremony #1: Palazzo Comunale, Prato, Italy

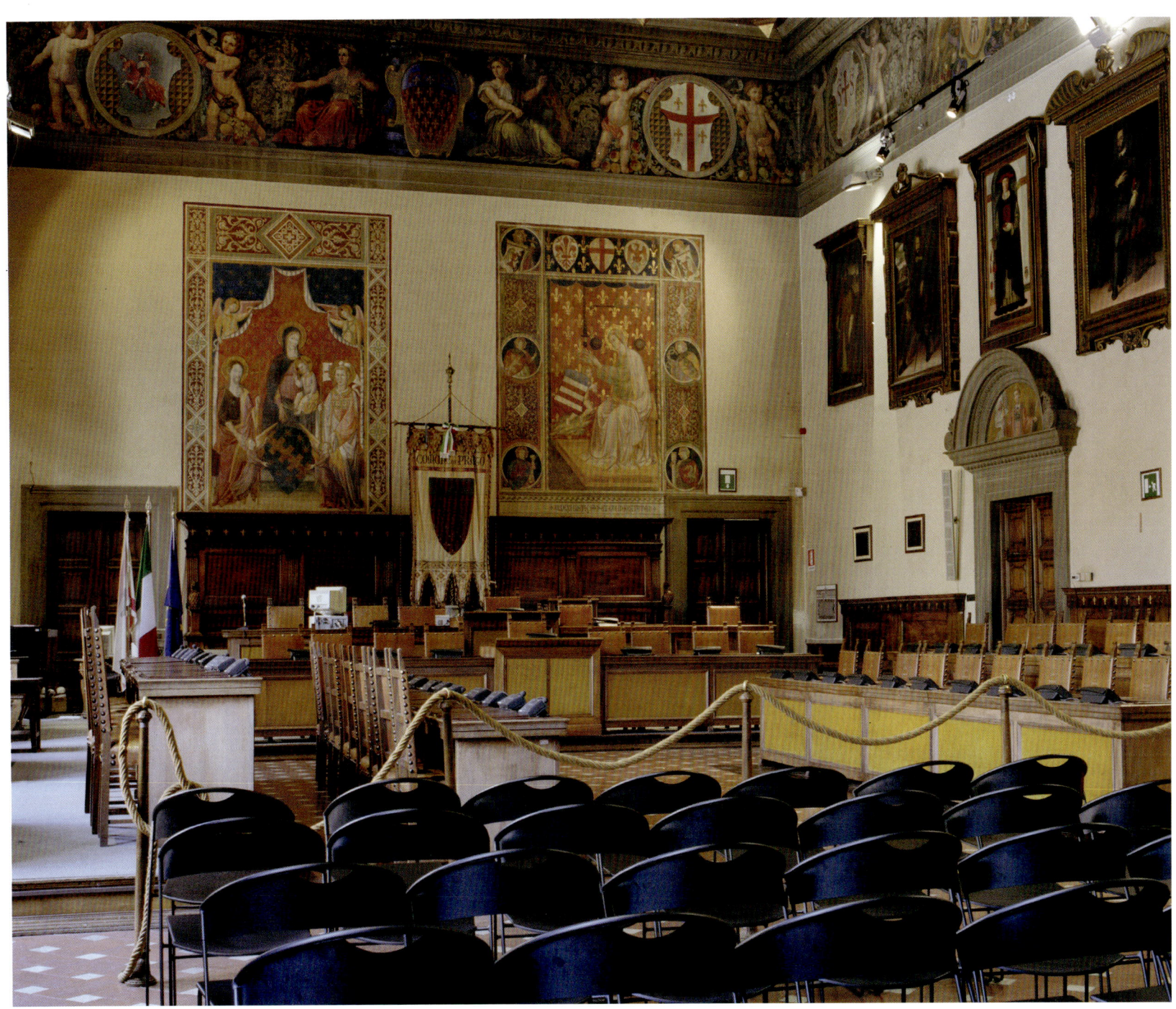

SITES OF CONVERGENCE

Governance #1: Palazzo Comunale, Prato, Italy

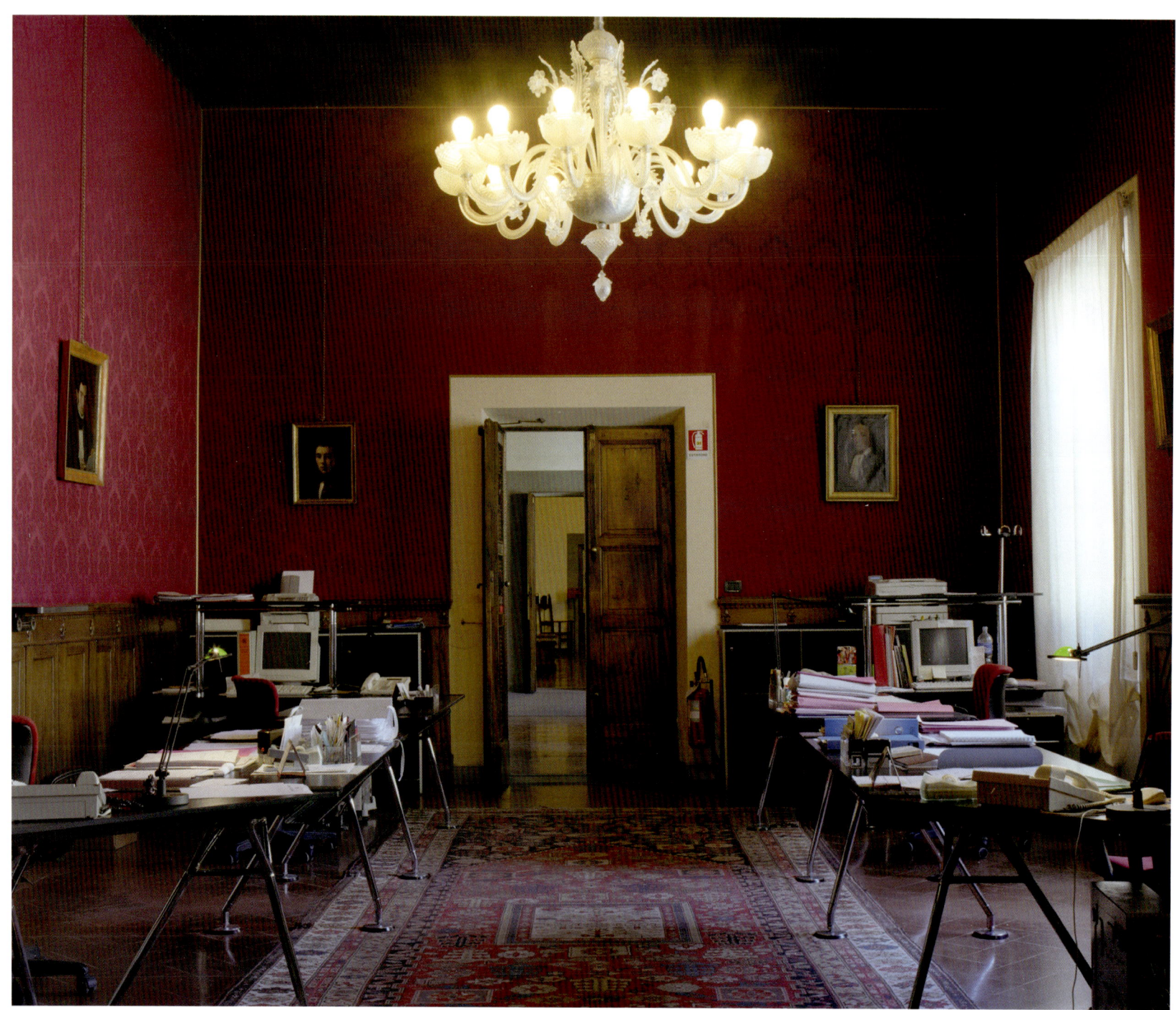

SITES OF CONVERGENCE

Administration #1: Palazzo Comunale, Prato, Italy

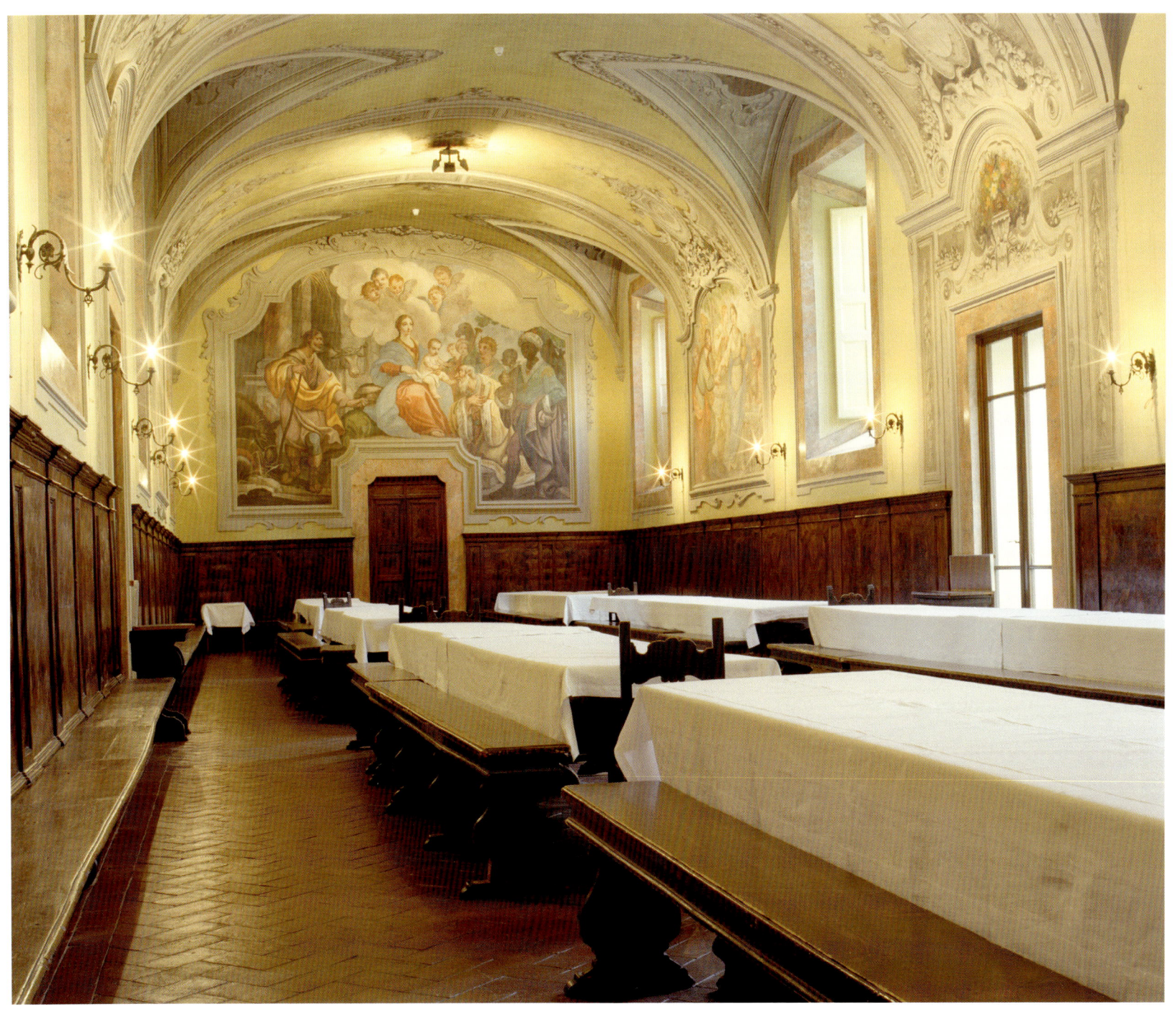

SITES OF CONVERGENCE 1020mm x 1220mm chromogenic prints, 2006

Nourishment #1: Cicognini College, Prato, Italy

Twenty-five years later, in 1992, academic research and teaching acquired another important locus in Prato. A former state technical school just north of the *centro storico* became home to the Polo universitario Città di Prato, or the Prato centre of the University of Florence, with teaching and research services managed by PIN S.c.r.l., a non-profit consortium jointly owned by the University of Florence, Prato's municipal and provincial governments, and other local institutions such as the Chamber of Commerce. The Polo universitario constitutes a literal precedent for the arrival of Monash's Centre in Prato. Certainly it was perceived as such in the local media. For example, in December 1998, the popular newspaper *Il Tirreno* reported Monash University's intention to found the Centre in Prato, presenting the story as good news for Prato's economy, and for the local government's project of advancing the city as a large university hub. With regard to Prato's commercial gain, 'the arrival of Monash' was also posited as an entrée to potential markets in the Australia, New Zealand and South East Asia.

Throughout 1999, the Centre working party at Monash in Australia sought financial support for the prospect of launching the venture at the Palazzo Vaj. And the question 'Why Prato?' appeared in a heading on page four of the investment brochure that argued the case. The brochure stressed the merits of Prato's regional location, first and foremost with reference to Florence, and to existing ties between Monash academic staff and a number of Tuscany's distinguished university presences: Villa I Tatti, Harvard University Center for Italian Renaissance Studies; The European University Institute; the University of Florence; the Georgetown University Centre at Fiesole. Interestingly, the investment brochure did not name the Prato Province. Now with the benefit of 10 years' hindsight, the youth of the province seems at least as significant as the undisputed relevance and attractions of Tuscany. As outlined above, a long view of the civic scene into which Monash was welcomed can show that the province's self-conscious efforts to differentiate its capital city from Florence had helped to make the Comune di Prato decidedly enterprising, strategically shrewd, and Europe-minded.

Within Monash senior management, these established traits resonated strongly with the language that would characterise *Leading the Way: Monash 2020*, the ambitious statement of intent for the university overall, which was adopted in July 1999. The chief themes of this document were innovation, engagement and internationalisation. Monash was resolved to spearhead the redefinition of Australia's tertiary institutions in expansionist terms, as a response to globalisation—its acceleration, challenges and opportunities for transnational mobility of people and ideas. In the light of this goal, a centre in Italy was part of a worldwide vision, and would enhance the university's profile in the northern hemisphere, specifically within the European Union (EU), a matrix for global networks and global citizenship. Hence at Monash in Australia, Prato rapidly came to be considered the desirable location for a European base, as much for the city's industrial and demographic history, as for its ability to attract international interest as a producer of contemporary culture and research. Moreover, by taking out a long lease on the first floor of the Palazzo Vaj, a young university stood to obtain a foothold situated amid the patrimony of western Europe's 'old world'; a part of the globe indivisible from the medieval Latin origins of the university itself as a corporate institution.

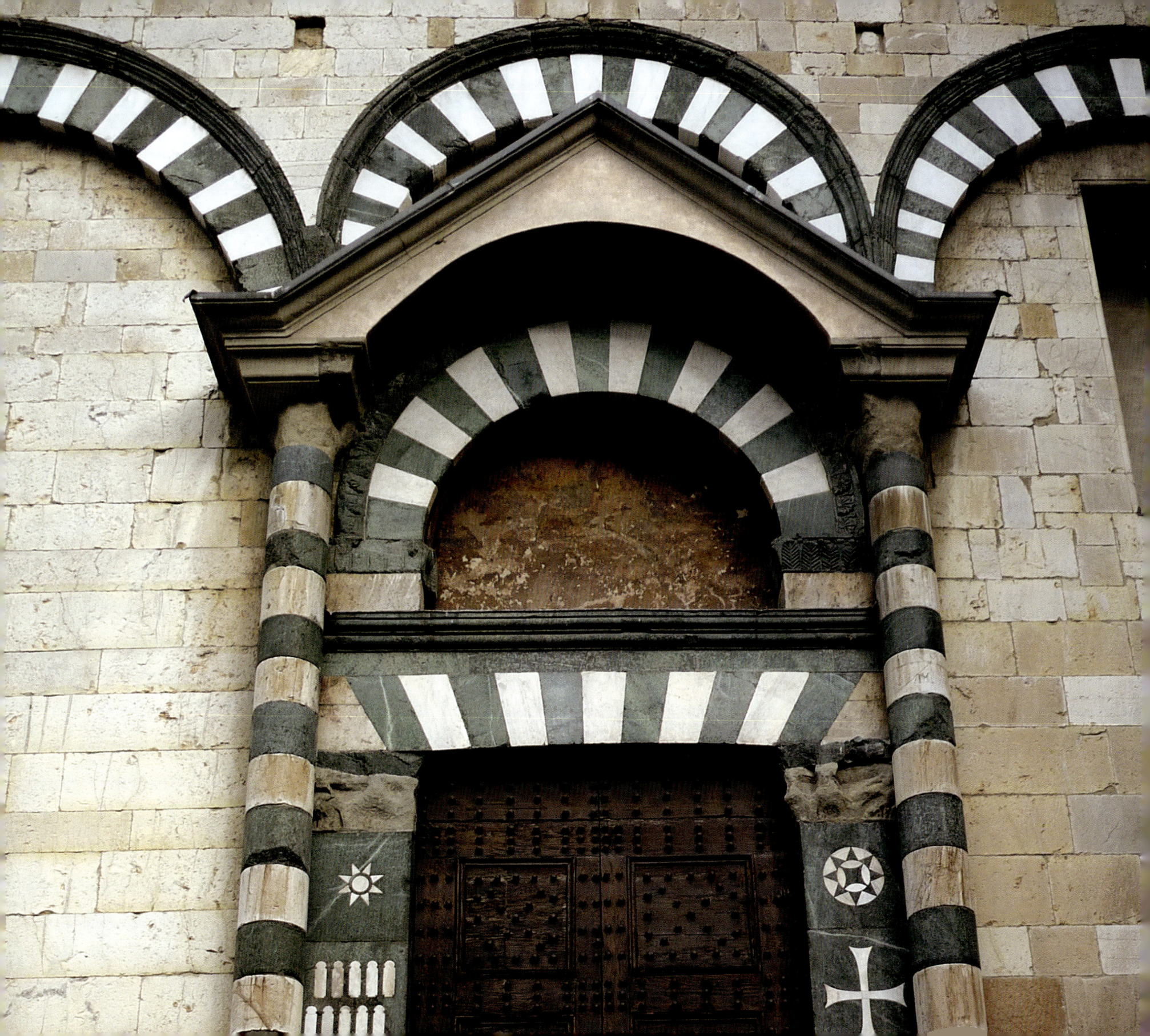

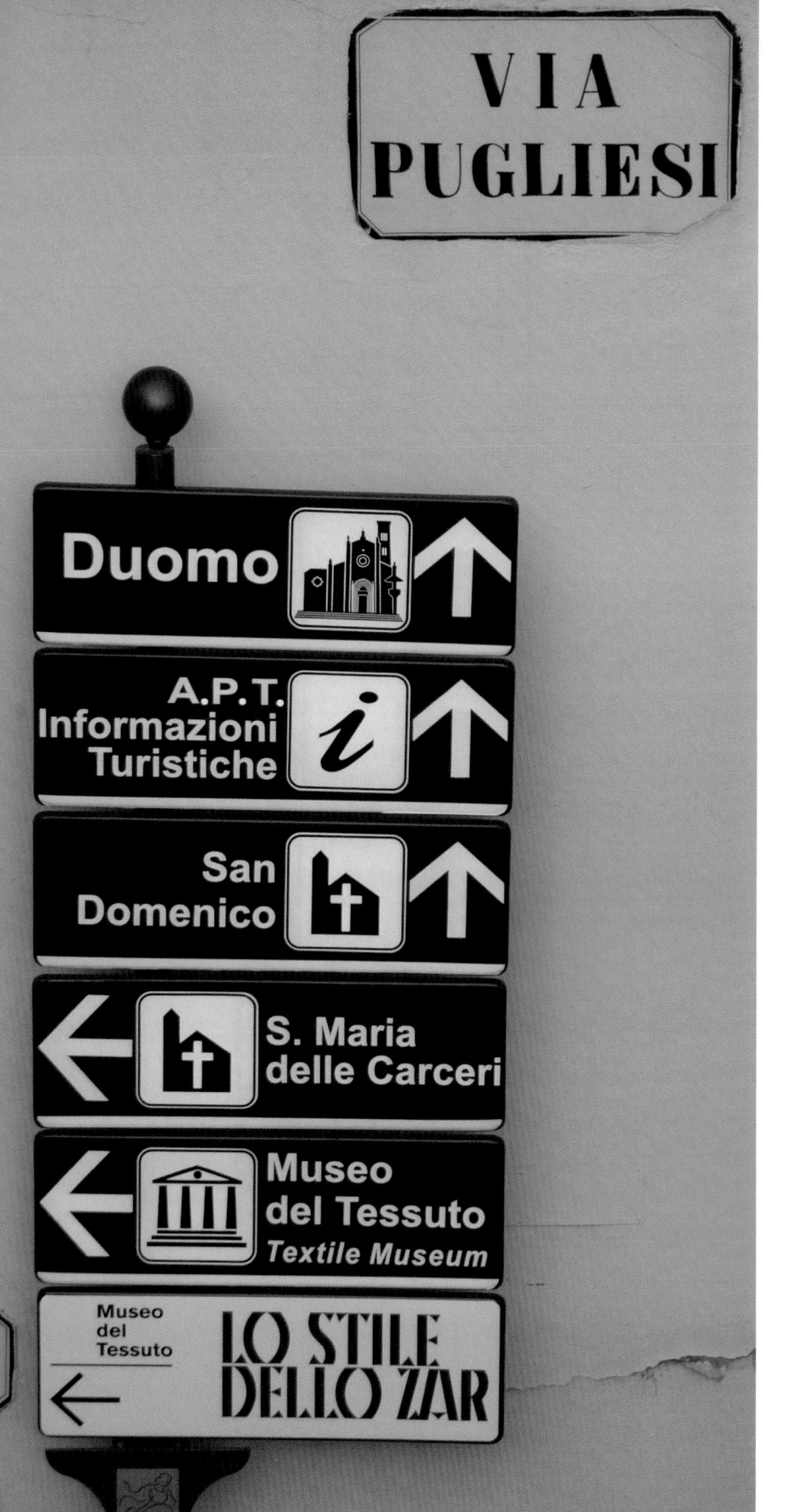

Conspicuously placed at the centre of Piazza San Marco—the major intersection between the *centro storico* and the wider city, the Bisenzio, and the central railway station—*Square Shape With Cut* (1974) has become a symbol for Prato as a city for modern and contemporary art. Concurrently the Metastasio Theatre has come to represent the modern and the contemporary in the sphere of the performing arts. Re-opened after re-modelling in 1964, during the mid-1970s the Metastasio was associated with provocative seasons directed by Luca Ronconi, one of Europe's great innovators of the era.

Like the renovated Campolmi textile mill that has housed the Textile Museum since 2003, Prato's Palazzo Datini attests to a civic strategy of bringing wide, new perspectives to bear upon local heritage. In this case perspectives of a scholarly nature were brought into conjunction with the thirteenth century residence built by Francesco di Marco Datini, the 'Merchant of Prato' so well known to economic and social historians as one of the outstanding business figures of his age. 1967 saw the foundation of the Istituto internazionale di storia economica Francesco Datini—known in English as the Datini Institute—under the leadership of Federigo Melis and the eminent historian of the Mediterranean Fernand Braudel.

The institute's brief was explicitly intended to attract researchers of international standing to Prato, and linked the State Archives of Prato and the Palazzo Datini with methodologies for preindustrial history of a vast sweep.

cloisters and frescoed chapels, ancient laneways and towers, coloured marbles and abraded brick facades. This is the picturesque, historical Tuscany that can be typified by the vista from the first floor terrace of the Palazzo Vaj.

The northwest side of Prato's hexagonal walls runs beside the Bisenzio river, which flows south into the Arno at the town of Signa. The Bisenzio was once a vital source for the textile industry that has been a defining feature of the area's economy since the early middle ages. Long based on the production of wool cloth, nowadays textile-related activity includes manufacture of natural and synthetic yarns and fabrics. Prato's spinning mills, weaving and finishing sectors supply world garment markets—high-end fashion markets in particular, for which 'innovation' is a byword. In the past decade, ready-to-wear clothing firms have helped to transform Prato's industrial profile, though textile production continues to propel the local economy.

Very closely tied to the recent history of the textile industry was a rapid rise in overseas migration to Prato during the 1990s, making Prato a manifestly multi-ethnic city. While immigrants from China, Albania, Romania and Pakistan are the most numerous, the Chinese community is by far the largest of the migrant communities resident in Prato. It is also notable as the largest Chinese community in any Italian province. Originating mainly from China's south-eastern provinces of Zhejiang—identified with the port city of Wenzhou—and Fujian, Prato's Chinese immigrants have visibly altered the city's social and cultural landscape. As immigration flows continue to increase in Europe, the integration of the Chinese and Italian communities is a matter of special topicality and concern at regional, provincial and municipal levels of government.

Overall, the promotional materials produced by the Agenzia per il Turismo di Prato—the tourist agency at the service of the Prato Province and its municipalities—do not draw attention to the city's multi-ethnicity. Or rather, this aspect of the city is broadly comprehended in an emphasis on balanced juxtapositions between the old and the new; between mindful conservation of the vestiges of the past, and a lively modernity. In the context of globalisation, such modernity denotes a European outlook. The Museo del Tessuto, the Textile Museum in the *centro storico*, is promoted in precisely these terms, as one of the city's up-to-date institutions of international importance, where the museum collection is inseparable from technological research and development. However, the key architectural image for Prato's modernity is the sharp-cornered metal roofline of the Luigi Pecci Contemporary Art Centre, located south of the *centro storico*. The 'Pecci Centre' was opened in 1994 as a museum, archive and laboratory for the art of the twentieth century and beyond. The origins of this institution point to a tradition of cultural entrepreneurialism that might be called a distinguishing facet of *pratesità*, or Prato patriotism—one that since at least the 1960s has sought fresh opportunities to assert the city's cultural independence from Florence, and an imaginative orientation towards the future. The Luigi Pecci Contemporary Art Centre was an initiative of industrialist Enrico Pecci supported by the Comune di Prato (the city government), and envisaged as a source of creative stimulus that would place Prato firmly on the European map of the artistic avant-garde.

A monumental sculpture by Henry Moore was purchased by the Comune di Prato with a similar motivation after the 1972 retrospective of Moore's work held at the Forte di Belvedere in Florence.

MONASH IN PRATO – MONASH IN EUROPE

By virtue of its location in Via Pugliesi, the Monash Prato Centre immerses its visitors in the many-layered stone streetscapes of Prato's 'old town', the *centro storico*. Newcomers to the Centre who are also newcomers to Prato are typically impressed by the relative absence of the crowds and obtrusive impact of mass tourism. And by this progressive Italian city of a scale so conducive to convenience and a sense of personal connection.

Annamaria Pagliaro, former director of the Centre, reminisced in 2011 about the search for a building in Tuscany that could serve as the headquarters for the proposed 'Monash University Centre in Italy'. A delegation from the Tuscan Region visited Melbourne in March 1998, and, as a result, the search began in earnest during the second half of that year. '[Founding director] Bill Kent chose the Palazzo Vaj in Prato. … He thought that the historical centre was a jewel, and that this was the appropriate place to be. In fact no one has ever thought otherwise because of the advantages of this little city'. The advantages of Prato are manifold, indivisible from the city of Prato's location, history, and demography; from the imagery and general disposition of the city as represented by local authorities.

Prato is located on the plain between the Florence and Pistoia in northern Tuscany, in the Bisenzio river valley. Subject to the jurisdiction of Florence since 1351, Prato gained the title of *civitas*, or 'city', when part of the town was recognised as a diocese in 1653. It was in 1992 that Prato and its countryside gained independence from Florence. *La città di Prato* became the capital of the newly chartered Provincia di Prato, or Prato Province—acknowledgement of a process of political and administrative ascendancy that began in the seventeenth century. Although the province of Prato is geographically small, the city of Prato is nonetheless the second largest in Tuscany, with a resident population of over 188,000 people.

The hexagonal outline of Prato's city walls, dating to the 1300s, nowadays delineates the *centro storico*. Here a remarkable concentration of civic and religious landmarks radiates from the Piazza del Comune. These offer a surfeit of evidence for past prosperity and aspirations: for the rise of the commune in north Italy during the middle ages; for the religious rituals epitomised by the veneration of the Virgin Mary's 'holy girdle', a symbol for the city and a sacred relic kept in the Cathedral of Saint Stephen, the Duomo. This is the enduring Prato of castles,

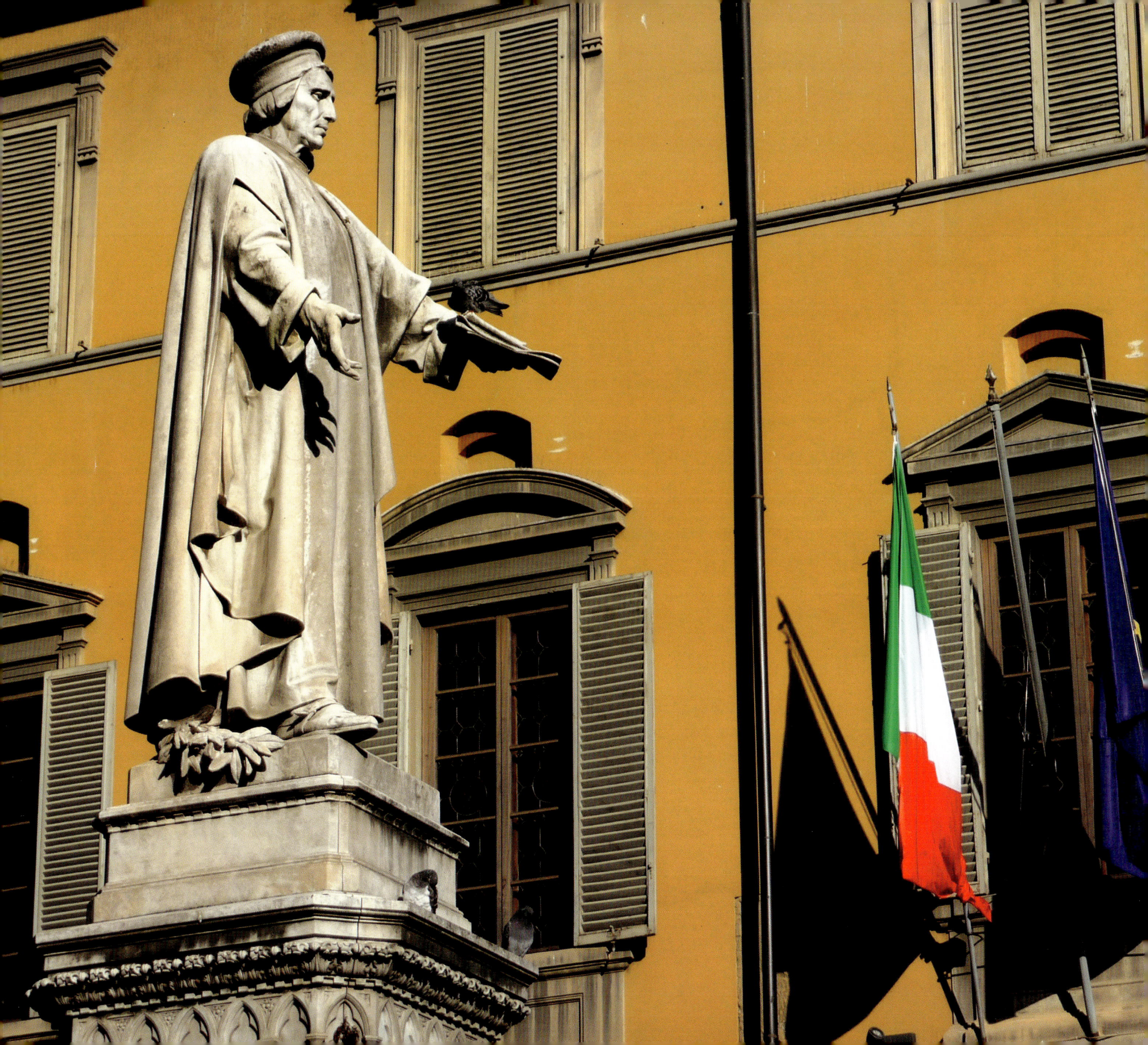

PART TWO
A Site of Convergence

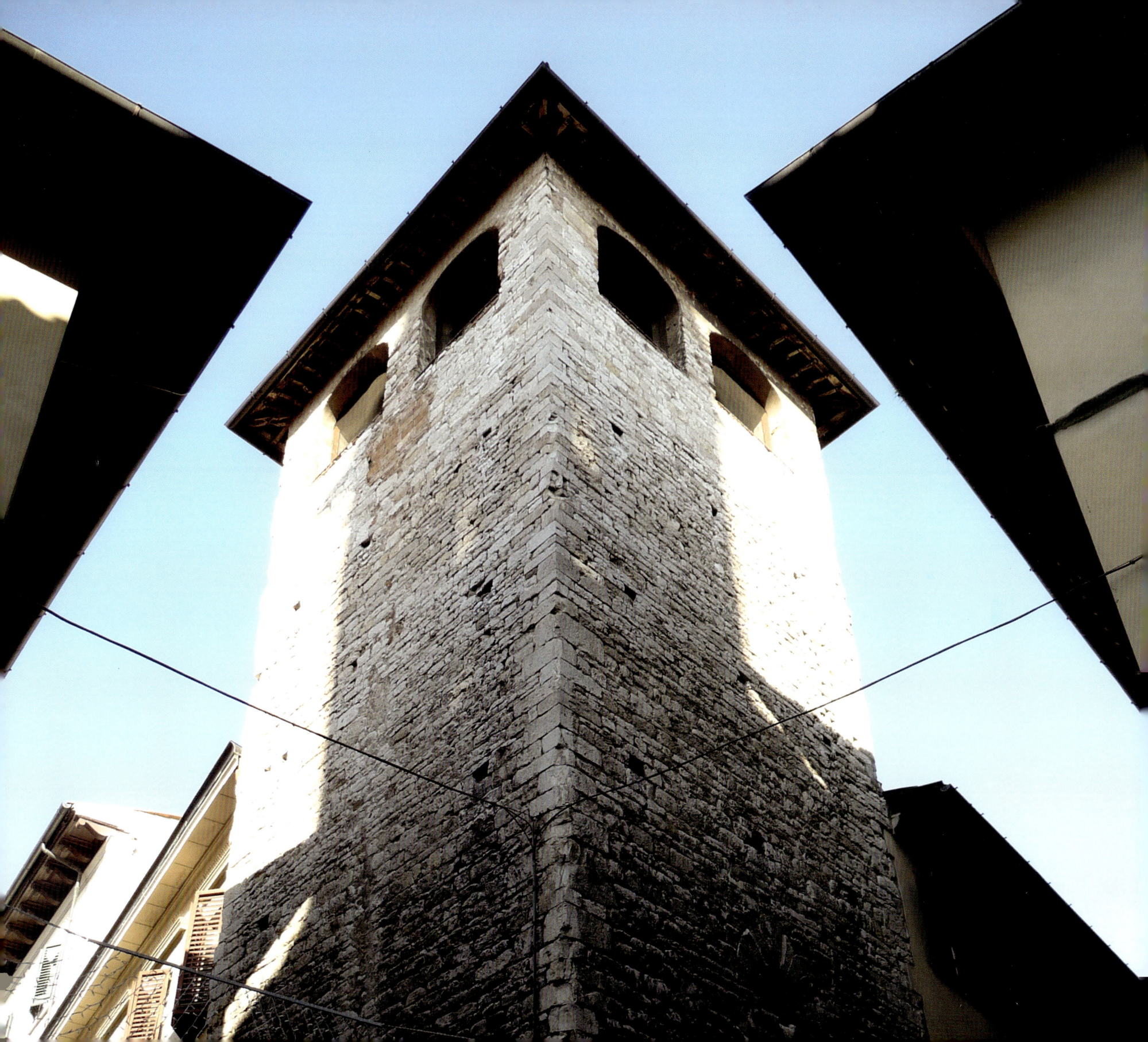

detailed studies of these spaces in all their accrued elegance and material vulnerability. They point up the constitutive role of the architecture and its embellishments in rituals that have long been focal for cooperative social relations: rituals of nourishment, governance and citizenship, religious worship, entertainment.

While working on *Sites of Convergence*, Duggan also undertook to photograph interiors of the Palazzo Vaj—her own expression of the pleasure invariably elicited by the building. Over several summer mornings, she entered the Centre before it had opened for the day, and worked her way clockwise around the 1500 square metres of the first floor (see the image essay beginning on page 44). Like the photographs of the more monumental places in *Sites of Convergence*, these images of the handsome rooms occupied by the Centre contemplate the character and decoration of the spaces, their amplitude, and the play of natural and artificial light. The artist's theme is similarly that of architectural spaces identified with civility and a vast European inheritance of knowledge and values. Thus Duggan's images propose the Monash University Centre as an additional 'site of convergence' in downtown Prato—therefore the title of this volume.

By depicting most of the rooms empty of their furniture, the artist has accentuated the Centre's tasteful blend of historical features with the wiring and technology necessary to a venue for study and teaching, conferences and public events. She has also endowed the spaces with an ambience remarkably still, warm, and full of expectation. Stacked chairs glimpsed in a mirror of the Salone Grollo make a telling contrast with the solemn rows of chairs in *Governance #1* and *Reverence #1*. That is, above all, Duggan's images of the rooms tenanted by the Centre portray as their most attractive quality their openness to different sorts of assembly and social interaction. As such they evoke the Centre's collegial atmosphere; the openness of mind and long sightlines required for collegial dialogue, a productive convergence of ideas.

Five years after photographing the Palazzo Vaj, Duggan was invited to return to Prato. Loretta Baldassar had named her the Centre's first artist in residence, presaging the commitment to an Artist in Residence program announced in 2010. Duggan's essay at the close of this publication discusses her association with Centre, through which she gained a sense of belonging to a dynamic intellectual community. The consequences for her creative practice were profound. This account is akin to a case study of the momentum of 'the Prato effect' in an individual's personal and professional life. Duggan's images and words can be described as a tribute to the formative vision of the Centre as a destination 'for the whole person'.

The section preceding Duggan's essay seeks to acknowledge the ways in which art and artists have been integral to the Centre's history. Through the past decade the work of visual artists especially has been a feature of Centre life, and Prato's vigorous cultural life. The midpoint of this volume is comprised of a collection of eight vignettes: personal perspectives on episodes from the Centre's establishment, or reflections on experiences of its thriving academic and conference programs. The contributors—not all Monash staff—are all Australians at various stages in their careers. Like so many academics, teachers, students, dignitaries, leading researchers and artists from around the world who converge upon the Centre, they hold it in special affection. The earlier pages of the volume recognise that the outward looking province and city of Prato, and the venerable Palazzo Vaj, have always been crucial to the richness of encounter desired for Centre visitors. Naturally they remain intrinsic to the Centre's contribution to knowledge, and to its international appeal.

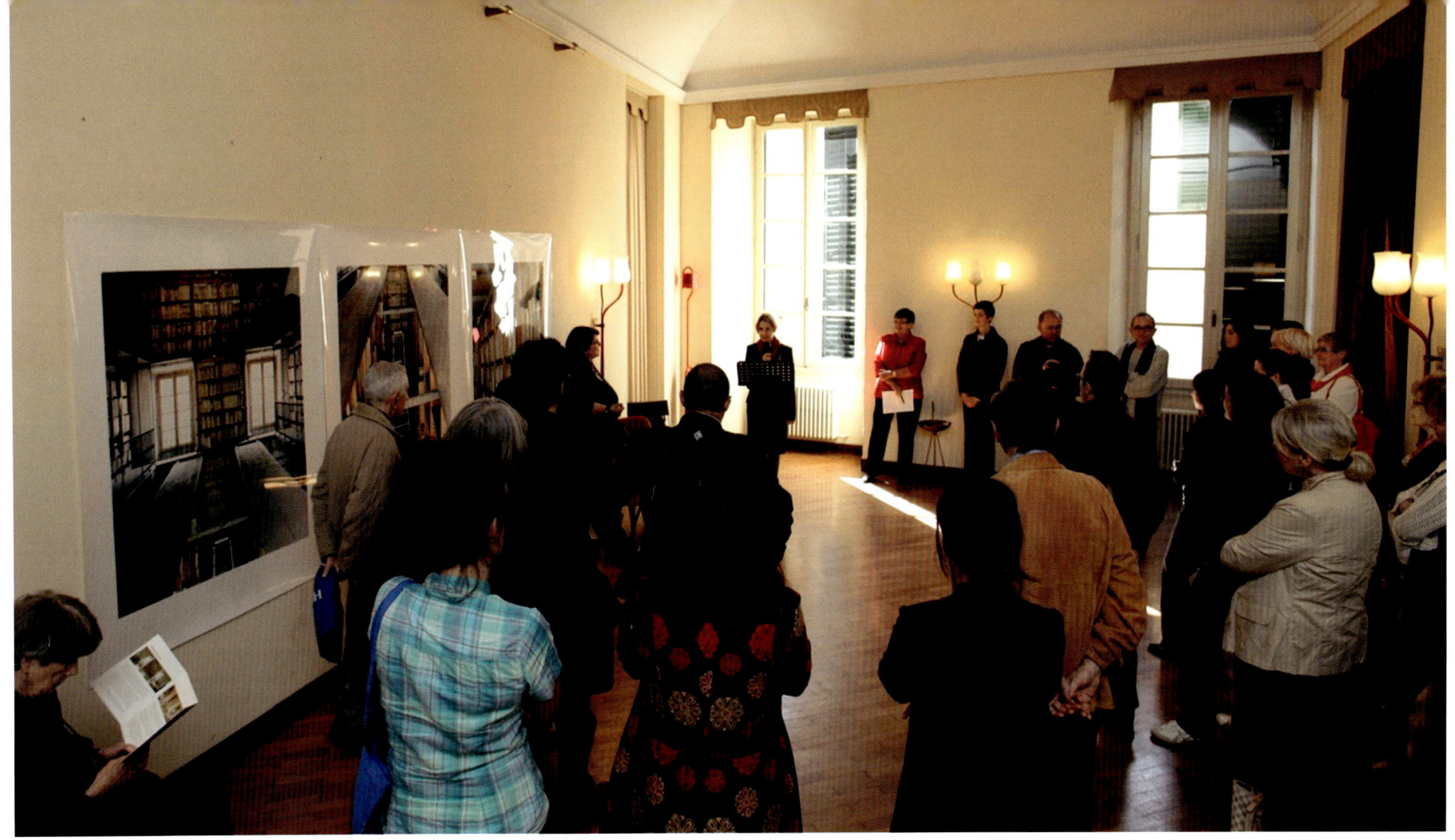

2010 opening of *Wondrous Possessions*. Photograph by Andrea Abati © Andrea Abati

Bill Kent's report dated 17 August 2004 declared, 'the Centre has just finished the most intense and varied conference period in its short life', and, some three pages on, 'during this period we have had more visitors than there are autumn leaves in Vallombrosa'. So by this time, 'the Prato effect' reflected a burgeoning confidence in the Centre's robustness, connoting also the rightness of its multifaceted purpose, its location and abode.

2004 was also the year in which Australian photomedia artist Jo-Anne Duggan travelled to Prato with her project *Impossible Gaze*, which was exhibited at the Centre for 12 months. She stayed in Prato researching a new folio of work that became *Sites of Convergence* (see the image essay beginning on page 24).

In the first series of images bearing this title, Duggan turned her intelligent and sensuous eye to historic interiors situated within walking distance of the Palazzo Vaj, inside the walls of Prato's ancient town centre. Her subjects included the Palazzo Comunale, seat of secular power in the city since the late thirteenth century; the frescoed refectory of the Cicognini College, Prato's oldest state school, and parts of the Dominican convent of San Niccolò, one of the best preserved monastery complexes in Tuscany. The resultant images are lavishly

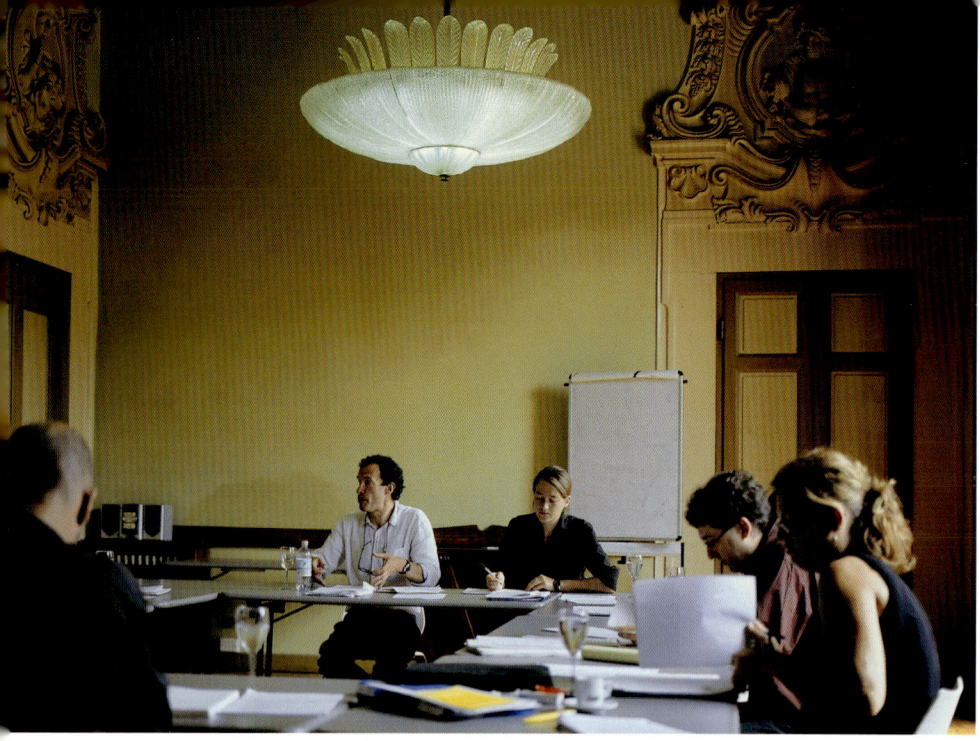
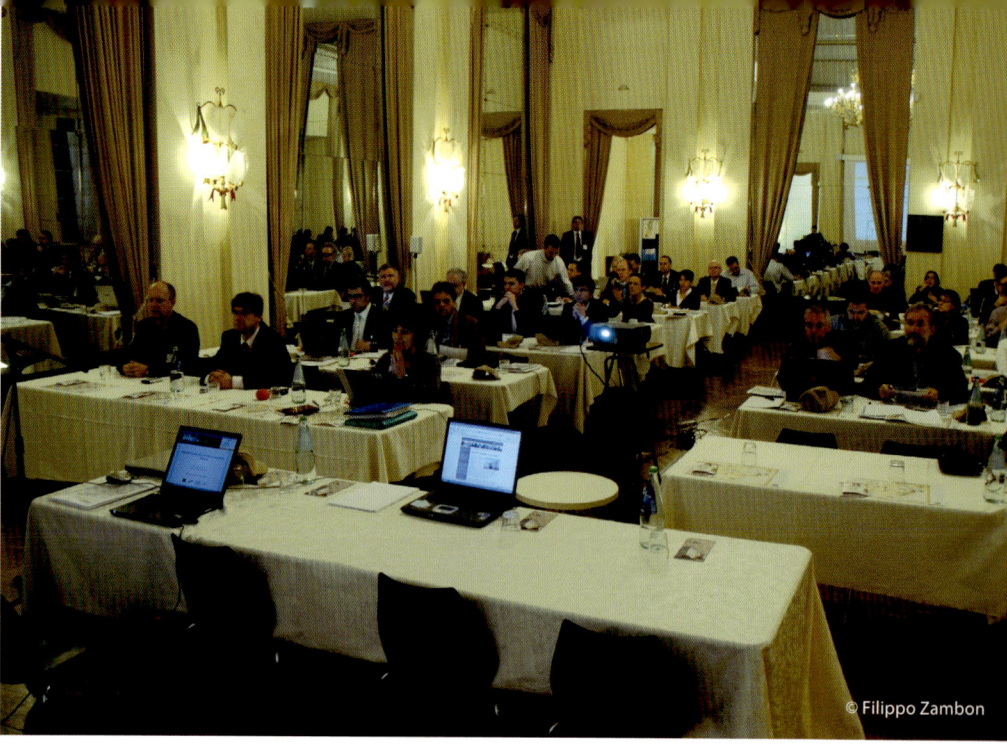

those on campus mixed easily across the boundaries of specialisms and departments, and across generations.

Bill Kent outlined an instance of such mixing in his director's report of June 2002:

> As I wrote this, [Visiting] Professor [David] Arnott walked into my office and said he had just had a long and stimulating discussion with one of the visiting New Zealand architecture lecturers about design theory. He added 'this is what Prato is about'. We are finding that the juxtaposition of scholars and students from different places and disciplines in a relatively small and pleasant space is generating intellectual excitement.

By 2004, when more than 10,000 people had visited the Centre for a course, conference or an event, Kent was apt to refer to this discernible excitement as 'the Prato effect'. 'The Prato effect' came to mean at once the diversity of people attracted to Centre, and the unexpected and indirect rewards—to the visitors themselves, to the Centre and Monash University, to public life in Prato—that could follow from their interaction. An elating conversation; ideas for future study; prospects for a further meeting, a symposium, a Memorandum of Understanding; publishing opportunities; a shift in perception; a friendship. Presumably the specific rewards or subtle kinds of inspiration afforded by contact with the Centre will continue to prove unexpected. However, the welcoming tone conducive to inspiration itself has been diligently cultivated by Centre staff. Reflecting on the years of the Centre's establishment, Cecilia Hewlett, executive officer and then associate director from 2001 to 2006, has emphasised that

> essentially … the Centre was made possible not because we had impressive, efficient administrative apparatus but because we put everything we had into making sure it was a positive experience for all those who came. […] We were trying to build a very vibrant intellectual community.

A CENTRE FOR THE WHOLE PERSON

L'INTERVISTA

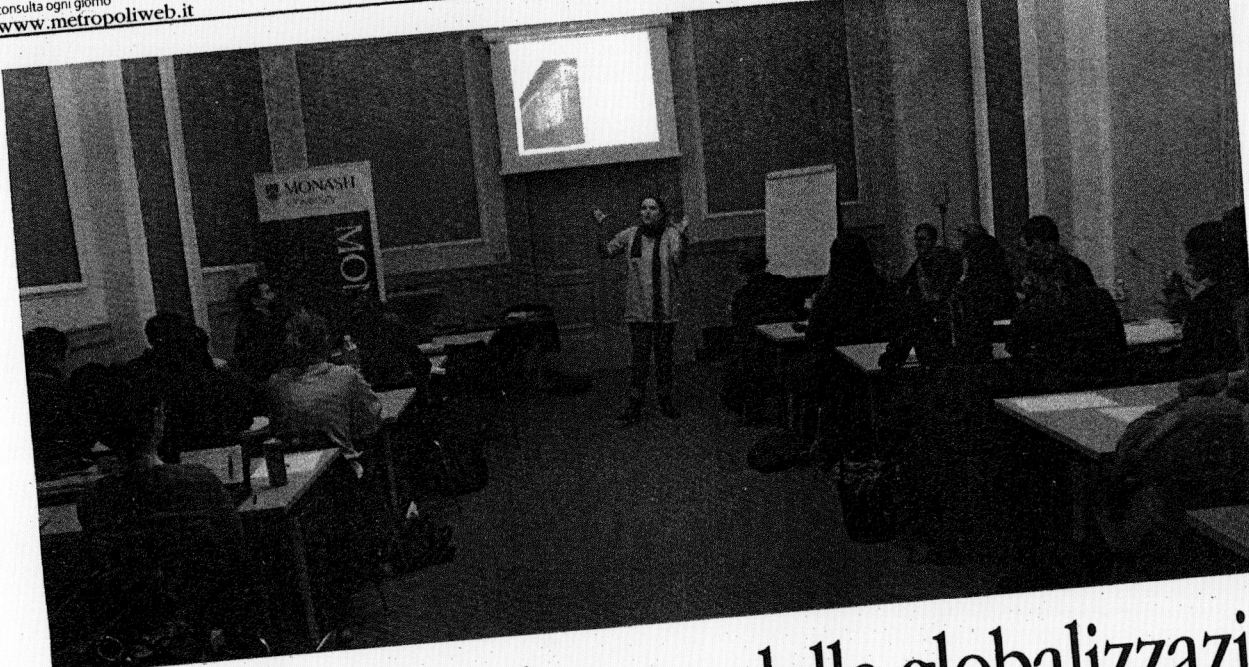

UN'AULA DELLA MONASH A PALAZZO VAJ
Qui si tengono le lezioni agli studenti che nell'Istituto sono circa seicento suddivisi in quaranta corsi. Sotto: la direttrice dell'Università australiana, Loretta Baldassar

Monash, il lato buono della globalizzazione

La direttrice dell'Università australiana che ha sede in centro: «Un convegno internazionale sull'emigrazione cinese»

FABRIZIO NUCCI

Un pezzo di università australiana nel cuore storico di Prato: la Monash University è ormai da nove anni una realtà di primo piano nella nostra città. L'unica vera sede europea della prestigiosa università di Melbourne si trova infatti a Palazzo Vai, in via Pugliesi, nello storico palazzo di proprietà dell'Arte della Lana. Un connubio quello tra Monash University e Prato che sta diventando di anno in anno più fecondo e soprattutto sta offrendo alla nostra città una chiave di lettura diversa al fenomeno della globalizzazione rispetto a quella cui siamo abituati. Il villaggio globale insomma non comporta solo immigrazione selvaggia ma anche possibilità di scambio e di arricchimento culturale impensabili solo fino a qualche anno fa. Di tutto questo siamo andati a parlare con la direttrice della Monash di Prato, **Loretta Baldassar**, antropologa italo australiana, che ci ha offerto un quadro dei rapporti tra il suo istituto e Prato e un'interpretazione del momento che sta vivendo la nostra città davvero molto interessante.

Partiamo da un po' di storia: come nasce il binomio Prato - Monash University?

«E' nato nove anni fa grazie al lavoro e all'impegno del professor **Bill Kent**, docente di storia del medioevo e del rinascimento di fama internazionale. E' stato lui a scegliere Prato, nel quadro di una strategia che vede la presenza della Monash University in ogni parte del mondo, con campus in Sud Africa e Malesia. Quello di Prato non è un vero e proprio campus ed offre corsi intensivi di arte e di segno, giurisprudenza in...

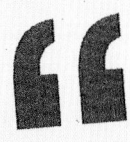

Vogliamo fare della nostra università una piattaforma neutra in cui discutere di immigrazione

...no sempre stati improntati alla massima collaborazione. Il Comune e la...

quello che sta vivendo Prato».

In effetti il problema dell'immigrazione visto da un paese come l'Australia che ha alle spalle due secoli di globalizzazione ante litteram assume un valore diverso rispetto a quello cui siamo abituati...

«Proprio così. La mia speranza è quella di accreditare la Monash di Prato come una piattaforma neutra dove poter discutere di immigrazione nella giusta maniera. Il trenta per cento dei nostri studenti è di origine asiatica e capita spesso che vengano presi per cinesi illegali perché non si è abituati a vedere il fenomeno immigrazione nella sua complessità e nella sua prospettiva di scambio culturale. La vera sfida che ci pone il tema dell'immigrazione è quella dell'inclusione sociale. In Australia ovviamente con duecento anni di immigrazione alle spalle questo processo è in fase avanzata: la comunità più numerosa è quella italiana. Io stessa ho origini italiane: mio nonno era di Treviso ed è stato un vero e proprio pioniere, come migliaia e migliaia di altri italiani. Certo il fatto che a Prato un'alta percentuale di immigrati sia clandestina rende tutto molto più difficile ed è chiaro che anche noi non abbiamo soluzioni in tasca».

In effetti Prato sta vivendo un periodo molto delicato...

«Non c'è dubbio. Anch'io vivo a Prato e se dovessi scrivere un libro su questa città lo intitolerei "Un momento difficile" perché è la risposta che mi danno tutti quando chiedo un giudizio sul periodo che stiamo vivendo. Capisco che i pratesi stentino ormai a riconoscere la propria città e abbiano l'impressione che il loro mondo stia crollando. Attenzione però a scegliere la strada sbagliatissima della non inclusione perché non porta da nessuna parte. All'asilo mio figlio di 5 anni che ancora non parla italiano ha trovato un ambiente bellissimo ma un suo...

ma. Abbiamo intenzione di organizzare un grande convegno internazionale che abbia come tema l'inserimento dei cinesi nei vari contesti internazionali, comparando ciò che accade a Prato con quanto sta succedendo in Canada, negli Usa, in Malesia. Questo convegno sarà l'occasione per invitare **James Kynge** il giornalista americano che ha scritto il best seller "China shakes the world", un libro che ha destato impressione in tutto il mondo. Kynge ha dedicato l'intero quarto capitolo del suo volume proprio alla realtà di Prato e quindi sarà molto interessante avere il suo contributo».

Quali sono i programmi della Monash per il 2010?

«L'attività didattica proseguirà con la speranza di ampliare ulteriormente l'offerta di corsi ed il numero di studenti. Un appuntamento importante che vorrei sottolineare è per il prossimo mese di maggio con l'Open day. Sarà una giornata davvero speciale in cui apriremo le porte della nostra se-

A maggio con il nostro open day apriremo le porte di Palazzo Vai alla città

de per farci conoscere meglio a tutti i pratesi. In quell'occasione inaugureremo anche la biblioteca dedicata al professor **Bill Kent** e la speranza è che anche lui possa partecipare all'iniziativa. Quella del rapporto con la cittadinanza è una delle sfide anche culturali che dobbiamo vincere. Credo che a Prato anche le istituzioni siano ormai consapevoli del ruolo che la nostra università può svolgere in questa città».

In effetti gli oltre seicento studenti che frequentano la Monash a Prato vanno oltre il semplice contributo al turismo...

«E' ovvio. La Monash di Prato ha una posizione strategica di grande valore: è l'unica sede europea e quindi è sicuramente la più idonea ad ospitare convegni a livello mondiale. L'Europa, è...

SEMINARI A PALAZZO VAJ

Appuntamento questo pomeriggio venerdì 22 gennaio alla Monash University of Melbourne (Palazzo Vaj, via Pugliesi 26), con il secondo seminario di cultura politica organizzato dal Pd di Prato e dalla Fondazione Istituto Gramsci di Roma. Il titolo dell'incontro di oggi è "Da una sponda all'altra. Europa e Stati Uniti tra vecchie eredità e nuove aspirazioni". I relatori sono **Giuseppe Maione** dell'Università di Bologna e **Federico Romero** dell'Università di Firenze. Do...

(the city government), the provincial government, and the Prato Chamber of Commerce for expansion into the Palazzo Vaj's ground floor. All told, Pagliaro greatly strengthened relationships between the Centre and local authorities in Prato and in Tuscany. Her warmth and tenacity in doing so were movingly commended in November 2008, at the reception held to mark her departure as director: Eleonora Maffei, the prefect of Prato—local representative of the Italian Government—presented Pagliaro with a silver medal in honour of her contribution to Prato; the mayor of Prato, Marco Romagnoli, presented her with the *Giglio di Prato*, an award comparable to the keys of the city.

Loretta Baldassar is Professor in the Department of Anthropology and Sociology at the University of Western Australia; she brought a fresh eye to the Centre's objectives and operations in 2009. Her directorship has seen revisions to academic and conference programming to ensure sustainability, and a focus on building the Centre's research capacity. The formal Artist in Residence program, and a year-long calendar of conferences in celebration of the Centre's tenth anniversary, are amongst many new ventures that have quickly gathered momentum since her commencement as Director.

> The Monash Prato Centre holds such inspiring promise for the future. […] The collegiality that it sponsors among students and among students and faculty, the unusually high level of learning and discourse, and the sense of enthusiasm for the scholarly endeavour that it supports mark the Prato Centre as an unmatched educational opportunity in Italy.

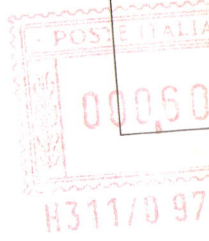

J. Duggan: 'Impossible Gaze' Series c-type photograph 1000mm x 1200mm, 2002

Jo-Anne Duggan
"Impossible Gaze"
Lo Sguardo Impossibile
Esposizione fotografica

Inaugurazione
10 giugno 2004, 18.30

Monash University Centre in Prato
Palazzo Vaj, Via Pugliesi 26, Prato
Tel: 0574 436 920

Esposizione: 10 giugno – 15 luglio
10.00-12.00   15.00-18.00

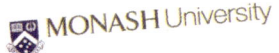

These remarks were made by the internationally prominent art historian John Paoletti in November 2010, by way of introduction to his Bill Kent Memorial Lecture, delivered in Melbourne. Paoletti's mention of collegiality highlights an attribute of the Centre that soon became perhaps the most persuasive, if unquantifiable, evidence of its flourishing. And proof of its appeal to the 'the whole person'. Anecdotally, it is easy to hear the Centre spoken about with obvious enjoyment. It is the atmosphere of collegiality that visitors tend to appreciate most, promoting feelings of loyalty and the desire to return. From one perspective, this atmosphere can be correlated with the Centre's European cultural context, in which face-to-face communication remains a preferred basis for the formation of interpersonal relationships. For Monash scholars and staff acquainted with the University's history, it is reminiscent of the more informal early days at Monash Clayton, the 1960s, when

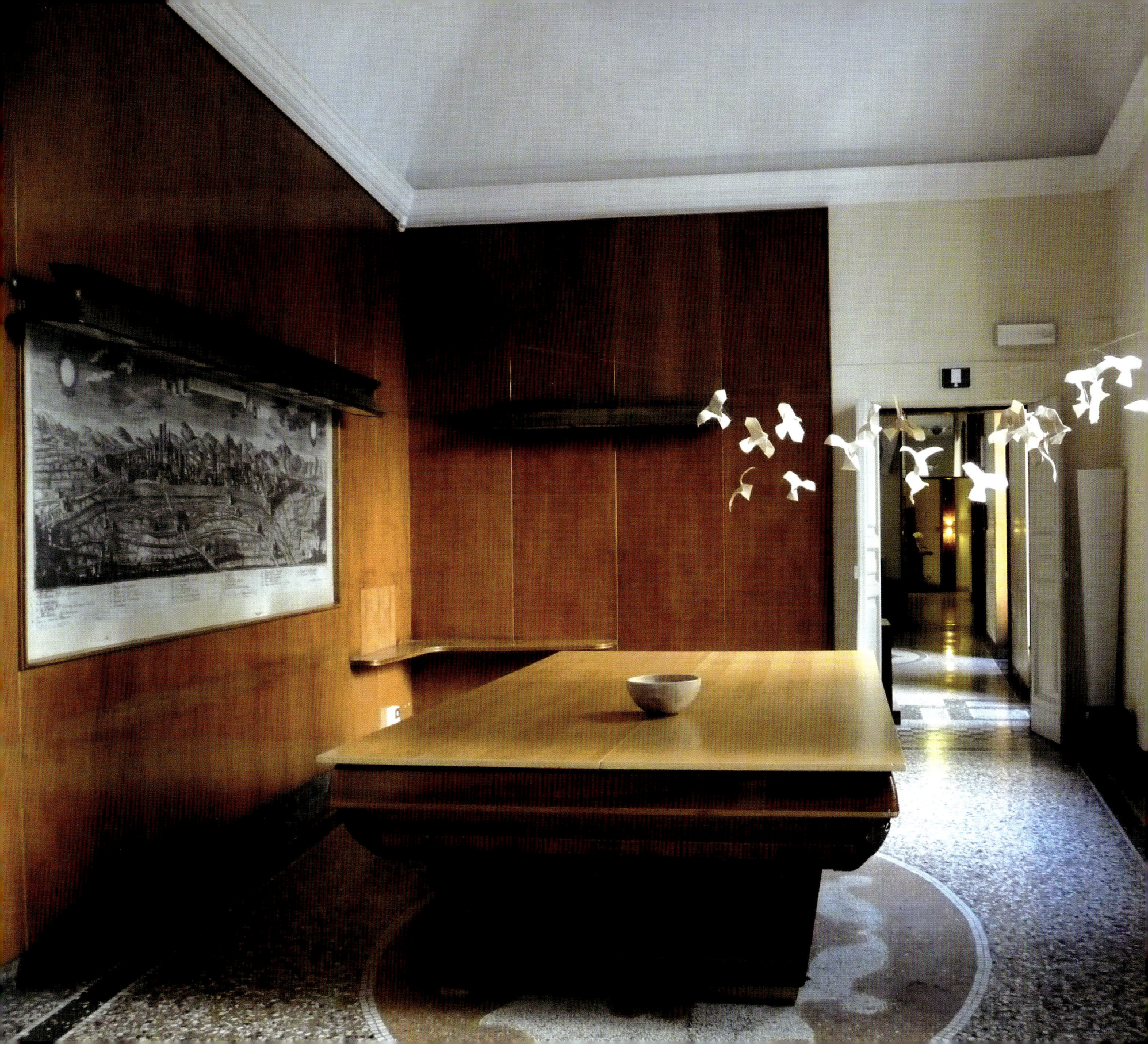

you have certainly 'brought it off'. During my time there, the Centre was host to three international conferences as well as facilitating and participating in the Xavier College immersion programme for secondary students of Italian, and hosting a concert of contemporary Australian music [...]. It was clear while I was in Prato that the Centre already has a high profile in the city [...].

Indeed, from its first months of operation, the Centre has been open to the city and province of Prato, while promoting new forums through which to foster 'Australia's connections with universities, governments, cultural organisations and industry in Europe', a pivotal aim. It has made possible a new way of organising meetings, workshops and conferences, increasing cooperation between Monash academic staff and international colleagues. From mid-2001, the Centre's academic programs have offered Monash and other students, including school students, the priceless opportunity for intensive periods of study in Tuscany. Over a decade of multiplying visitors and activities, the Centre has earned international regard as an extraordinary educational resource in Italy and Europe. Of course such regard is inseparable from the dedication of the Centre's staff. And from the repute, efforts and talents of the Centre's three successive directors: Bill Kent (2000–04); Annamaria Pagliaro (2005–08) and, since 2009, Loretta Baldassar—each a tireless champion of the Centre and its scope.

Bill Kent, Professor of History and eminent scholar of Renaissance Italy, was an iconic figure. His devotion to building goodwill towards the Centre was as strenuous as it was genial and imaginative. It seems now that his combination of passion and drive bore fruit with remarkable speed, in every vital sphere: 'at home' amongst Monash senior management, administrators, faculty deans and students; more widely in Australia; within scholarly and professional communities in Europe, and locally in Prato. During the five years of his directorship, a daring experiment became a thriving international enterprise. In 2004, in recognition of Kent's achievements as director, Monash University commissioned for the Centre a striking portrait by the celebrated photographic artist Jacqueline Mitelman, and the Bill Kent Prato Research Fellowship, tenable at the Centre, was created in his honour.

Dr Annamaria Pagliaro is a specialist in Italian literature of the nineteenth and twentieth centuries. At the time of her appointment as Centre director, she was convenor of Italian studies at Monash Clayton—and already deeply familiar with the Centre's aims and development. Tuscan-born, Pagliaro had been involved in liaison with officials of the Tuscan Region as part of a working party during the Centre's prehistory in the late 1990s. Later, she assisted with the negotiations for Monash's tenancy of the Palazzo Vaj. It was during Pagliaro's directorship that the Centre obtained financial assistance from the Comune di Prato and Italian communities'. He also outlined the University's rationale for a distinctive presence in Europe, characterising the Centre as 'the Italian expression of Monash's vision to be a leader in the worldwide advancement and application of knowledge'. With campuses already established in Malaysia and South Africa, and the Monash University London Centre based at King's College, the Prato Centre represented Monash's fourth overseas 'gateway', and a first in Italy for any Australian university.

The Monash University Prato Centre is the only foreign university presence in Prato; in-principle support from the regional, provincial and municipal governments has never wavered, nor has active endorsement from Australia's ambassadors to Italy. The blue Monash banner is now a well-recognised signpost in the heart of the historic city, and the Centre's pertinence to the character of contemporary Prato is widely acknowledged. Without doubt, Bill Kent's observation, made in 2008, that 'the Centre has on the whole received an excellent press, in Italy, Australia, and beyond', continues to hold true.

Following the Centre's Open Day of 20 May 2010, Lucia Pecorario's report for the Prato edition of *La Nazione* remarked on the growth of the Centre's 'integration and collaboration with the city' of Prato—in addition to growth in 'international conferences, research activities, and academic programs' during the past decade. Titled 'Monash, What a "Business" For Our City', the article opened with a commendation of the Centre as a drawcard for visitors from all over the world, and for its 2009 contribution to the Prato economy of more than EUR 2.5 million. In such press, local ownership of the Centre as a success story is clearly conveyed. Andrea Lulli, since 2001 a member of the Chamber of Deputies in the Italian Parliament, conveys a similar pride by association, where his official profile notes him as 'the first point of contact for the arrival in Prato of the prestigious Monash University'. Lulli was previously Prato's councillor for economic development, and amongst those whose keen political advocacy helped the founding of the Centre at the Palazzo Vaj. On behalf of the local government he had written to Bill Kent in August 2000, 'With this letter we confirm the interest of the Comune di Prato, discussed with you personally, in Monash University's establishing itself in our city. For our part we will make every effort possible to reduce the expense incurred by the University in leasing Palazzo Vaj'.

For those closely involved in arrangements for the Centre's opening ceremony, the intense excitement surrounding the occasion was shadowed by the news of the 11 September terrorist attacks in the USA, and the widespread anxiety that ensued. In practical terms, the attacks and their immediate aftermath seemed to discredit the concept of internationalised university study and research, or at least its premise of uncomplicated international travel and mobility. In fact, the direct impact of the 11 September crisis on Centre programming proved much smaller than expected.

During the Centre's first years, another, less circumstantial reason for alarm came from awareness of previous attempts, over decades, to create an Australian academic or scholarly base in Italy. Ros Pesman, at that time pro-vice-chancellor for the College of Humanities and Social Sciences at the University of Sydney, reflected on such precedents in a letter to Bill Kent, after her first visit to the Centre in October 2002: 'I would have to rank myself among the sceptics when I first learnt of the Monash Prato project—all those years when so many scholars and committees have tried unsuccessfully to set up an Australian Centre in Italy'. Nonetheless, Pesman's letter continued,

A CENTRE FOR THE WHOLE PERSON

As announced in the Prato edition of the newspaper *Il Tirreno*, the formal opening of the Monash University Prato Centre at the Palazzo Vaj was an 'inauguration in grand style'. On 17 September 2001, over 120 guests gathered in the Centre's glittering Salone for a unique pre-dinner function. The speeches of commitment, well-wishing and thanks were complemented by music from the Monash University Music Ensemble, and a viewing of two exhibitions. Displayed in the rooms adjacent to the Salone were the prehistoric specimens of *Dinosaurs of Darkness*, and Australian contemporary paintings, prints and installations selected from the Monash University Collection. Those present for the occasion included members of the Italian Parliament Franca Bimbi and Andrea Lulli; mayor of Prato Fabrizio Mattei; Carlo Calamai, representing the lessor of the Centre's premises, the Prato Wool Guild; Murray Cobban, Australian ambassador to Italy; Sir James Gobbo, the Centre's distinguished patron, at that time commissioner for Italy for the Victorian Government; Tom Hazel, representing the Centre's benefactors Rino and Diana Grollo; Monash chancellor Jeremy Ellis, Monash vice-chancellor David Robinson, Monash academic and administrative staff, as well as a group of undergraduate students.

Recollecting this milestone in 2010, founding director Bill Kent affirmed that the program was designed to 'give a flavour of what was possible' for the Centre. More precisely, it was intended to invigorate guests intellectually and artistically by bringing about a variety of encounters. During strategic planning in 2002, this intention for the Centre was summarised in the phrase 'a Centre for the whole person'. In 2008 Kent published a detailed account of the background to the Centre's establishment in the edited collection *Australians in Italy: Contemporary Lives and Impressions* (a volume derived from a symposium held at the Centre in 2005). This essay and archival documents make clear that, at least from 1997, the proposed Centre was expansively conceived as a multifaceted institution for students, artists and academics, political and business leaders. By September 2001, the Centre had been hosting events for some 10 months, including, in May of that year, the international conference 'Multiculturalism and Immigration: Italy and Australia, Two Experiences Compared', held in collaboration with the Tuscan Region and Prato's provincial and city governments. Hence at the opening, Kent could freely describe the Centre as 'a venue for learning, teaching and research in the service of both the Australian

The Australian Wed. 23 May 2001

Education

Italian palace of ideas

The dream is to create an intellectual Silicon Valley for modern Europe.
David Rosenthal reports from Palazzo Monash at Prato

'SMALLER than a campus, less expensive — but intellectually and educationally more ambitious," is how Monash University's new centre at Prato near Florence is described by its director, Bill Kent.

The embryonic institution flagged these ambitions last week by staging a conference on migration and multiculturalism, issues at the core of Australia's historical links to Italy.

"We thought there was a place for a different sort of overseas centre, not a campus that just taught undergraduates; something that might even become a sort of academy overseas," says Kent, a historian of renaissance Florence who taught at Monash's Clayton campus for 25 years.

Monash in Prato opened its doors last November and forms part of the university's growing overseas network; a smaller version started in London early last year while a full Monash campus in South Africa — there is another in Malaysia — began taking students this year.

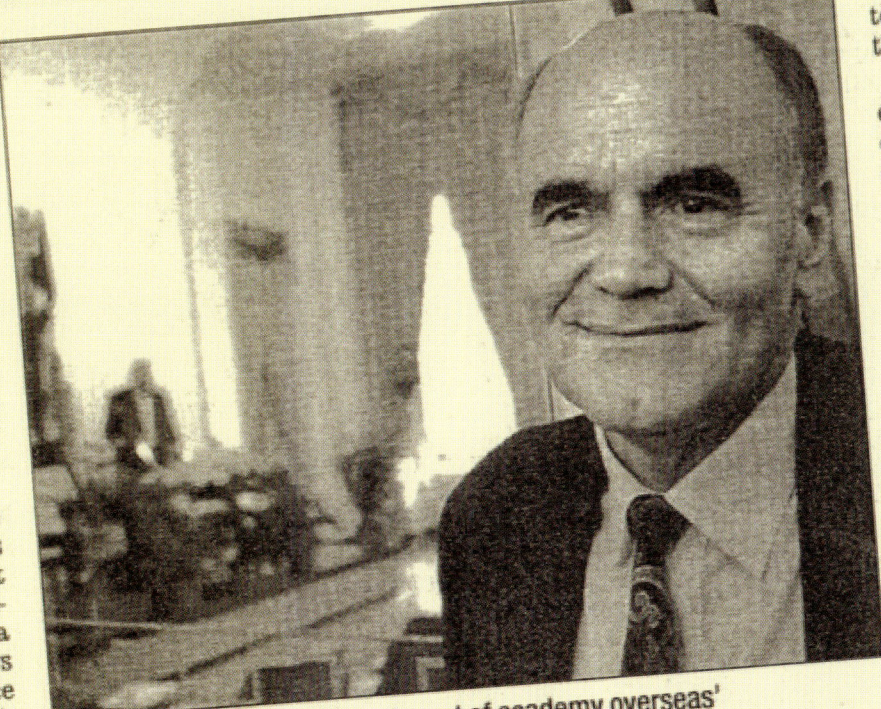

Lofty ideals: Kent envisions 'a sort of academy overseas'

Network, which deals with student equity and access issues.

Design and renaissance history courses will run this year; next year will bring additional courses in small business, Italian language and five law faculty programs, which will involve input from Italian aca-

However, he warns that if Monash really wants students to have an overseas experience as part of their degree, it will have to "bite the bullet" and increase existing levels of subsidy for travel and accommodation.

Holding the Multiculturalism and Migration: Italy and Aust-

the conference. "There is much to learn from countries going through this before us."

Claudio Martini, the president of traditionally left-wing Tuscany, says Italy stands at a crossroads: "On one side there's the unhistorical attitude of those who refuse every form of diversity and who hide behind the claim to conserve a poorly understood idea of national identity; on the other there is a welcoming culture of acceptance and a favourable attitude to the sharing of cultures."

Views such as Martini's are unlikely to dictate Italian policy in the near future. The Centre-Right, which swept into power on May 13, has an anti-immigration coalition partner in the Northern League, compared by several Australian speakers at the conference with the One Nation party. It appears unlikely, for example, that rules on citizenship, which requires a 10-year wait and in practice is usually obtained only through marriage, will be eased.

And although few expect the House of Liberties alliance under Silvio Berlusconi to try to purge Italy of its "clandestines", recent laws that set up deten-

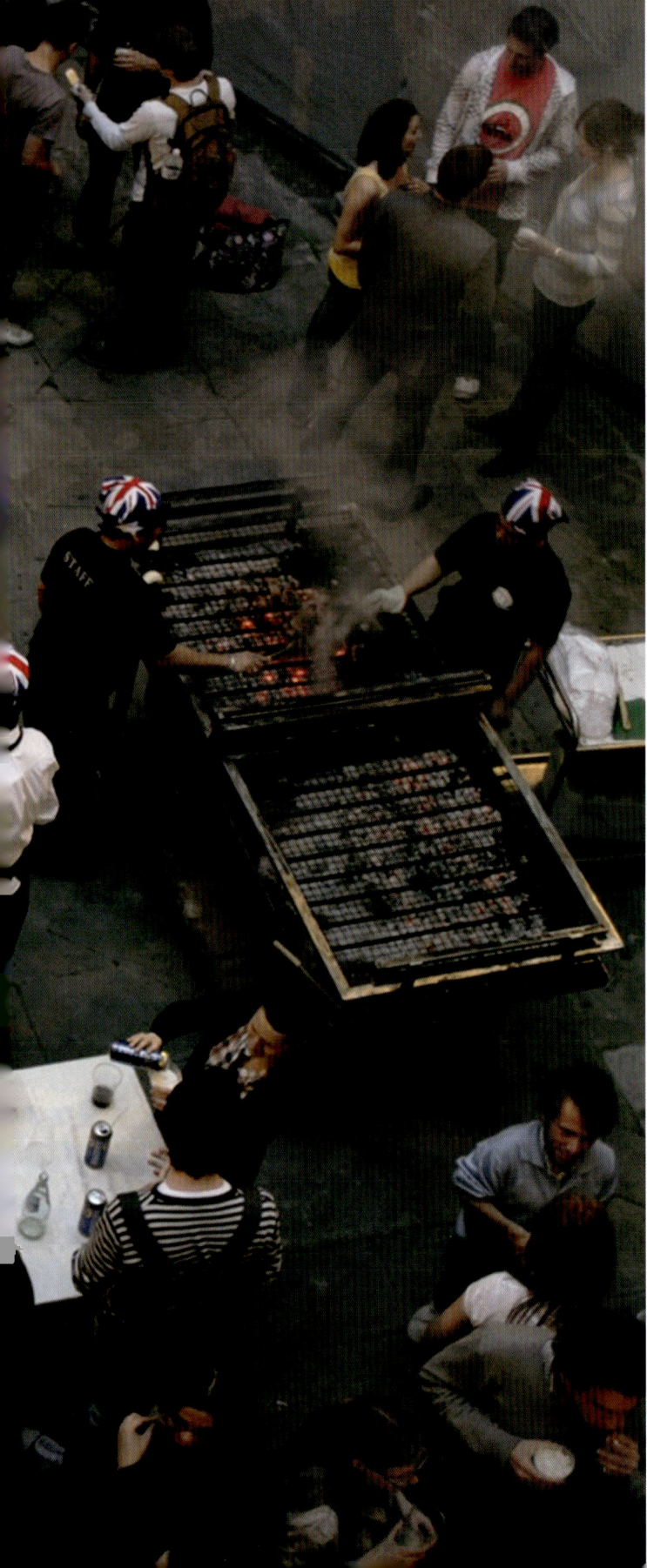

and local businesses. The Centre has an agreement with over 40 establishments—cafès, restaurants, bakeries, food stores, museums and theatres—which offer special discounts to Centre visitors and students.

Since 2006, data on the Centre's activities has been recorded electronically in a central database. Previously, founding director Bill Kent and associate director Cecilia Hewlett maintained hardcopy files with the discipline of expert historians. As of 2011, the application process for organising activities allows additional information to be recorded on the database, such as conference outcomes and sponsorship. A planned introduction of more sophisticated processes and software will make possible greater data extraction and analysis. For example, the two year cycle of medical conferences produces a cyclical spike in the participant numbers for this area of activity. However, in 2010, for the first time, the overall total in the category 'international conference participants' decreased, despite a 2009 increase (from 2008) in the number of conferences held at the Centre. This represents a basis for the Centre's present strategy to favour smaller, more intensive research workshops over 'blockbuster' style conferences. Given that the Centre's operations are running close to maximum capacity, especially in the peak periods of April to July and September and October, record-keeping and resulting trends continue to inform strategies for the Centre's future directions and continued success.

Cultural events hosted at the Centre are mainly organised by prominent local associations and institutions, such as FareArte, a nonprofit cultural organisation housed at the Palazzo Vaj; the Scuola di Musica 'Giuseppe Verdi', one of Italy's largest local government music schools, and the Teatro Metastasio, the Public Repertory Theatre of Tuscany. Events include concerts, presentations and exhibitions. Frequently the exhibitions originate from Australia, as was the case, for example, with *Aborigena: Contemporary Australian Aboriginal Art from the Gabrielle Pizzi Collection* in 2003; Jo-Anne Duggan's *Impossible Gaze* in 2004–05; Kevin Shaw's *Mates Collection* of photographs from the Kimberley in 2007 and 2010, and *From Here to Eternity: Contemporary Tapestries from the Victorian Tapestry Workshop* in 2008.

The category 'individual and group research' comprises Monash and non-Monash researchers and academics—key contributors to the vigour of the Centre, typically on sabbatical, who spend varying periods of time based at the Palazzo Vaj. They take advantage of the Centre's proximity to significant archives, libraries and museums, as well as academic institutions like the European University Institute (situated on the outskirts of Florence at San Domenico di Fiesole), in order to research and write while maintaining close connections with their European counterparts.

'Visitors' consists of recorded numbers of participants in all of the above areas of activity; it excludes walk-in visitors, or those with appointments—who are often noteworthy institutional or government figures. Currently the Centre does not require visitors to register at the point of entry, hence participant lists (for conferences and courses) and event plans forwarded to the Centre prior to the commencement of activities are the sources for these numbers. As required by the Centre, at least half of the conference participants are international; that is, not originating from Australia. Predominantly from Europe, conference participants also travel to the Centre from the Americas, the Asia-Pacific, Africa and the Middle East. Students enrolled in academic programs are chiefly Australian 'domestic' students (in some cases, Australian international students, who are mainly from Asia), with the exception of the Law program, which accepts one third of enrolments from Monash partner institutions in Israel, North America, France and Italy. Participants in events involving the wider public are the most difficult to tally. However, as mentioned, most cultural events are organised locally, therefore the *pratesi*—the people of Prato—are the visitors featured in this category.

Initiatives such as the annual Open Day help relationships between the Centre, the city of Prato, and the Prato public to flourish in different ways; they have been developed as part of a commitment to local engagement that is emphasised by the present Centre Director Loretta Baldassar. The Centre's first Open Day in 2010 saw over 500 visitors welcomed to Palazzo Vaj to learn about the presence of an Australian university in Prato. This was also the occasion for the launch of the Centre's Artist in Residence program, and the opening of the Bill Kent Library, a reference and research collection for European Medieval and Renaissance studies housed on the ground floor of the Palazzo Vaj. Like Open Day, the Monash Prato Card aims to foster rapport at the local level by encouraging an ongoing relationship between Centre visitors

10 Years in Numbers

Cathy Crupi Manager, Monash University Prato Centre

In 2001, the year of the Monash University Prato Centre's official opening, two undergraduate courses and four international conferences took place at the Palazzo Vaj. Since then, the Centre has continued to grow significantly—in 2010 alone, it hosted over 5000 visitors, 30 international conferences, 38 academic programs and 25 cultural events. In 2006, development of the annual program resulted in the Centre's physical expansion: from 2006 onward, in addition to the first floor of the Palazzo Vaj, Monash University has also leased the ground floor.

The Centre focuses on four areas of consolidated activity: academic programs, international conferences, cultural events, and individual and group research. 'Academic programs' refers to undergraduate as well as postgraduate courses and seminars that have an average duration of one month. For the most part, these programs are offered by Monash faculties. Nowadays an increasing number of academic programs are offered annually or biennially, such as the award-winning Monash Law at Prato Program; the undergraduate and higher degree units offered through Monash's Faculty of Art and Design—the Centre's longest running teaching program, begun in 2001—and the Faculty of Arts program, which includes studies in Italian, History, Archaeology, Criminology and Music.

Especially for the purposes of tracking statistical information, the broad category 'international conferences' encompasses research workshops, meetings, symposia and round tables hosted at the Centre that have an average duration of three days. Biennial conferences and symposia, the largest of these in the medical field, attract a wealth of international experts. Due to the Centre's strategic location in Europe, these gatherings achieve an increased accessibility and visibility for collaborative research in a large variety of disciplines and specialist subjects. Major conferences in the 2010 calendar ranged from 'Definitions of Statelessness' (organised by the United Nations High Commission for Refugees) and 'Heart and Mind: Psychogenic Cardiovascular Disease' (in collaboration with Australia's Baker IDI Heart and Diabetes Institute), to 'Mobility, Social Inclusion and Transnational Identities: Social Realities and Representations in Italy and Beyond' (in collaboration with the University of Warwick), and the '29th National Congress of the National Group of Solid Earth Geophysics' (organised by the Prato Research Foundation).

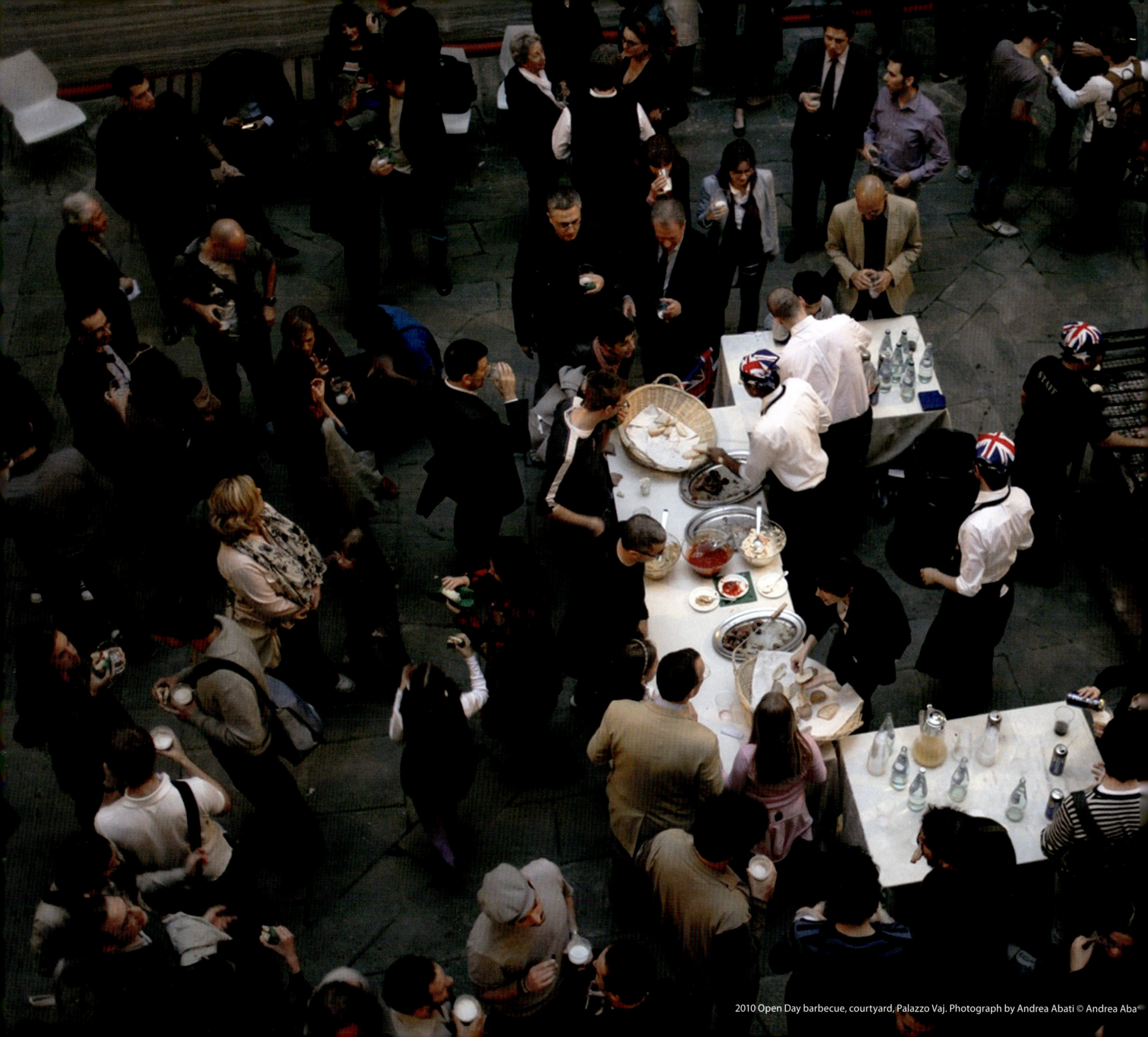

2010 Open Day barbecue, courtyard, Palazzo Vaj. Photograph by Andrea Abati © Andrea Abati

PART ONE
The Monash University Prato Centre

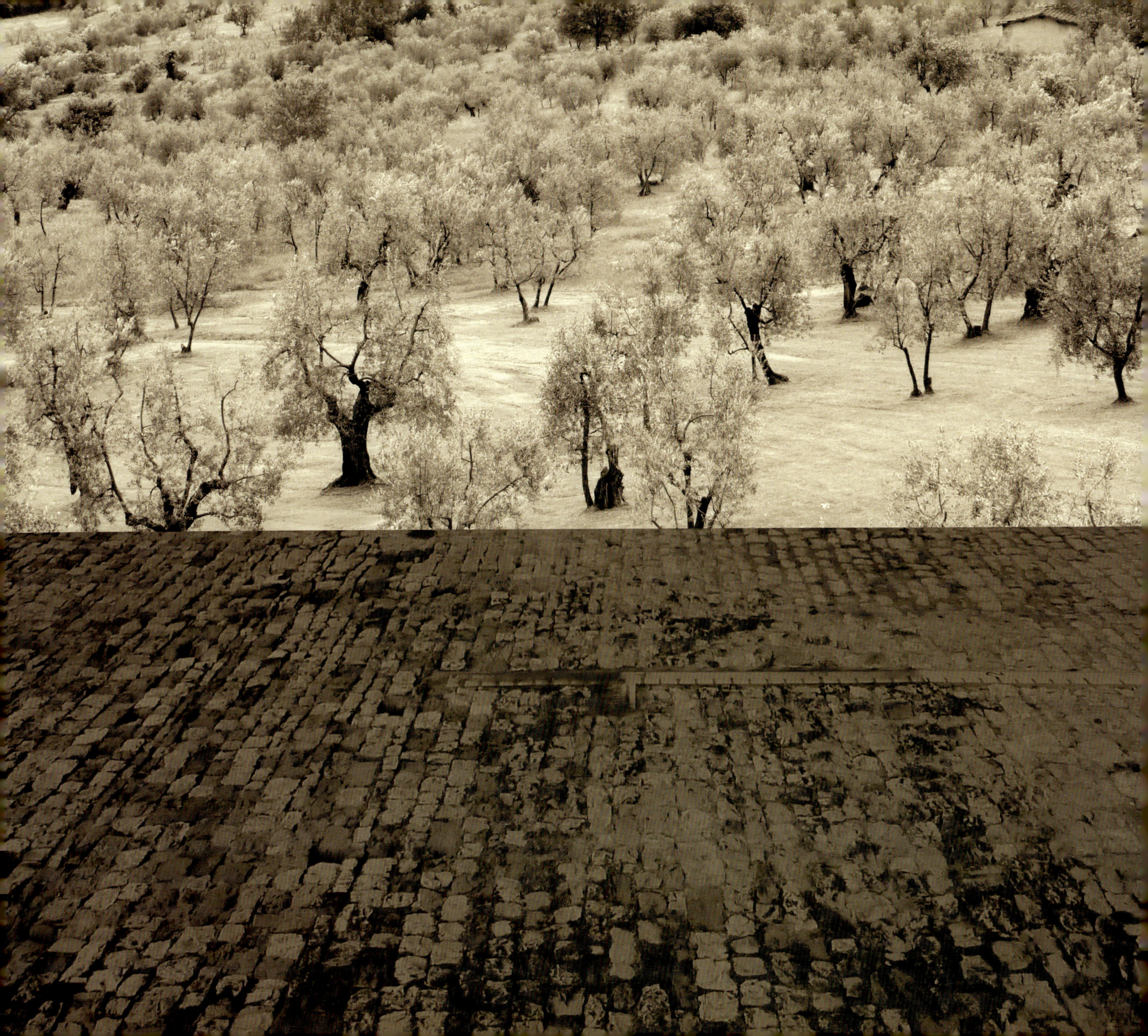

At Monash University, Annamaria Pagliaro, director of the Centre from 2005 to 2008, graciously agreed to a long interview by telephone, at the beginning of a day's intensive teaching at the Centre. Cecilia Hewlett, now Director of the Office of the Deputy Vice-Chancellor (Education), unstintingly fostered this project, as did Helen Fletcher-Kennedy, Office of the Deputy Vice-Chancellor (Education).

Bill Kent, founding director of the Centre, died in August 2010. Any with a connection to the tenth anniversary of the Centre's official opening profoundly regret that he did not live to share in the formal celebrations of this milestone, and mourn his absence. But Bill's personal enthusiasm for the idea of this publication brought excitement to the venture when its parameters were still in outline. At that early stage, he recorded an illuminating interview for the project with immense grace and fortitude. I thank him for his faith.

Without exception all those who were contacted during research for this project welcomed news of the initiative. Demonstrating the goodwill intrinsic to 'the Prato effect', all were delighted to reflect on their experiences of the Centre's history and programs. Special thanks to the contributors of vignettes, whose involvement has been of inestimable value, not least for the stimulus it afforded. John Paoletti granted permission to quote from the introduction to his lecture, 'Learn My Language: Strategies of Medici Patronage in Renaissance Florence', presented in Melbourne on 9 November 2010.

For their generous participation I also thank Kit Wise, John Nieuwenhuysen and Sahar Sana. Thanks too to the following people for helpful discussions: Matthew Absalom, Graeme Davison, Rae Frances, Peter Howard, Kate Murphy, and Elizabeth Sellars.

Nathan Hollier, Manager of Monash University Publishing, and all his colleagues, were quickly receptive to a proposal for this volume. Nathan, Sarah Cannon, Joanne Mullins, Kate Hatch, and Les Thomas make such a fine team. I thank them for their investment of talent and meticulous skill, which has made this elegant publication possible; I thank them for their collegiality, and patient handling of the process. Production of excellent quality was made possible through financial support from the Office of the Deputy Vice-Chancellor (Education); particular thanks to Jeffrey Bender, Project Manager in this Office.

At Colour Factory, Phillip Virgo, Shane Waghorne and Linsey Gosper achieved the highest possible standards for Jo-Anne's artwork. Efficient assistance with other image-related queries and permissions has been provided by Andrea Abati; Peter Bartelt (Monash University Design and Publishing); Blaine Cooper, Jon Oldmeadow and Lillian O'Neil (Safari Team); Kirrily Hammond (Monash University Museum of Art); Grant Smith (Gallery Gabrielle Pizzi); Anthony Wallis (Aboriginal Artist's Agency Limited), also Robert Burke, Kevin Shaw and Renata Summo-O'Connell. The collaboration of Dryphoto Arte Contemporanea regarding Andrea Abati's photographs of the Centre's 2010 Open Day is also acknowledged.

Neville Chiavaroli, Victoria Hamilton, and Ros Pesman each very kindly gave friendship, encouragement and the timely benefit of their expertise. Jo-Anne wished to express wholehearted personal thanks, above all, to Kevin Bayley. My own are to Sudaya.

Cynthia Troup

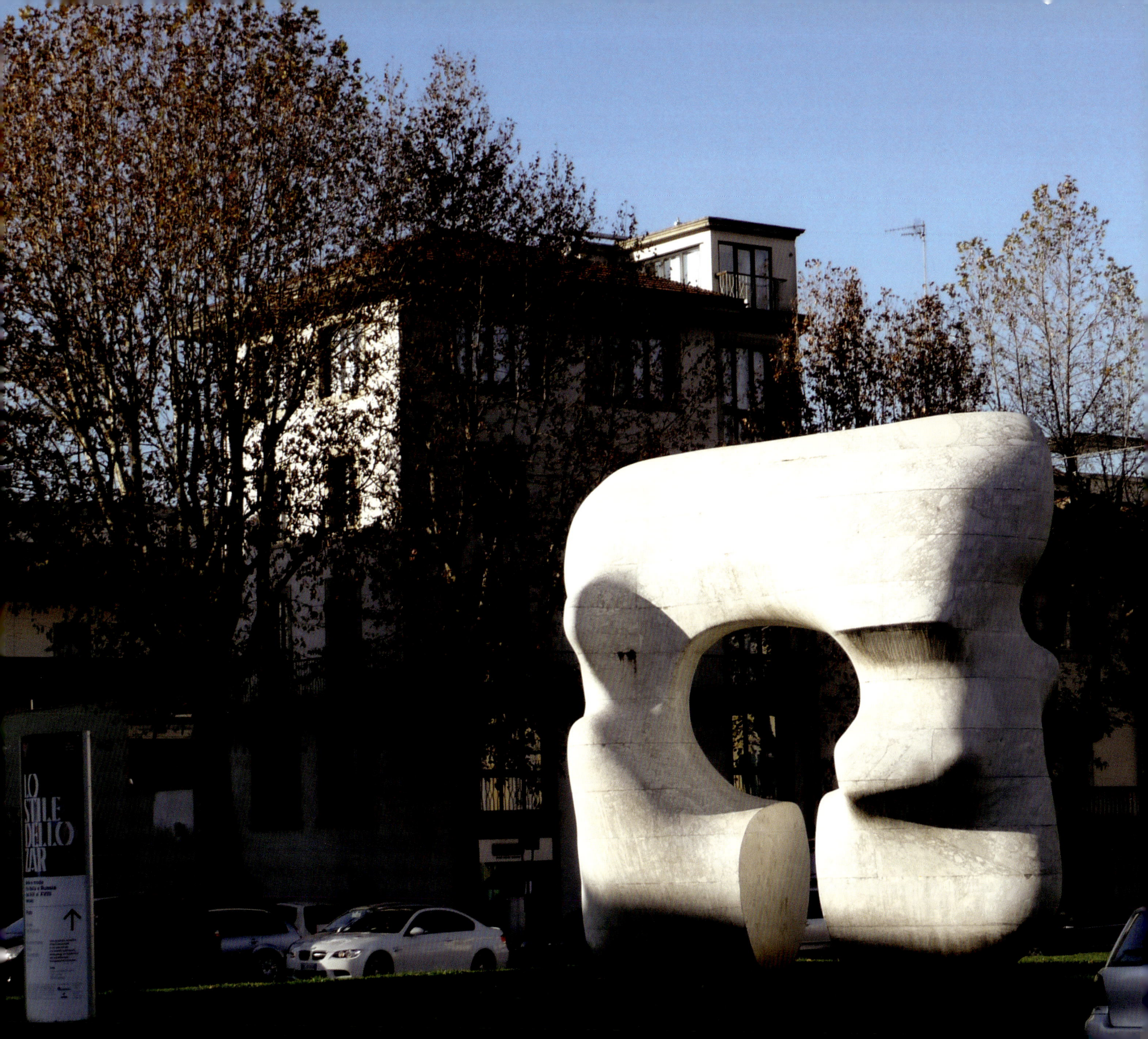

ACKNOWLEDGEMENTS

In keeping with the multifaceted nature of the Monash University Prato Centre's programs, this publication was planned as a collaboration between Jo-Anne Duggan and myself. Early in December 2010, Jo-Anne recollected her first conversation about the project with Centre Director Loretta Baldassar.

> We talked over steaming cups of hot chocolate in a café near the Palazzo Vaj. It was a frosty December afternoon in 2009. We were meeting to discuss the forthcoming inaugural Artist in Residence program for 2010. However, we came to speak about a tenth anniversary publication, and how it might reflect the breadth of vision associated with the Centre. I could imagine a publication rich in images, emphasising the unique sense of place that pertains to the Centre. Of course I saw the need for more than one perspective—as a start, a dialogue between images and text.

Jo-Anne died early in March 2011. She had been diagnosed with cancer a year before. In the intervening months she applied her energies to this project with extraordinary diligence, courage and good humour. Very very sadly Jo-Anne did not see the contents and layout of the present volume even in draft form. All those who have worked to bring the publication to fruition hope that the results do some justice to her creative concept, her tenacity—and to the splendour of her art. I express the following also on her behalf.

This project could not have been undertaken without the endorsement of members of the Prato Advisory Group (PAG) which guides the Monash University Prato Centre's activities, chaired by Professor Stephanie Fahey, Deputy Vice-Chancellor (Global Engagement). Sir James Gobbo AC is patron of the Centre, and readily agreed to contribute a preface to this volume. From the beginning Michael Simmonds, Office of the Deputy Vice-Chancellor (Global Engagement), provided unwavering support of all kinds, for which I am most grateful. Thanks to Melinda Pipan, Project Officer, Office of the Deputy Vice-Chancellor (Global Engagement) for her attention to detail in administrative matters during the first months of the project. Thanks to Monash University Archives for source material.

I thank Loretta Baldassar for the opportunity to respond to a unique proposition, for her trust in the ensuing process—and for recording an interview en route between Prato and Perth. The present staff of the Centre have been unfailingly helpful in response to emailed queries and requests for material, providing vital assistance. The willing collaboration of Centre Manager Cathy Crupi, and Research Officer Narelle McAuliffe have been greatly appreciated. Donata Batisti, Architectural and Facilities Consultant, drafted a floorplan of the Palazzo Vaj for reproduction; Leonardo Tinti, Network and Systems Administrator, rendered technical assistance with image transfer.

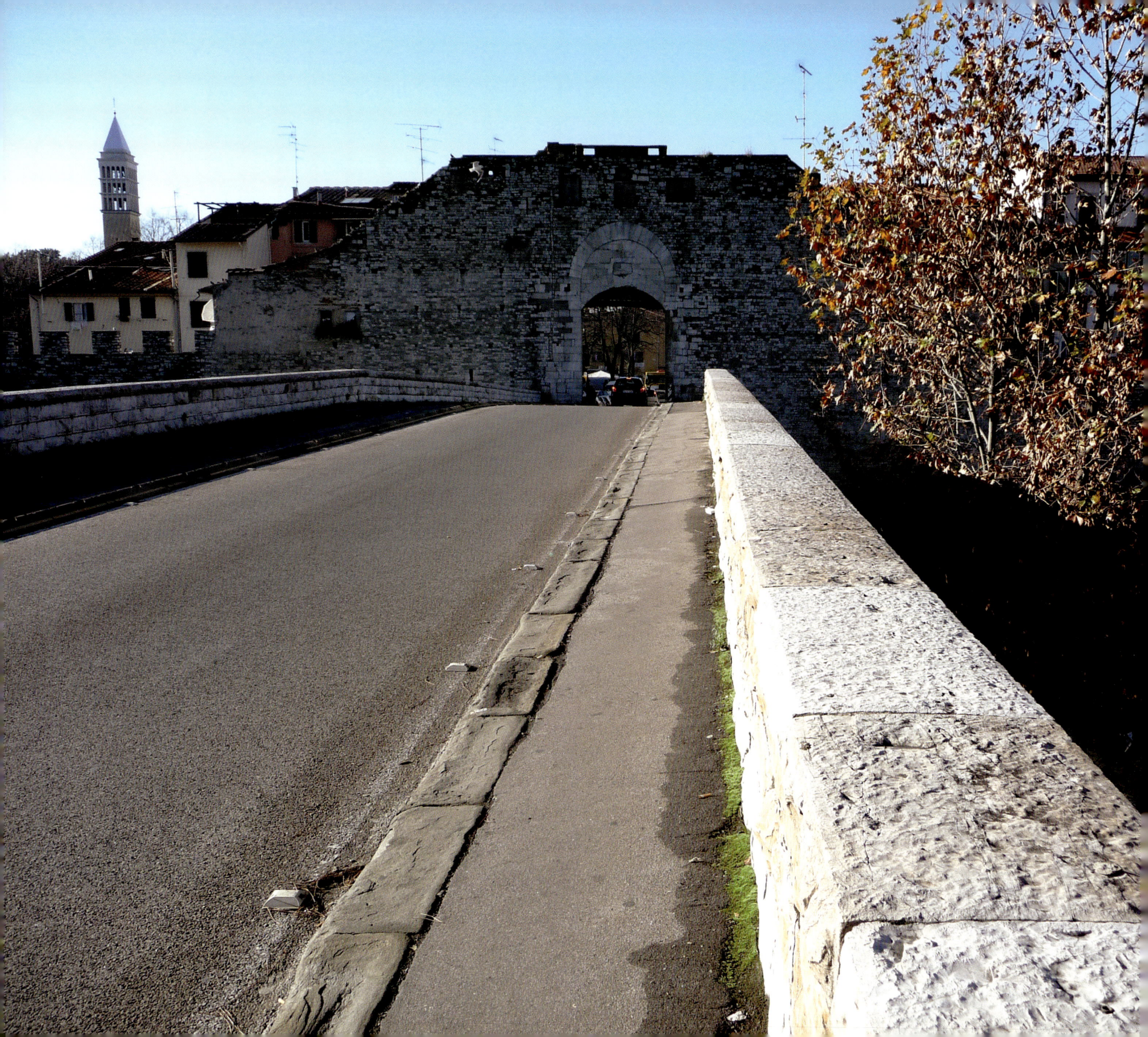

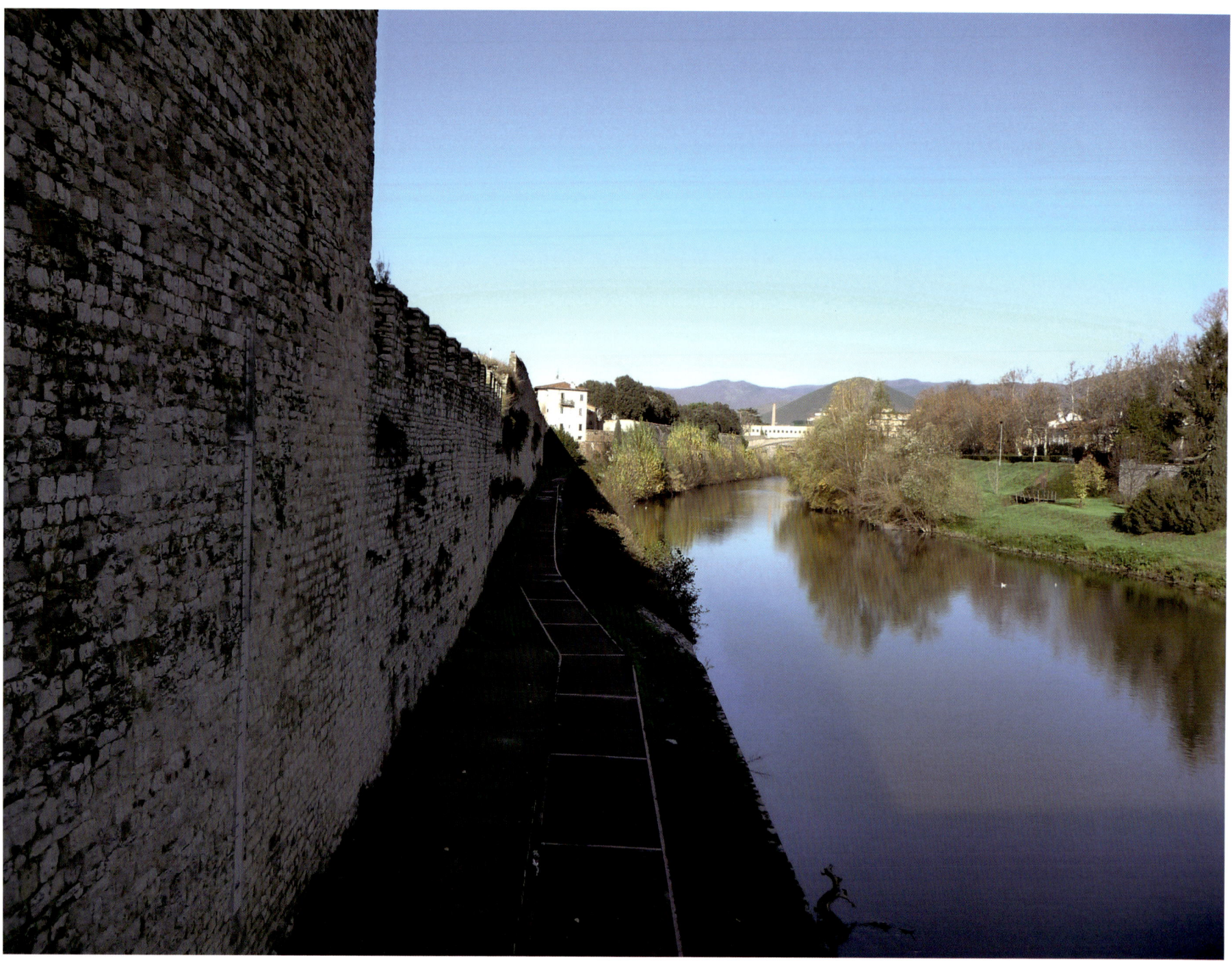

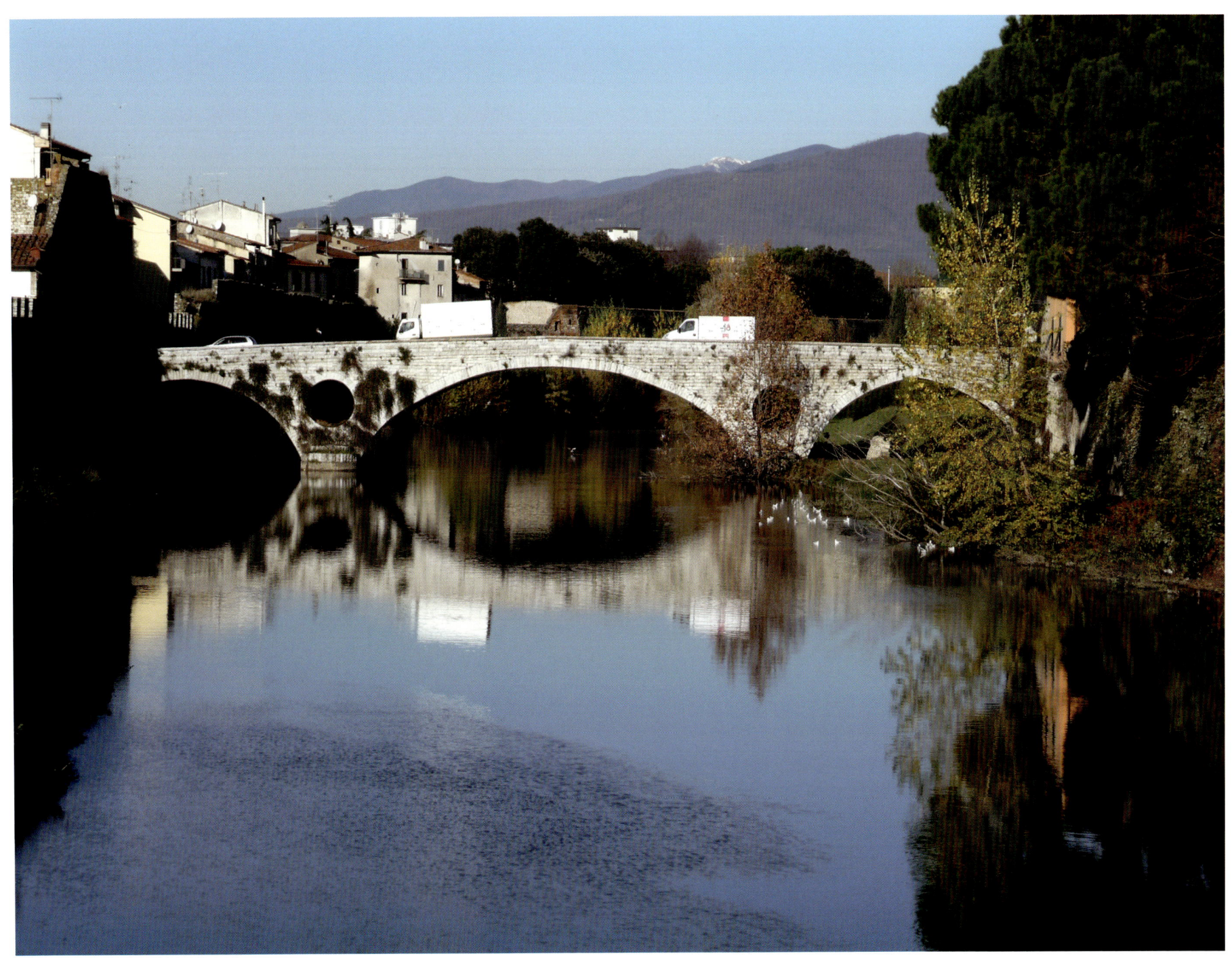

PREFACE

As FOUNDING PATRON of the Monash University Prato Centre, I am delighted to accept the invitation to write a preface to this work celebrating the Centre's tenth anniversary. I recall vividly that ten years or more ago, in spite of Professor Bill Kent's persuasive advocacy, the proposal to establish the Centre seemed a very ambitious one. The challenge was not only to secure a fruitful and widespread involvement of Monash University but also to attract both Italian and other university participation. As this publication clearly illustrates, the Monash Prato Centre has succeeded admirably in meeting these challenges.

The title of this celebratory volume, *A Site of Convergence*, aptly conveys the way in which the Centre sees itself. In this it reflects how the cities of Tuscany, indeed all Italy see themselves. Though close to other major centres of industry, commerce and culture, each city is proud of its own role and contribution. The Centre in Prato, though probably closer in travel time to Florence than Monash is to the centre of Melbourne, can be considered an enterprising site of convergence that successfully draws on its distinguished neighbours. The Centre has in addition succeeded in bonding with the local authorities and cultural and commercial institutes of Prato. This bond is special as Monash is the only overseas university in Prato.

The Centre has brought about new, ongoing links between Australia and Italy in areas that go beyond the customary roles in language, arts and history played by the many overseas universities that have study centres in Italy. I refer to Monash contributions in the area of comparative law and evidence and court procedures, and more particularly in the field of population and multicultural studies.

This publication provides engaging personal perspectives from researchers, teachers and other visitors to the Centre. These and the description of the Centre's many diverse activities are a valuable affirmation of the original project, and a sure base for future growth and achievements. Congratulations to all those who have contributed to this thoughtful publication marking the tenth anniversary of the Monash Prato Centre.

Sir James Gobbo AC, July 2011

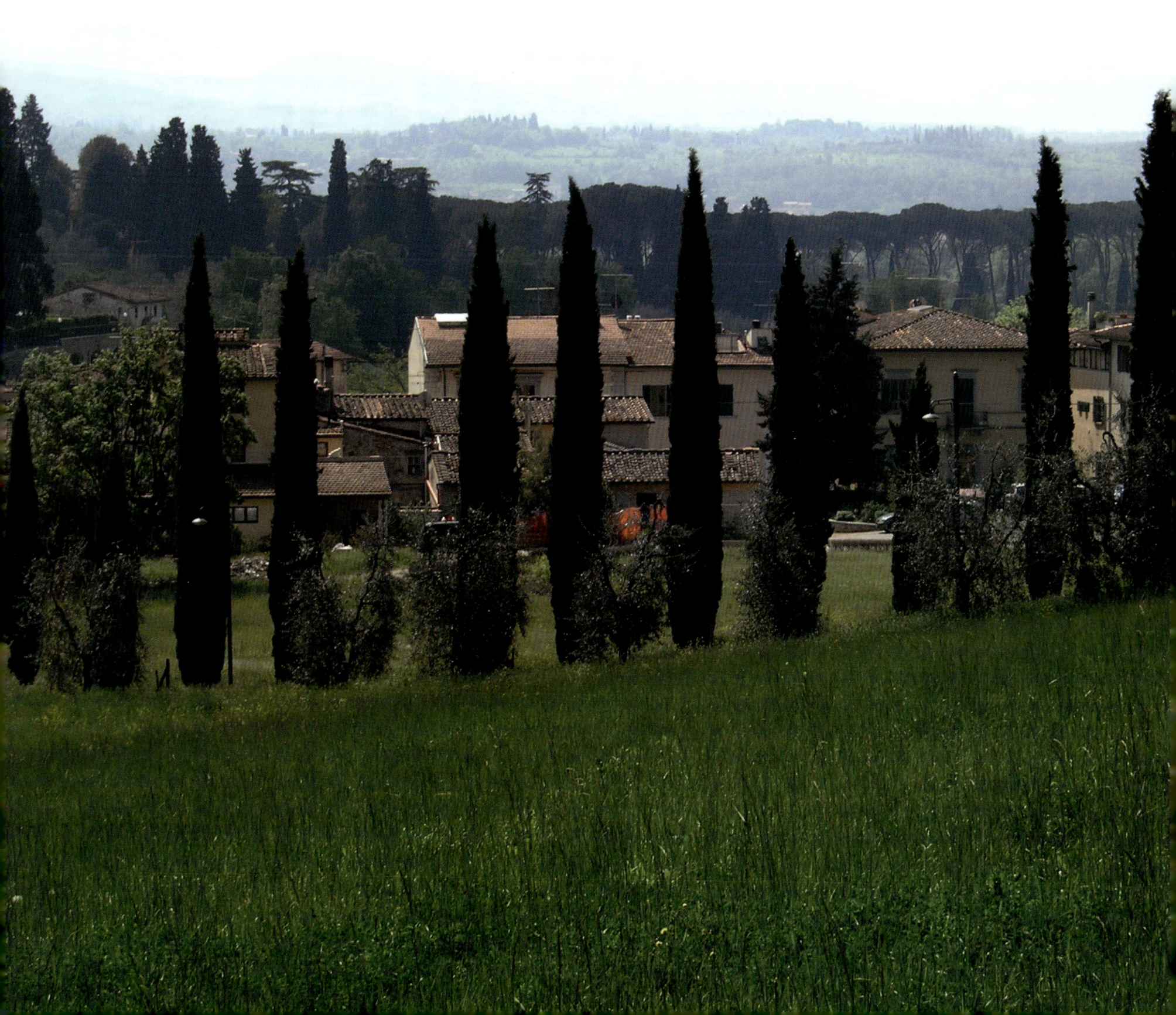

CONTENTS

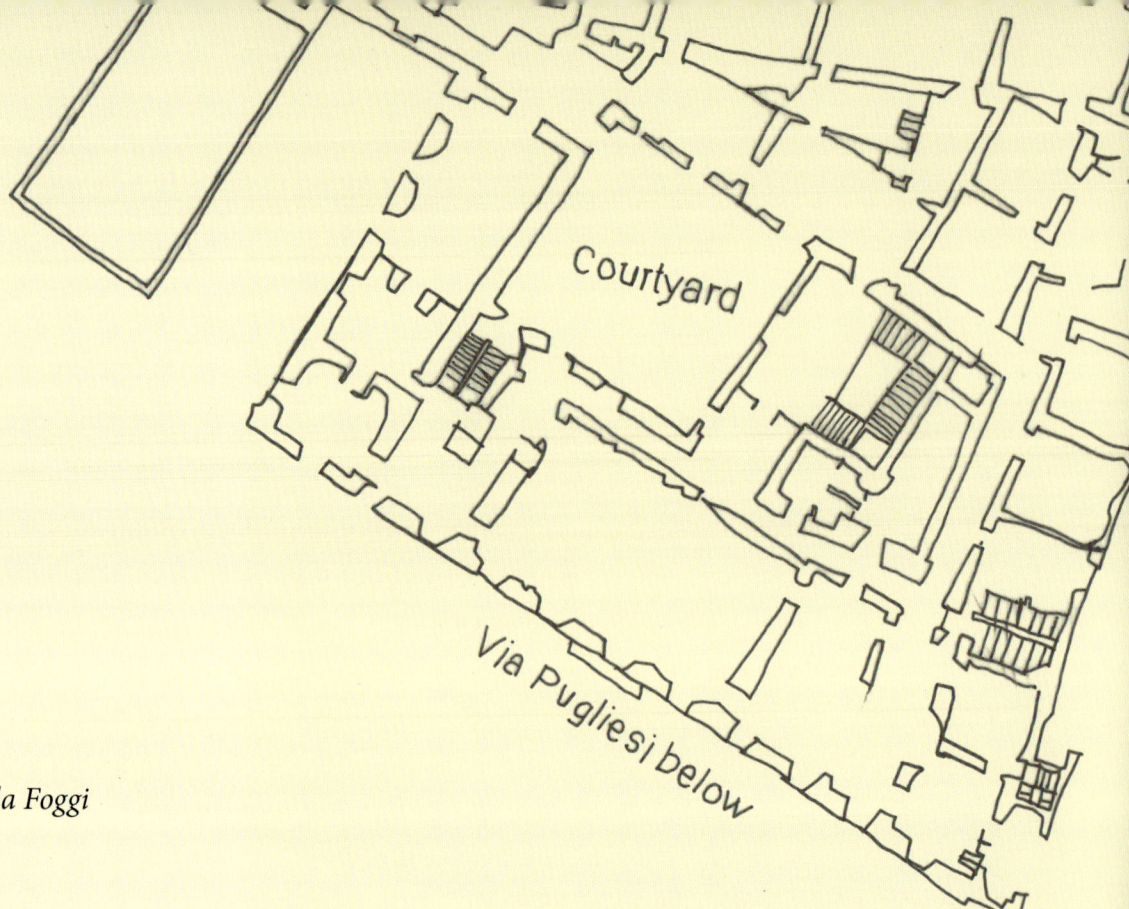

PREFACE   Sir James Gobbo AC

ACKNOWLEDGEMENTS

PART ONE: THE MONASH UNIVERSITY PRATO CENTRE

- 3   Ten Years in Numbers   *Cathy Crupi*
- 7   A Centre for the Whole Person

PART TWO: A SITE OF CONVERGENCE

- 19   Monash in Prato—Monash in Europe
- 35   Palazzo Vaj: A Brief Historical Sketch   *Rossella Foggi*
- 39   'Keeping House' at the Palazzo Vaj

PART THREE: MULTIPLE PERSECTIVES

- 53   Camaraderie and Collaboration
- 56   A Pioneering Project   *Renn Wortley*
- 58   Budgeting for a Remarkable Pace   *Terry Masocco*
- 60   Art History in Prato   *Bronwyn Stocks*
- 62   'The New World of Medicine' and Beyond   *Leon Piterman*
- 64   Global Context for a Law Degree   *Marianna Linnik*
- 66   Memories and Communities in Prato   *Justine Heazlewood*
- 68   Teaching Dante From Contemporary Prato   *Clare Monagle*
- 70   From Perth to Prato: A Life-Changing Experience   *Fiona Millimaci*

PART FOUR: A CENTRE FOR ART AND ARTISTS

- 75   Context for the Artist in Residence Program
- 82   Imagination and the Immediacy of History   *Jo-Anne Duggan*

BIBLIOGRAPHY

IMAGE ESSAYS BY JO-ANNE DUGGAN

- 24   Sites of Convergence
- 44   Piano Nobile, Palazzo Vaj
- 84   Before the Museum
- 90   Wondrous Possessions

Monash University Publishing
Building 4, Monash University
Clayton, Victoria 3800, Australia
www.publishing.monash.edu

© Copyright 2011
All rights reserved. Apart from any uses permitted by Australia's Copyright Act 1968, no part of this book may be reproduced by any process without prior written permission from the copyright owners. Inquiries should be directed to the publisher.

This book is available online at www.publishing.monash.edu/books/prato

   ISBN: 978-1-921867-18-7 (pb)
   ISBN: 978-1-921867-19-4 (web)

Cover image: Jo-Anne Duggan

Design: Les Thomas

Printed in Australia by Griffin Press an Accredited ISO AS/NZS 14001:2004 Environmental Management System printer.

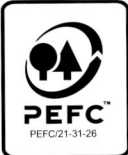

The paper this book is printed on is certified by the Programme for the Endorsement of Forest Certification scheme. Griffin Press holds PEFC chain of custody SGS - PEFC/COC-0594. PEFC promotes environmentally responsible, socially beneficial and economically viable management of the world's forests.

Note to the reader

This volume has been published in anticipation of 17 September 2011, the date which marks ten years exactly since the formal opening of the Monash University Prato Centre—and a day of celebrations at Prato.

Images throughout this publication have been used with express permission. Unless otherwise indicated, all photographs are by Jo-Anne Duggan, are copyright protected, and have been reproduced with the permission of the Estate of Jo-Anne Duggan.

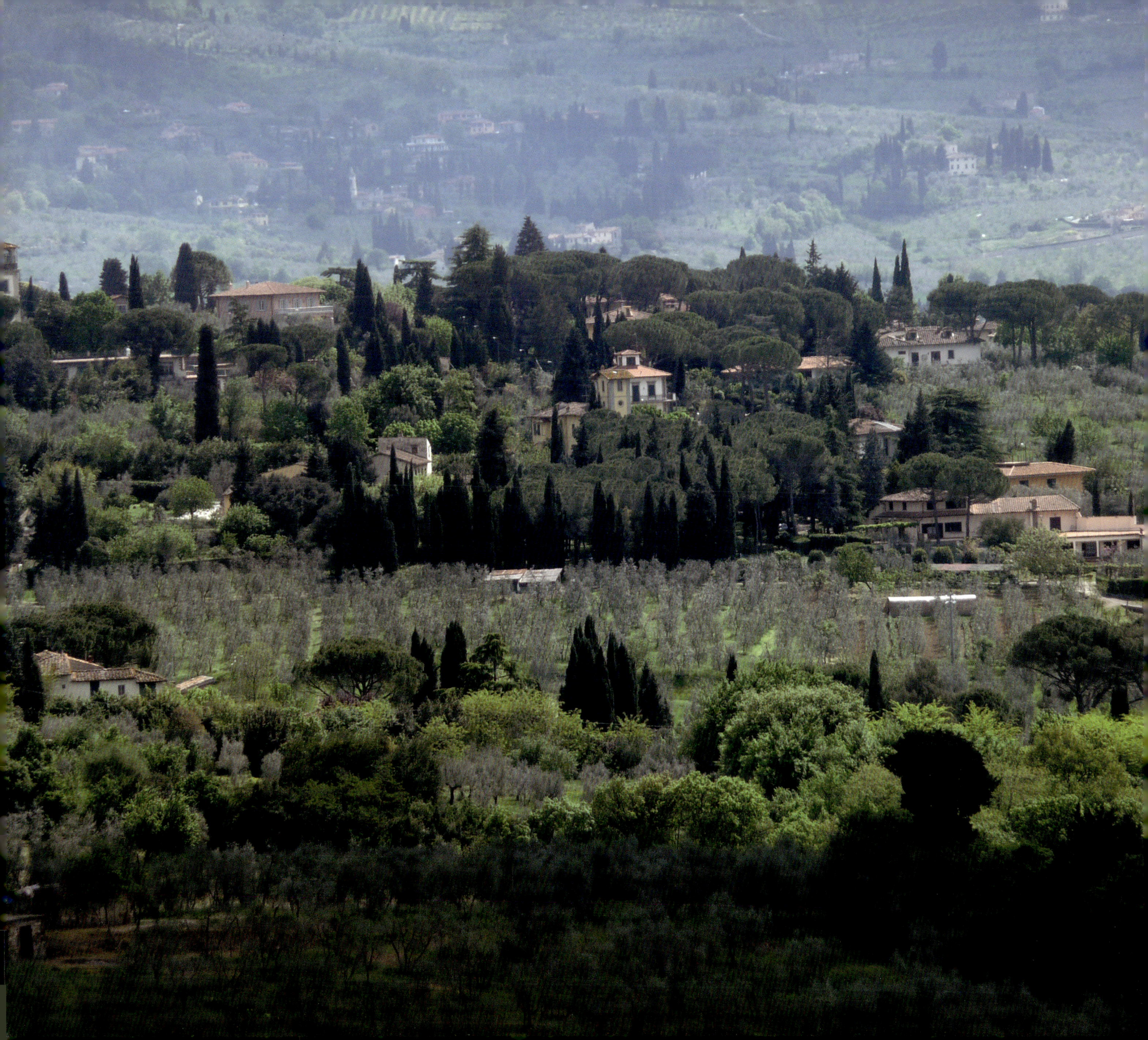

A SITE OF CONVERGENCE

Celebrating 10 Years of the Monash University Prato Centre

CYNTHIA TROUP WITH JO-ANNE DUGGAN

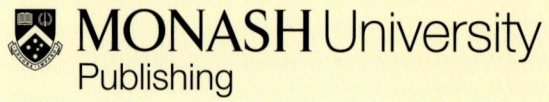